THE AGE OF COMFORT

The
AGE
of
COMFORT

When Paris Discovered Casual—
and the Modern Home Began

JOAN DEJEAN

BLOOMSBURY

New York   Berlin   London

Published by Bloomsbury USA, New York

All papers used by Bloomsbury USA are natural, recyclable products made from wood grown in well-managed forests. The manufacturing processes conform to the environmental regulations of the country of origin.

Library of Congress Cataloging-in-Publication Data

DeJean, Joan E.
The age of comfort : when Paris discovered casual—and the modern home began / Joan DeJean.—1st U.S. ed.
p.   cm.
Includes bibliographical references.
ISBN-13: 978-1-59691-405-6 (hardcover)
ISBN-10: 1-59691-405-X (hardcover)
1. Design—France—Paris—History—17th century.   2. Design—France—Paris—History—18th century.   3. Design—Human factors—France—Paris.   4. Interior architecture—France—Paris—History—17th century.   5. Interior architecture—France—Paris—History—18th century.   6. Human comfort—France—Paris.   I. Title.
NK949.P27D45 2009
306.4'812—dc22
2009006602

First published by Bloomsbury USA in 2009
This paperback edition published in 2010

Paperback ISBN: 978-1-60819-230-4

1   3   5   7   9   10   8   6   4   2

Typeset by Westchester Book Group
Printed in the United States of America by Worldcolor Fairfield

In memory of Kate Keating, who dreamed of writing about eighteenth-century French painting.

CONTENTS

The Age of Comfort

ALMOST EVERYONE I know believes that we have a right to expect a high degree of comfort, above all, in the place where we can control it most easily, in our homes. Oh, we always differ a bit about what is most essential to our well-being. I know people who will go to any lengths to find sheets with the absolute highest thread count, others who are willing to spend a fortune on the most luxurious bathroom they can afford. And I know still others ready to go on a quest for the perfect sofa—just the right shape, with the best support and perfect upholstery. These differences, however, seem meaningless next to the shared belief that comfort is our birthright.

Our comfort-driven life is a phenomenon with little precedent in Western history. In fact, the first period after antiquity when comfort became both desired and possible on anything like a large scale began in Paris in the early 1670s. It was there and then that comfort and informality first emerged as priorities in domains ranging from architecture and fashion to furniture design and interior decoration. It was there and then that the modern home began—from the rooms we still use on a daily basis to the furniture we see around us every day, to what now seem obvious decorating choices, such as plain white ceilings. Fields as diverse as upholstery and plumbing were thrust from the stone age into the modern age: inventions from the sofa to running water to flush toilets appeared in private residences. The architects, the craftsmen, and the inhabitants of Paris during the century (1670–1765) I refer to as the age of comfort can be said to have created a blueprint for today's home and the way we live in it.

The home and life in it were reinvented, furthermore, virtually overnight, as a result of little more than a half century of extraordinarily intense creativity in design, art, and architecture. This was one of several moments in the history of Paris—and perhaps the most powerful one of all—when the city became a center of cultural, artistic, and social ferment. Paris was transformed into a giant design workshop in which inventions in the arts and crafts and innovative technologies were tried out. That transformation began with developments that originated either at court or among the wealthiest individuals in Paris in the final decades of the seventeenth century and then gradually spread down the social and financial ladder. As a result, by the mid–eighteenth century, the ideal of a comfort-driven life had won widespread acceptance.

This was also the first moment ever when the history of comfort can be accurately re-created. Earlier periods have left us only a few scattered artifacts and the occasional eyewitness account. Before the early eighteenth century, there was no systematic attempt to document inventions designed to make life easier.

Certain individuals always try to communicate a sense of why and how daily life in the world they see around them is becoming different from what it was only a short time before. They record for posterity the kind of prosaic phenomena all too easily overlooked. At the turn of the eighteenth century, such cultural chroniclers began to write about an area that had never before attracted significant attention: ordinary things that suddenly seemed extraordinary because they were rapidly taking on radically new designs. Chairs and tables and beds and bedrooms began to receive extensive coverage in letters, in diaries, in newspapers—and even in guidebooks. Tourist guides to Paris actually told foreign visitors about the most impressive bedrooms and baths in the city and encouraged them to try to get a glimpse of their furnishings and décor. Artists began to depict the way individuals were engaging with redesigned objects, the way in which they used new conveniences. There has never been a moment in which individuals were so openly thrilled with creature comforts and so eager to tell the world about them.

The creators of those comforts were every bit as eager to record their accomplishments for posterity. Thus, for the early eighteenth century and for the first time ever, we have ample and amply detailed contemporary documentation not only about public architectural projects, but about private ones. The foremost architects of the day realized that residential architecture was taking on unprecedented significance. They therefore published the plans of homes being built in Paris's new neighborhoods almost before the paint was dry on their walls. For the first time, new designs in furniture and bath fixtures were documented in detail and in print; they were most often documented in more than one source. For the first time, artisans and craftsmen published accounts of how such fields as furniture making and upholstery were changing. For the first time, we have abundant advertising from contemporary periodicals in which merchants and craftsmen (from those who sold fabric to those who made plumbing fixtures) provided detailed accounts of the specific wares they offered for sale.

From today's perspective, however, what is most impressive about this period is that its most characteristic inventions once again play an equally central role in our definition of comfort. The sofa—probably the most important piece of furniture in homes today, the form of seating that has conditioned many of our most basic postures—came into existence between 1685 and 1710. It was at the turn of the eighteenth century that cotton—soft, light, and supple, the material we put on our beds and choose for our most comfortable clothing—began to be used just as it is now. One of the arrangements now seen as basic to home design—the pairing of private bedroom and private bath—was introduced in the early decades of the eighteenth century, shortly after both the private bedroom and the private bath had been invented.

In addition, in all areas amazingly high standards—standards easily up to those operative today—were immediately enforced, with the result that, within only a decade or two, designers and craftsmen managed every time to get it just right. Objects that we would barely recognize in their previous incarnations were transformed into ones we would still be delighted to own and use. From bathtubs to armchairs, from toilets to casual daywear, there was nothing even remotely primitive about any of comfort's new accessories. One minute, there were armchairs that appear laughable today because they're absolutely stiff and unpadded and seem crudely made; the next, they had been replaced by models trendy designers are still copying three centuries later.

In the 1670s, when this ferment began, those with wealth and influence thought only of magnificence. Their residences were known for their splendid façades, huge interior spaces, and showstopping furniture. Only such visible proofs of an owner's status mattered, for the demonstration of rank was the primary task assigned architecture by all who could afford to plan their homes. No one considered how daily life would actually unfold behind those imposing façades. Architects paid virtually no attention to practical considerations such as lighting, heating, and storage space. No one had ever thought of positioning any specialized furniture, such as a night table, near a bed. And all forms of seating, from armchairs to stools of ease, were made of hard, bare wood, with at most a removable cushion or a thin layer of fabric or tapestry for padding. Nothing in the home had been designed to promote comfort and convenience. The representative figure of the age of magnificence that reached its apogee in the 1680s, Louis XIV, was responsible for the construction of perhaps the grandest and least comfortable residence of all time, Versailles. Of him, his second wife and closest confidante during the final decades of his life, the Marquise de Maintenon, remarked: "He never even thinks about discomfort; all that counts for him is grandeur and magnificence."

Stiff seating guaranteed that everyone remained bolt upright, a position perfectly suited to the rigid etiquette and protocol that governed the lives of anyone with any degree of social status. It was considered absolutely essential always to be seated and positioned in the most imposing manner possible, inconceivable to appear in public attired in anything but one's most elaborately formal clothing. For women, a gorgeous outfit that was not rigidly corseted was simply unheard of. Only in this way would one be seen as powerful and influential.

If you had status or aspired to it, you could never, ever be casual, for you were always on display. Architecture thus did not plan for privacy any more than for comfort. It was undoubtedly because Versailles was the ne plus ultra of grandeur and formality that life there inspired a desire that had never been a priority for the elite, the desire to relax and be casual. The sea change that ended the uncontested rule of magnificence began as a palace revolution when first a royal mistress, the Marquise de Montespan, and then Louis XIV's children, legitimate and illegitimate, their wives and husbands, and his grandson's wife joined forces to promote a way of life based on a new set of values: comfort, informality—and privacy.

Only a few decades later, even Versailles had been transformed. For Louis XV, son and grandson of the first members of the royal family to share these values, grandeur and magnificence still counted, but other concerns were at least as important. To begin with, comfort mattered to him, and it mattered a great deal. When he was still a very young king, he had Versailles's massive walls ripped open in 1728 to install the plumbing for its first bathrooms; he repeated the procedure a number of times until he felt that his architects had gotten the concept right. And he had his personal space appointed with fixtures next to which his predecessor's closestool would have seemed ridiculously primitive. In 1751, the royal mistress who more than anyone else shared and encouraged his passion for an easeful way of life, the Marquise de Pompadour, had a new bidet delivered to him at Versailles. It had gilt bronze mounts and was veneered in rosewood with an elaborate marquetry in a violet-tinged wood depicting sprays of flowers. These matched the pattern on the blue-and-white-flowered fabric covering the padded backrest, the handrest, and the removable cushion that concealed a porcelain bowl for washing. Louis XV's bidet perfectly represented the new conception of comfort: a mundane object made simultaneously flawlessly functional, luxurious, and aesthetically pleasing.

Perhaps the most spectacular change of all, however, came in the realm of behavior. Louis XV took it for granted that he had a right to a second existence, parallel to his official one, and that he could live this other life outside the public eye. Whereas Louis XIV had reserved almost no space for his unofficial life, his great-grandson created an entire parallel universe for himself at Versailles—a second dining room and so forth. Insiders knew of these interior rooms; access to them, however, was tightly controlled via a system of hidden entrances and back stairs. The interior world came to occupy roughly as much space as the official Versailles, but it was all completely invisible to visitors. This meant that Louis XV was able at virtually any moment to escape from the intimidating vastness of the public spaces.

For this reason, Louis XV was not obliged to be as formal as possible at all times. He was able instead to throw off the demands of protocol and to live a simpler, more casual life. He even tried to make that model of domestic discomfort, Versailles, homey. Thus, in 1726, a private kitchen was added because the newly married king wanted to study the art of pastry making with the château's master pastry chef. (He continued to hone his skills for a decade.) On the terraces on Versailles's roof, hidden from the view of those in the gardens, he had an aviary—a chicken coop, really (a giant one, but a chicken coop all the same)—constructed so that he and the Marquise de Pompadour could indulge their passion for raising chickens and other birds. He was a new kind of monarch, one who clearly relished every moment spent living informally in the comfort of what he could view as his personal space.

He was also a product of his age: the trends evident in Louis XV's Versailles were first visible in the 1690s in Paris. Before then, the definition of a dream home had nothing in common with what we now desire. By the 1720s, however, when Louis XV began to transform Versailles, many of the features people look for today—from cozy bedrooms to hardwood floors—had been invented. Fabulous homes were still a demonstration of their owners' rank, but comfort had become as important to them as it was to their monarch. A newspaper article from the mid–eighteenth century explained that after a half century of transformation, many things basic to daily life, from furniture to clothing, "no longer resembled in the slightest those our fathers used." The inspiration for so much radical change? "To make things more comfortable."

Modern comfort was invented by visionary architects and designers and by some of the most brilliant craftsmen of all time. Credit for its invention is also due to their very wealthy and demanding clients, probably the first truly socially diverse clientele for architecture: aristocrats (particularly young royals both male and female) and royal mistresses, but also immensely wealthy financiers, real estate developers, and even a famous actress or two. (Never before had a significant number of women been clients for major architectural projects. They deserve credit for many crucial aspects of today's definition of comfort.) Individuals who, in an earlier age, might never have met and would certainly never have become neighbors in the most exclusive neighborhoods in the world made high-end real estate what it still is today, something that makes people everywhere dream big dreams. They were the clients architects long for, individuals willing to bankroll new technology, to pay for what is now known as architect-designed furniture, to try out radically new room designs and floor plans.

During the final decades of the seventeenth century, wide acceptance began to be won for the idea that activities ranging from sleeping to bathing to relieving oneself should take place not in front of others, but in solitude. Architects devised new rooms, specialized rooms, each devoted to one of the newly private activities. They created the original modern bedrooms and the original modern beds. It then became the norm to sleep in private and, for some, to sleep alone. Other new rooms housed the first modern conveniences, bathtubs and flush toilets. And as soon as individuals came into contact with specialized rooms and new conveniences, as soon as they came to believe that much of their lives should take place out of the sight of others, for the first time since antiquity, comfort, cleanliness, and relaxation became widespread priorities in Western life.

The clearest proof of the way life was being revolutionized came from the fact that French became the first modern language to develop a vocabulary to designate the concept of comfort. The earliest indications that change was in the air appeared in the 1670s; they all featured the same two words, which, while not new, began to be used in a new way and to be given new prominence. The adjective *commode* and the noun *commodité* originally implied convenience and cleanliness, above all in the public realm; city services such as street cleaning were the original *commodités*. From the 1670s on, the words were increasingly used in the domestic realm, to refer to personal hygiene, for example, and to designate all that produced a sense of well-being and ease.

As soon as new models for architecture, furniture, and dress gained prominence, *commode* and *commodité* came to signify well-being in one's surroundings, the value these new models embodied. Homes, garments, chairs, and carriages all began to be evaluated in terms of their *commodité*. The words were on everyone's lips and were the buzzwords for the new age; they were testimony to the fact that the desire was becoming widespread to have one's possessions and one's immediate environment increase one's sense of ease.

As the newly comfortable architecture and furniture created in Paris spread through Europe, the vocabulary went along with them. When, for example, English architects evoked a new ideal for architecture, the quality of being convenient, they spoke of "commoditie." The French language had given the world the original modern vocabulary of comfort. The words used in English today, comfort and comfortable, derive from another French word, *réconfort*, help or assistance. "Comfort" and "comfortable" began to take on their modern meaning only in the late eighteenth century; prior to that time, they signified help or consolation, in the manner of today's "comforting." Among the first to use "comfortable" in the new way was that longtime resident of Paris and great admirer of the eighteenth-century French way of life, Thomas Jefferson.

In January 1678, the term *commodité* and the new concept of comfort went public. The French newspaper with the largest readership in Europe published a supplement, called an "extra," to broadcast a news flash: "In France today, people only want to live comfortably." The paper's editor, Jean Donneau de Visé, was describing a new trend in ladies' fashion: the women of the French court had decided that they wanted relief from the highly constricting *grand habit,* or grand outfit, de rigueur at Versailles; from then on, when they were away from court, at home or out and about in the city, they planned to adopt more casual and less confining dress. And sure enough, as that increasingly formidable style-setting machine, the French fashion industry, swept across Europe in the next decades, persuading more and more women to follow French styles, for the first time ever high fashion began to try to make women comfortable rather than help them put on the most magnificent show possible. And the trend soon snowballed.

Forty years later, the editor of a Dutch periodical reported from Paris that "comfort now seems to be the only thing that Parisian women consider when they plan their outfits." By midcentury, casual dress was well established even at that temple of magnificence and formality, Versailles. A court insider described the moment in 1752 when a prominent physician failed to recognize the wife of the heir to the throne because she was "more than dressed down."

Proclamations of the need for comfort were hardly confined to the world of women's fashion. In 1728, Charles Etienne Briseux opened his *Modern Architecture* by announcing point-blank that in France "no one" cares about "magnificence"; clients no longer beg for the most impressive façade possible or the grandest reception rooms. Now, people ask architects for one thing alone: "to enjoy all the comfort that money can buy." By defining modern architecture as an architecture that delivers comfort, Briseux laid claim to a new territory: henceforth, any project worthy of the name modern would be comfort-driven.

For the previous generation of architects, the phrase *modern architecture* had no meaning. No architect thought of being modern, only of living up to the ideals of great—that is, classical—architecture. Then, in the first half of the eighteenth century, architects broke with the model of Italian Renaissance architecture and proclaimed themselves modern. Architects and theoreticians such as Jean Courtonne in 1725, Jean Mariette in 1727, and Jacques-François Blondel in 1737 and 1752 trumpeted the news that modern French architecture had invented an "art completely unknown to the ancients," the art of making homes comfortable.

Before the desire for comfort began to be expressed, dwellings—from modest houses to grand palaces—were composed almost exclusively of a few big spaces, spaces largely both undivided and undifferentiated. People would set up a table and eat just about anywhere, for example; if they owned a tub, they generally bathed in the warmest room in the house, the kitchen. Then, in the final decades of the seventeenth century, the original modern architects took on highly visible projects for the most architecturally progressive members of the French royal family and for exceedingly wealthy individuals from the world of finance. So many innovations originated with these projects that they can be seen as the foundation of what was soon to be named modern architecture. The first formal sign of the way architecture was being redefined came in 1691, with the publication of the original edition of the treatise destined to become the bible of eighteenth-century European architecture.

Augustin Charles d'Aviler's 1691 *Lessons of Architecture* marked the original appearance in print of the distinction that most clearly set French eighteenth-century architecture apart from what had preceded it: between *appartements de parade*, public space or reception rooms, and rooms to which architecture had never before paid attention, what d'Aviler called *appartements de commodité*, the interior rooms in which individuals actually lived, or in d'Aviler's words, "that which is less grand and more used."

As soon as *commodité* officially entered the vocabulary of architecture, two extraordinary generations of French architects set about a revolution in domestic architecture, the first ever systematic redefinition of the notion of a home. The most influential architects for the first time concentrated their energy no longer on the creation of imposing façades and on a building's exterior grandeur, no longer on showstopping reception space. They focused instead on interior architecture, rooms in which people could carry out their daily lives, and on splendors that would rarely be seen by those outside the family. And splendors the new conveniences certainly were: the cost of indoor plumbing alone was initially beyond the reach of all but the most privileged. For the first time, architects put private needs first and designed homes around the demands of family life, relaxation, and friendship. For the first time, as Briseux noted, they had clients willing to spend any sum to buy comfort. And in no time at all, it became a commonplace to criticize what had previously been the most fabled monument of French architecture, Versailles, as "the least livable" and "the most uncomfortable" palace in Europe.

Renowned architects, also responsible for public monuments such as what are now Paris's Place Vendôme and Place de la Concorde, set about helping their clients feel comfortable in their homes, about making them feel, well, at home in them. And thus it was that in the course of the first half of the eighteenth century, private space gradually took over territory previously reserved for public space. "Comfort" rooms proliferated; the size of rooms decreased and their number increased as rooms became more specialized. Each of the new smaller spaces was from then on reserved exclusively for an activity such as sleeping or bathing that before had been performed in spaces that were at least semipublic.

The new values of *commodité* were simultaneously transforming related domains, first of all home furnishing. Previous ages had used furniture above all for its display value: the best pieces in the house were only for show. Indeed, there was remarkably little furniture in the rooms in which people actually lived. Then came the new comfort rooms; they seemed to cry out for new furniture, both in the sense of more pieces and in that of new kinds of furniture. Furniture design thus took on its modern identity. Designers—and there were many truly great ones; the eighteenth century is often referred to as the golden age of furniture design—began to imagine their clients' lives and to invent pieces that would fit their needs. Architects began to design furniture expressly to work with all the decorative and design elements in a given room. Never before or since have so many kinds of furniture been added to the repertory. Unlike the huge buffets and desks for which people had previously been willing to spend vast sums, the finest furniture now was often small, designed for convenience rather than ostentation.

Small tables were the darlings of the eighteenth-century furniture industry; they were intended to be moved around wherever they could prove useful. Night tables became de rigueur for a comfortable bedroom. Many variations on the small table were imagined—for coffee, for sewing, for snacks. There were tiny desks as intricately inlaid as jewels. In the new comfort-driven home economy, individuals were willing to spend a fortune for something destined to be seen only by family and close friends, as long as it was exquisite and as long as it made their lives easier.

For the first time, architects and furniture designers tackled a problem ever since considered basic: home storage. The chest of drawers, known appropriately as the *commode*, was invented in the 1690s to provide a more elegant and efficient alternative to the trunk. There was also the most elegant solution of all: built-in storage—everything from kitchen and dining room cabinets to library shelving and the original medicine cabinets.

The most significant transformation in home furnishing of all took place in the area of seating. Prior to the late seventeenth century, there was remarkably little seating in a home, and what little there was was hardly inviting. There was essentially only one kind of chair, a plain, straight-backed, sturdy model used all over the house. There were benches; there were stools; and in some countries people simply sat on the floor on large cushions.

The armchair was introduced in the seventeenth century. Early armchairs featured an overwhelmingly tall, wide, straight back and were clearly meant to be imposing rather than easeful, a sort of informal throne and the ideal seat for the age of magnificence. Then, at the exact moment when architecture and dress were moving onto new terrain in France, the grand armchair began to be reconceived. In the 1670s, the first *fauteuils de commodité*, or comfort armchairs, were delivered to Versailles. These were hinged so that their backs could recline and marked the beginning of the end for straight-backed, rigid seating.

The clearest sign that seating's function was being reimagined was still to come. During the final two decades of the seventeenth century, a double-size armchair was invented. Known as a *canapé*, this was the first piece of furniture intended to provide comfortable seating for more than one person. The original *canapés* were fairly stiff affairs, but the concept caught on, and the double armchair soon morphed into a far more radical form of seating: the sofa. The original sofas were the first furniture ever to feature upholstery on all surfaces—front, sides, and back; all surfaces were also padded. These were pieces intended to cushion every body part that touched them, the first furniture designed to facilitate relaxation.

Prior to the sofa's invention, an upholsterer was above all someone who covered the walls of rooms with fabric or tapestry (hence their French title, *tapissier*), to decorate them and also as a barrier against the cold. Upholstery fabric was used mainly for elaborate bed hangings and curtains—once again, to protect against the cold and also to provide some measure of privacy. Fabric was little used on seating, and only very occasionally did it cover a thin layer of padding. All that changed at the time of the sofa's invention. People began to want ample, fixed padding, and they wanted it literally on all forms of seating. Thus, when the flush toilet was invented in 1710, its well-cushioned seat was compared with a sofa's ease. As a result, within decades virtually all the techniques for upholstering furniture now in use had been invented, and the upholsterer began to play a vastly expanded role in the world of interior decoration.

The sofa captured the spirit of the new age and set off a design revolution. The armchair was quickly transformed from that huge, rigid icon of magnificence into a sofa for one, all curves and soft cushions. Indeed, by about 1760, every kind of seating known today had been perfected. In 1769, the first great theoretician of furniture design, André Jacob Roubo, claimed that all the creativity had been inspired by one thing alone: the desire to make people comfortable.

The leading designers of the age conceived of their work in scientific terms. Roubo repeatedly stressed that comfort was not just a matter of adding more stuffing: support, especially support for the lower back, was essential, particularly for those who spent a lot of time in a seated position. New models were thus proportioned and rounded to follow the body's contours. Designers favored models with a gentle backward slope.

In 1741, Nicolas Andry de Boisregard published the first in-depth study of human posture and invented what he called "orthopedia," the science of preventing disorders of the human skeleton; to this end, he considered proper seating essential. He explained that bad posture was a result of straight-backed seating with insufficient lumbar support and advocated the kind of slightly inclined position that most modern researchers consider least stressful for the lower back. Roubo shared his concern with making comfort ergonomically sound; he illustrated with precision the exact degree to which the back of each type of seat should be slanted so that people would never again be forced to sit bolt upright, what Roubo described as "a most stressful posture for the lower back."

"Orthopedic" now conjures up visions of something that, while good for our bodies, is decidedly unattractive. The original orthopedic seating, however, was both so gorgeous and so appealing that in the course of the eighteenth century, it challenged straight-backed, rigid seating all over Europe. Fundamental behavioral patterns were driven out along with the old chairs as new furniture designs revolutionized first the practice of sitting down and then the very way in which people moved.

Until the sofa's invention, the right to be seated was at the center of the rigid etiquette that governed the age of magnificence. Everyone knew the unwritten codes of who was allowed to sit in various circumstances, as well as the type of seating to be assigned to them. At Versailles, very few were allowed the privilege of sitting in the presence of the king or members of the royal family. And of those, most were assigned the most rudimentary and least comfortable form of seating: *pliants,* folding stools. Almost no one was awarded the coveted armchair, the seat of royalty: to be given an armchair meant that one was being received as an equal. This privilege was among the most hotly sought after by the young royals. The wife of Louis XIV's grandson, the Duchesse de Bourgogne, caused an uproar known as "the affair of the stools" when the king's son passed her over for an armchair.

And French etiquette was not the worst. The Marquise de Sévigné—the ultimate court insider, whose wonderfully vivid letters chronicle the emergence of a comfort-driven life in the last decades of the seventeenth century—recounts the clash of protocol that took place when the king and queen of England arrived at Versailles in January 1689. The queen asked Louis XIV if she should follow "French custom" or "English custom" when she met his family, for, as Sévigné explained, "in England no one has the right to sit down."

All this began to unravel with the invention of comfortable furniture. Not even four years after the original sofa had reached the Trianon, a gorgeous tiny palace on the grounds of Versailles, the king's marvelously trenchant sister-in-law, the Princesse Palatine—whose equally vivid letters record her constant rearguard struggle to prevent the proponents of comfort from changing the ways of magnificence—announced to her German cousins that etiquette was dead: "At Trianon . . . all the men now sit down in the presence of M. the Dauphin and Madame the Duchesse de Bourgogne; some of them are even stretched out full-length on sofas. . . . You can't imagine what it's like here because it no longer looks at all like a court."

Once "orthopedic" upholstered furniture had created an alternative to stiff, rigid bearing and posture, comfort fanatics at Versailles and Paris took the well-padded expanses of the original sofas as an open invitation to behavior totally unprecedented in modern Western history: casual, relaxed lounging about. Beginning in the 1680s, paintings and engravings prove that men and women alike transformed their posture and body language. They began to stretch their legs out in front of them on sofas, to tuck one leg under them as they curled up with a good book, to drape their arms nonchalantly over the sofa's rounded frame, and to sprawl out on the new seat's cushions and curves with what surely seemed wild abandon. Then, like the new architecture and the new fashions, the new art of what one commentator named "comfortable well-being" spread across Europe in the course of the eighteenth century. Bit by bit, the rigidity of what has been called "the English icon style"—seated bolt upright on stiffbacked chairs, staring straight ahead—gave way before breezily casual ease.

One of the gestures that quickly became essential to the insouciant look, that of flinging the folds of loose garments across newly expansive furniture, was greatly facilitated by the kinds of fabrics that were a major part of the visual surface against which the age of comfort unfolded. Between 1670 and 1710, the world of textiles underwent one of the most significant transformations in its entire history. Heavy, stiff, and formal fabrics went the way of magnificence and were replaced for many settings and occasions by breezily light silks, known as gauzes or mousselines, and, above all, by cottons imported all the way from India. These new fabrics swirled about the body, encouraging a more relaxed style of movement.

In seventeenth-century palaces, deep, regal hues prevailed. The new fabrics ushered in brighter, more casual color schemes: vivid tints, dramatic juxtapositions of color, and often large expanses of white. Asian cottons and silks also featured motifs new to the European scene—lots of airy florals, sprays of greenery, exotic birds and animals. Within decades, stripes and checks had become common in what d'Aviler first described as the rooms that are most used. Cotton textiles were found literally all over the new comfort rooms—on the walls, at the windows, to upholster the seating, and on the backs of those snugly ensconced in cozy, lumbar-supporting armchairs. Over time, all this proliferation—of new kinds of spaces, new types of furniture, and new uses for textiles—led to the creation of a new field: interior decoration.

The grandest interiors had of course always been decorated, even when the ornamentation was a rather minimal affair. The person responsible for the decorating scheme could be from one of a number of fields. In Versailles's Grand Gallery, now known as the Hall of Mirrors, for example, chief royal painter Charles Le Brun headed the decorating team. Interior decoration acquired a name, its modern identity, and status as an independent field only once modern architecture had come into existence. Originally, it was truly interior decoration—that is, the decoration of the most interior spaces in which private activities took place. It was also born because of the new world of choice that began at the turn of the eighteenth century.

Prior to that moment, choice in decoration was relatively minimal. You could choose between a chair or a stool; you could choose the type of wood from which it was to be made. By the early eighteenth century, you could choose from among several kinds of armchairs, and as far as the sofa was concerned, well, don't ask. So many models were quickly created that even Roubo himself admitted he had trouble keeping up with them. How much padding did you want? Where did you want it—for example, on the armrests, too? You could now also select the fabric in which your chair was to be covered (and you weren't limited to one choice alone: ingenious systems were devised that made it possible easily to switch the summer fabric for one that gave a room a new look for winter).

If you used fabric on your walls, should it match that on the furniture? Did you want curtains on your windows or not? (Certain designers felt that this made for *un très bel effet*, a very striking look.) And did you want the new, large-paned windows? Did you want hardwood floors instead of tiled—and if so, should the parquet be in the newly fashionable "Versailles" design? With so many options suddenly available and with the rapid spread through society of the concept of home decoration, it was inevitable that professionals would step in to take charge.

Through it all, dress, the area in which the desire for comfort had first appeared, followed suit. Beginning in the 1670s, a series of radically new styles based on a kimono-cut took first Paris and then Versailles by storm. They were voluminous, requiring many yards of fabric, so the sofa's expanses must have seemed tailor-made to show off all that textile. They were also loosely fitted, which meant that the version for women did not require the kind of absolutely rigid undergarments that were the necessary underpinning of court dress. Women wearing dressing gowns were thus literally free to stretch out and lounge about.

When the kimono-cut was introduced, it was known as a *robe de chambre*, a dressing gown. Men fell in love with its informality and comfort every bit as much as women did. They often paired their kimonolike gowns with soft velvet caps, sometimes topped with a tassel to make them more exotic still. In 1681, a "multi-colored" (probably a mix of red, blue, and violet) floral print dressing gown in Indian cotton ("padded" so that it would be warm enough for winter) was delivered to Versailles. The Sun King, the most majesty-obsessed man in the world, had fallen for comfort's charms.

Dressing gowns were naturals for the intimate spaces that were the hallmark of modern architecture, but soon their proponents were too pleased with their relaxed fit to want to dress differently when they went out. February 1699 in particular marked a triumph for proponents of comfort and informality: a band of young royals, led by the Duchesse de Bourgogne, wife of the king's grandson, arrived at a ball at Versailles dressed in Indian cotton *robes de chambre*. The Princesse Palatine, ever ready with a one-liner at any failure to uphold the standards of magnificence, quipped that, thus attired, people "looked as if they were ready for bed." Her remark gives a good sense of the generational conflict provoked by comfort's arrival on the scene. It's hard to imagine how someone used to the traditional ways—having spent her life always in the public eye, dressed as formally as possible, sitting in the proper manner on stiff chairs—must have felt at the sight of those being groomed for the roles of king and queen of France cavorting about in casual garments of flowered cotton, stretching out on well-rounded and padded seating that hadn't even existed a few years earlier.

That sense of culture shock would have been even more profound because all the transformations I have been describing took place not only quickly, but virtually simultaneously. It's impossible to say, for example, if the use of new fabrics or new furniture was the primary influence on the unprecedented body language of the age of comfort—or even if the desire for greater freedom of movement might not have been the impetus behind the design revolutions that took place in various fields. The new school of architecture with its emphasis on space with controlled access may have been the spark that set it all off. Developments in these different domains are so thoroughly intertwined that the age of comfort seems to have started in one great outpouring of creative synergy.

The new way of life was founded on a major redefinition of the notion of luxury. In the age of magnificence, luxury meant spending almost for the sake of spending, to create about one's person and one's home an aura of imposing splendor that positively cried out one's rank to the outside world. By the mid-eighteenth century, that great monument both to Enlightenment philosophy and to contemporary accomplishments in sciences, arts, and crafts, the *Encyclopédie*, defined luxury in terms unthinkable a century before—"the use that one makes of one's wealth to make life more enjoyable"—and declared: "All men in all societies understand luxury. Primitive men own hammocks bought with the skins of wild animals; Europeans have their sofas." Luxury was thus seen no longer as spending purely for show, but as spending to make daily life more pleasurable and more easeful. Comfort had become the greatest luxury.

The innovative designs and technologies that made life more pleasurable were expensive, often hugely so. At first, they were thus beyond the reach of all but the wealthiest individuals. Over time, their cost came down; cheaper models were also created, thereby making it possible for the less opulent to adopt many of the new luxury's inventions. In 1751, for example, Françoise de Graffigny, another prolific letter writer quick to spot every change in the contemporary design world, moved into her dream home in Paris. Though Graffigny was by no means of low birth, a disastrous early marriage to a spendthrift had left her the equivalent of a modern working woman; she became a writer to support herself. By 1751, she was reasonably successful—by no means well-to-do, but well able to make ends meet. Her new flat proves that by the middle of the eighteenth century, a single woman of modest means had standards inconceivable only

decades before. Graffigny had, for example, a bedroom with an adjoining
(*en suite*) toilet room, a dressing room "positively full of" storage space whose
"convenience" she marveled over, and a writing room or boudoir. She had a
good deal of comfortable seating, including two "delightful" sofas, used patterns borrowed from Asian textiles to cover her walls, and "of course" had
parquet flooring.

We'll never know how far or how quickly the new values might have spread.
By the time of Louis XV's death in 1774, France was no longer the exclusive
tastemaker for Europe, as it had been at the start of his reign. France's power in
the world of design and style had been on the wane since the period, in the late
1750s and early 1760s, of its loss of political and economic influence as a result
of the Seven Years' War, which ended France's position as a major colonial
power in the Americas and established England as the dominant colonial power
in the world. When the French Revolution destroyed many of comfort's monuments great and small, as well as infrastructures on which Parisians had relied
for the functioning of their conveniences, it closed the door on France's absolute dominance in the history of comfort. The finest residences that were
preserved usually became public monuments—the National Archives, for example. In the process, their small private rooms and their luxurious amenities
were gutted and turned into public space.

Certain aspects of the comfort-driven life simply disappeared. Nineteenth-
century women's clothing, for example, may well have been more straitlaced
than seventeenth-century court dress; upholstery became overstuffed rather
than beautifully orthopedic. And when everyday conveniences such as the
flush toilet were reimagined in nineteenth-century England, they were spartan
and purely functional, and the standards of craftsmanship and design evident
in every detail of their eighteenth-century French precursors had disappeared.
The notion of making these everyday fixtures truly comfortable rather than
merely utilitarian reemerged only in the final decades of the twentieth century,
when there was, for the first time since the eighteenth century, a client base
large enough to make their production viable.

In the long run, however, rather than the sofas or the sportswear or the bathtubs then created, it is the life changes brought about as a result of the age of
comfort that remain as its legacy. There is, to begin with, the very concept of
a private life. That phrase acquired its modern meaning by the 1730s. In 1769,
a French historian, Le Grand d'Aussy, outlined the first ever *History of Private
Life*, conceived as the history of architecture, furniture, dress, and leisure activities, which together, he claimed, offer an explanation of a country's national

character—in other words, we are the way we are because of the homes we live in, the way we dress, and the manner in which we relax.

The long-term effects of the shift in focus from public to private life can also be viewed in a less positive light—think of today's increasingly obsessive preoccupation with personal life and with absolutely everything that goes on in space perceived to be intimate. Some have argued that the beginning of private architecture was also the beginning of the end for the public realm and the effective use of the public space and formal settings in which public life unfolds.

In the short run, however, it is plain that individuals found the new focus exhilarating. The eighteenth century witnessed an incredible flowering of personal literature of every kind. Individuals clearly had new tiny writing desks set up in every interior room so that they could set pen to paper whenever and wherever inspiration struck. There were most obviously personal letters—the eighteenth century is the golden age of personal correspondence—and also first-person novels, memoirs, even the original autobiographies.

Many of the memoirs then published recount what was evidently still a novel experience, that of getting to know the private individual behind the public persona. The most interesting such accounts concern the man at the center of public life in France, Louis XV. All were written by individuals with important functions at court; all agree that had the new private rooms not existed at Versailles, no one would ever have been able to see beyond his well-maintained façade. The king's private rooms were known as his "interior suite" (*appartement intérieur*). Every anecdote concerning the private man—his kindness, what made him laugh, what made him sad—contains a key phrase: *dans l'intérieur*, meaning that it was only in his interior suite or in private that the king revealed himself.

In his particularly telling memoirs, Versailles insider Comte Dufort de Cheverny often plays on the double meaning of "interior"—the inside of a building and what is inside a person, one's inner life. He suggests that those interior rooms allowed the king's interior life to flourish, that because of them, he developed what we now refer to with a word not yet available to Dufort de Cheverny, as a personality. That word was first used in its modern meaning only in 1776, in the supplement to the *Encyclopédie*. Until then, people turned instead to a variety of terms, many of which—such as *déshabillé*, or casual dress— echo suggestions by Dufort de Cheverny and Le Grand d'Aussy that because of the new architecture, furniture, and dress, during the age of comfort individuals had been able both to explore their interiors and to know themselves as never before, and also to make known to others the combination of character traits and qualities that made them individuals.

At the turn of the eighteenth century in France, a new kind of image emerged when artists portrayed individuals enjoying their homes, relaxed and at ease, truly with the look of comfort. It was certainly a look unlike anything ever seen before. In the 1720s and 1730s, Jean-François de Troy in particular painted canvases that portray both the innovations of the age of comfort and the way life had changed in response to them. None of them represents the zeitgeist of the age of comfort more successfully than the painting known as *The Declaration of Love* (see color plates).

The woman's little smile and the nonchalant tilt of her arm and hand suggest someone well pleased with herself, sure that she's living the good life. Her well-being, the painting indicates, is produced first of all by her clothing: her typically French outfit falls softly about her in loose, casual folds. Her body is neither bound in nor confined. The gown's neckline, so artfully undone that its negligence seems almost accidental, calls attention to the absence of rigid undergarments. The glowing, gleaming expanses of fabric lend elegance and opulence to the interior; they also enhance the impression of comfort. There's nothing harsh or stiff, just the smoothest velvet, the most gossamer silk, and, on that fat pillow under the woman's nicely rounded arm, the softest cotton. These two are dressed for lounging about.

Furniture is also essential to their state of ease. It's hard to imagine a piece of furniture curvier or vaster than the sofa on which they are relaxing. It's so nicely padded that the woman can take advantage of the freedom of movement her clothing makes possible and positively luxuriate on it, ensconced in its plushness. She reclines back with her legs stretched out in front of her; he's also on the diagonal, gently leaning in toward her. The sofa envelops them with its enormous back: it's as if a piece of furniture had given them the sense of being tucked away in a tiny world unto itself.

We also have glimpses of the room beyond their little sofa world. It's a small space, intimate architecture that shelters and favors their closeness. And it's also exquisitely decorated. The tip of the woman's shoe peeks out fetchingly from underneath her dress, as though to point out the beautifully patterned parquet flooring. The swirling lines of the sofa's intricate carving echo those of both the frame of the painting hung above it and the room's paneling. Such decorating synergy is obvious in the interplay of textiles as well. The velvet of the man's coat almost merges into that of the curtain; the woman's dress is color-coordinated with the cushion; the pattern of its silk is in harmony with those on the sofa and on the wall above. We are left with an image of individuals literally at one with their interior.

In contrast, two decades after de Troy painted his 1725 vision of human inti-

macy enhanced by a well-designed interior, Arthur Devis created a diametri-
cally opposed view of the interaction between a couple and their home, one
that shows that in 1747, England had not embraced comfort (see color plates).
This space is much larger than the cozy room that favored intimacy, but that's
only part of the problem. Despite the presence of fine fabrics and expensive
objects, the room appears stark and curiously underfurnished. And the relation
between the two people in it also seems stark: it's as if they were not a couple,
but two distinct individuals who simply happened to be in the same space—
intimacy seems out of the question.

Devis's painting was in fact the portrait of newlyweds, Mr. and Mrs. Richard
Bull, in their new, recently decorated home. The look cultivated by the Bulls
reflects in a number of ways the growing influence in 1740s England of just the
artfully free and easy French style celebrated in *The Declaration of Love*. Note,
for example, the frames on the two paintings in the room, all whimsical, asymmetrical curls; those swirling shapes show how the French rococo, soon to be
baptized by Thomas Chippendale "the modern taste," a phrase borrowed from
the French, was beginning to invade England. The large, room-brightening
windows visible through the doorway were also a French invention. Even the
idea for Richard Bull's pose—in profile, gazing at his wife, with his legs crossed
at the knee, and holding a book nonchalantly—was, it seems, copied from a
French artist.

The English couple, however, certainly didn't get the French look right. Both
the feel of the Bull interior and the feel of the Bulls in their interior are worlds
apart from an authentic French experience. They look ill at ease in their surroundings, as detached from the room and the objects around them as from
each other. It's not that they aren't elegantly dressed, not that they don't have
beautiful things, not that their possessions haven't been arranged with care. It's
just that nothing seems in synch.

Their possessions seem intended purely for display, to impress others rather
than to put their owners at ease. Mrs. Bull's thoroughly English dress, with its
close-fitting, tightly boned bodice, for example, was designed to enforce the
rigid posture that was considered a proof of social status. She was bound in,
forced to sit bolt upright. Nor would the seating the couple had chosen have
encouraged anyone to lounge. For all their elegant legs and silk damask upholstery, the straight-backed chairs are stiff and unyielding. The Bulls obviously
wanted nothing to do with the sofa's expansive, well-cushioned surfaces and
the behavior such furniture made possible, behavior that the English condemned
as "lolling about."

Then there is the matter of the room's décor, which, while carefully contrived, is hardly harmonious. The wall paneling, for example, has straight lines and square corners and therefore fights rather than complements the curving legs on the chairs and table and the swirls of the frames. The textile patterns—in their clothing, the upholstery, the rug—do not work in concert. The rigid arrangement of decorative objects—the Oriental porcelain on the mantel, the busts on brackets on either side of it—does nothing to soften or personalize the space. And the rather spartan plank flooring contributes to the room's rigidity. In short, the components in Devis's rendering of an English interior scene do not add up to an ensemble. Small wonder that the man and the woman in it seem no more meant for each other than, say, the wall paneling and the picture frames. The painting suggests that stark and imposingly formal décor, architecture designed for show rather than for comfort, stiff seats, and equally stiff dress combine to create an atmosphere in which the home owners cannot sit comfortably, much less share intimacy of any kind.

De Troy's canvas can also be seen as testimony to the ways in which comfortably appointed private space was facilitating the development of an interior life. The drapery, the swirling carving, and the soft, seductive tints—indeed, all the components of the room's interior decoration—together produce an ensemble so unified that we understand why this couple appears exceedingly content: they are as much in love with their surroundings as with each other. De Troy's painting seems a paean to the potential for intimacy in a home designed and decorated with comfort as well as elegance in mind. In fact, the cozy seductiveness of this interior scene could even be said to suggest that the pair is able to fall in love with each other precisely because architecture, furniture, clothing, textiles, and interior decoration have put them so fully at ease.

In 1723, a new expression entered the French language: *tomber amoureux*, to fall in love. It clearly won immediate acceptance, for it was already recorded in a dictionary in 1726. It was followed in short order by related expressions such as *coup de foudre*, literally a lightning bolt, French for love at first sight. People had of course fallen in love before de Troy's couple declared their feelings while demonstrating how to take advantage of one of the original sofas. This couple, however, belonged to the first generation able to speak about the heady experience of "falling" in love. (The original dictionary entry compared it to an attack of "apoplexy.")

Did the new interior architecture and interior decoration really promote a newly intense interior life? Numerous contemporary writers and artists suggested, as de Troy's painting does, that the French language needed a new vocabulary for love precisely because this was the case. In France in 1725, a new concept, comfort, was working its magic. A man and a woman make contact;

they gaze into each other's eyes; he's taken her hand—in part, at least, thanks to the sheen of the interior world around them.

What follows is the story of how each of the domains—from architecture to interior decoration, from fine furniture to comfortable high fashion—that made possible the posture and the atmosphere depicted in de Troy's painting developed at exactly the same moment and created the age of comfort.

CHAPTER ONE

A Short History of Modern Comfort

THE INVENTION OF modern comfort was a vast, and vastly costly, enter-prise, one that transformed first the look of royal residences and then the cityscape of Paris, and did so, furthermore, in fast-forward mode, so rapidly that contemporaries kept repeating that it was all happening as if by magic.

At the origin of such spectacular change, however, we find motivations that still keep the world of high-end real estate turning: children convinced their parents and grandparents to update the family home by adding modern conve-niences; wives and lovers and daughters-in-law persuaded wealthy, powerful men to build new homes that were not mere status symbols, but true artistic statements. And the greed—land grabs, real estate speculation, fortunes made overnight based on insider-trading information—all that now seems business as usual.

Cherchez la femme, as the saying goes. Rarely has this been so true. The age of comfort was bookended by the taste and in particular the taste for comfort of two exceptionally influential royal mistresses—the Marquise de Montespan and the Marquise de Pompadour—women who shared a passion for architec-ture, interior decoration, and fashion and a vision of how to integrate them to create a total look. The new age began with the woman who convinced Louis XIV, a magnificence-obsessed man if ever there was one, to consider the advan-tages of another way of life.

Françoise Athénaïs de Rochechouart, Marquise de Montespan, was, like most royal mistresses, stunningly beautiful. Her contemporaries went on endlessly about her fabulous figure, her hair, her perfect and perfectly white teeth (not at all a given in the seventeenth century). Like the other women who played a long-term role in the Sun King's life, she was no child, twenty-six when she became involved with the twenty-nine-year-old monarch in 1667, nearly forty when their relationship ended in 1680, fifty (and apparently still able to turn heads) when she finally left the court in 1691. Also true to pattern, she spent money with a vengeance.

In other ways, however, the marquise charted new territory. Most French kings had had mistresses, all of whom had been objects of fascination at court. Only a handful of royal mistresses, however, had had both the staying power and the force of character necessary to exercise real influence. Montespan was among the most exceptional of this small group—in the nearly twenty-five years she spent at court, she never outranked but easily eclipsed the rather timid and dowdy Spanish-born queen. Montespan gave the king a true second family and thus a parallel life, one that initially unfolded largely outside the public eye. In addition, in areas from fashion to architecture to interior decoration, the Marquise de Montespan invented a new category: the royal mistress as tastemaker.

Everyone immediately recognized Louis XIV as a king who, in the words of the Duc de Saint-Simon—whose voluminous memoirs of life at the Sun King's court are positively crammed with juicy detail—just "loved to build." (Saint-Simon also said of him that "he had a compass built into his brain" and that he drove architects crazy until their results were a perfect match with what his inner compass told him.) Like his great-grandson Louis XV after him, Louis XIV built best when he worked in tandem with a woman who fully shared his passion. His partnership with Montespan began with the first construction completed on the grounds at Versailles, the Porcelain Trianon.

At first, Montespan was forced to share the king with her precursor, Louise-Françoise de La Baume, Duchesse de La Vallière. That arrangement ended in the winter of 1670, shortly after the birth of Montespan's first son. (The king already had four legitimate offspring at this point; the queen gave birth to her last child in 1672.) The Trianon, built expressly for Montespan, was seen as a celebration of her new status. Its construction was completed so quickly that contemporaries called it a fairy-tale palace. By the time the spring blooms in its celebrated gardens were making their first show, the Duchesse de La Vallière had entered a convent in Paris and Montespan had the king to herself.

Since the king insisted that Montespan be consulted about everything, contemporaries immediately saw the exquisite tiny love nest as the beginning of a beautiful design partnership. At Trianon, she succeeded in persuading the man who set the gold standard for the décor of pomp and splendor that less could be more—plain white ceilings, for instance, rather than elaborate frescoes and stuccowork. Such choices explain why the Trianon can be called the origin of modern taste in interior decoration.

In less than a decade, the marquise bore the king eight children, four of whom survived. In 1673, she convinced Louis XIV to do the unthinkable and have the first two of them declared legitimate. (They could not inherit the throne, but they could, and did, marry into the greatest French families.) She then decided that she needed quarters that reflected their new status, so work began on the Château de Clagny.

Montespan personally presided over the construction site, giving orders to some twelve hundred workers. This was the kind of power a royal mistress, and indeed women in general, rarely possessed. The Marquise de Sévigné quipped that it was like watching "Dido building Carthage." Because it seemed to spring up overnight, contemporaries saw Clagny as an "enchanted," "magical" palace. Architects soon pronounced it a new beginning for architecture, as well as the first dwelling in which comfort had not been sacrificed on the altar of magnificence and the building in which the creation of rooms for everyday life became "a new art form." They also gave credit for these innovations to Montespan; they explained that earlier residences by Jules Hardouin Mansart, Clagny's architect, were remarkable only for their "imposing grandeur" and were "completely lacking in comfort," "almost uninhabitable," mere "beautiful prisons."

Clagny's new *commodités* had many repercussions, to begin with, on the king's way of life. The Sun King developed there his particular brand of regal relaxation. He invited guests for informal meals, elegant little snacks, during which—oh, scandal!—he made up the guest list based on personal preference rather than rank and sat down at table with his guests without elaborate ceremony. All of this would have been unthinkable in a traditional palace setting.

Montespan repeatedly had herself portrayed in a pose that illustrates perfectly the informality she brought to the king's life. In every version, she is stretched out, usually on a daybed, the kind of furniture she helped make fashionable. In this one, she shows off her fashionably negligent outfit, her fashionably plush seating, and, in the background, one of Clagny's most fabled features, its gallery or enclosed walkway. She is surrounded by pliant cushions and soft fabrics. Everything is elegant; everything is comfortable and relaxed.

Louis XIV was so taken with Clagny's gallery that he absolutely had to have an even better one: thus it was that Versailles's Grand Gallery, now known as the Hall of Mirrors, came to be. He was also obviously taken with Clagny's private interior rooms. In 1678, as part of the remodeling necessary to build the Hall of Mirrors, he ordered Mansart, the architect for Trianon and Clagny, to create for him what was called a *petit appartement du roi*, a small apartment

This is one of the numerous portraits of the Marquise de Montespan in which she shows off the kind of casual behavior that new kinds of furniture were making possible, behavior that her contemporaries considered scandalous. For this portrait, she poses in front of the Château de Clagny, one of the places where the casual style was invented.

or suite of rooms. The term *small suite* was among those soon used to designate a home's private living quarters. The 1678 decree thus marked an early step on the road to architectural intimacy. That step was taken at a most opportune moment.

In August 1678, the Treaty of Nijmegen was signed, putting an end to the Franco-Dutch war that had exhausted Europe for six years. The decade that followed was a time of great financial prosperity for France, and a huge share of the wealth then spread around was spent on architecture and the decorative arts. This was, to begin with, the most important decade in the construction of the apex of French magnificence, Versailles. The same decade, however, also witnessed the creation of modern casual dress, the invention of the sofa, and the moment when cotton textiles first became a standard option in clothing and decoration. The foundations for the age of comfort were thus being laid even as the age of magnificence was in full flower. Rarely has the contrast between two ways of life been so evident. And then, five years after that *petit appartement* was added to Versailles, interior architecture began to play a major new role in the Sun King's life.

On July 30, 1683, the queen of France died. In record time, probably as early as the following September, the king entered into a second marriage that had to remain secret since the bride was hardly of appropriate rank, with the Marquise de Montespan's successor, Françoise d'Aubigné, Marquise de Maintenon. (It was as if romantic love had invaded Versailles.) Now, Maintenon's arrival at court is an amazing tale: royal children always had an official governess; Montespan and Maintenon were old friends; Montespan had Maintenon appointed governess to the king's legitimated children. Thus it was that in the mid-1670s, Montespan was supervising the construction of Clagny while Maintenon was supervising the education of her children. This is how she came to know the king and his legitimate offspring as well. All this produced in the end an extended family so complicated that it scandalized court observers and had repercussions that were, well, interesting. For example, after Maintenon had replaced Montespan in the king's affections, she retained a soft spot for the children she had raised, and they openly returned her affection—all the while apparently harboring hopes that in the event of Maintenon's death (she was three years older than the king), their mother might regain her royal lover's affections.

The king's second marriage was played out, Charles and Camilla–like, mostly on the margins of the court: since Maintenon could not play the queen's role at official functions, Louis XIV took to spending more time in their smaller rooms. This architectural intimacy started a chain reaction in the course of which basic daily activities were modified. The first piece of furniture ordered specifically for Maintenon was delivered within months of their marriage: one of the first sofas ever made, it featured a particularly high back, to guarantee that she be seated in all the latest comfort.

And then came Marly, Versailles's alter ego, the place where members of the royal family went to get away from it all, in times of mourning and whenever they needed to close ranks against the outside world. The château was planned before Maintenon had replaced Montespan. Marly began to be furnished and to be used as the place where the entire extended family could be together, however, only after the queen's death.

In Marly's décor, a casualness unimaginable at Versailles became the order of the day. Cotton was massively used as an upholstery fabric—in 1686 alone, six bedrooms were decorated entirely in bright, Indian cotton prints. And the color scheme! The overall effect was light and soft—there was lots of white, and a new tint was used everywhere: *aurore*, dawn, described as a glowing shade of yellow, carefully nuanced in order to suggest the gradations of the sky at dawn. It was very much, in other words, the light and breezy Montespan look. The consequences of such interior décor were all too predictable, especially for anyone familiar with Montespan's portraits. The king's sister-in-law was soon complaining that "at Marly protocol and etiquette were completely done away with. . . . In the salon, anyone, even the lowliest officer, was . . . stretched out full-length on sofas. The very sight of it all disgusted me."

In the late 1680s, Louis XIV was surrounded by an ever expanding group of young royals, two generations of them, most of whom had very modern ideas about the home and family life; he sought to create environments in which they could feel at home. He rejected, for example, Mansart's proposed redecoration of the Château de la Ménagerie because he found the style "too serious": "Make it all fresher," he commanded. "Bring me new sketches. . . . I want to see youthfulness apparent everywhere." Among the elements included in the young look the Sun King imposed at the Ménagerie were still another color scheme that imitated Montespan's style, breezy white cotton curtains, lots of comfortable seating. Many of the young royals subsequently re-created the same "youthful" style in their own residences.

There was, to begin with, the heir to the throne, the dauphin, known to all simply as Monseigneur, Your Highness. He was, by all accounts, an intensely guarded individual. Saint-Simon claimed that he had managed the impossible: "Even though he stood on the edge of the throne, he always maintained a private life," so much so that "the only things known about him are details." An impressive number of the most telling details we do know relate to the dauphin's role as tastemaker; time and again, he made cutting-edge design choices. It's clear, for instance, that he played the crucial role in the sofa's invention: every model that marked a decisive leap forward was created for him. He was also the first to understand the sofa's potential to center a room. In 1685, just as the new seating was coming into existence, he bought a seven-foot-long model, with four armchairs, all upholstered in blue velvet to match—the first modern living room furniture.

Monseigneur was so fixated on his privacy that he had furniture design moved forward in another key way. In 1686, he commissioned from the greatest furniture designer of the age, André Charles Boulle, a coffer designed so that its secret drawers with a complex locking mechanism would face the wall, thereby guaranteeing that they could remain truly secret. This early example of storage furniture with locking secret compartments was the ideal design for the private man and the age that invented the notion of truly private space.

Louis XIV loved to build; his son loved to furnish and to decorate. Monseigneur worked with the finest designers, and his favorite was the best of them all, Jean Bérain, the man whom many see as the original modern interior designer. The dauphin was constantly having his living quarters updated in the latest style. His wife, Marie-Anne de Bavière, was the perfect match for a prince who preferred to be offstage. The Marquise de Sévigné described her with phrases not often applied to those who breathed the rarefied air of the French court: "She was a real person," completely "natural." She may, in fact, have been a bit too natural at times: on one occasion, "the Sun King's majesty was nearly shaken," when during a court ceremony the dauphine couldn't keep herself from giggling at something she found particularly "ridiculous." But the king was so fond of her that he just laughed it off afterward. It was undoubtedly much easier to forgive her giggles when she became, in quick succession, the mother of three sons.

In 1687, the private prince and the natural princess commissioned a portrait by Pierre Mignard to commemorate their unusual way of life. Contemporary royal group portraits display dynasties, all the generations gathered together to convey to the world an impression of political stability. They chose instead a family scene, what we would call a nuclear family gathered together, the parents surrounded by their three boys. It's all very cozy: the princess is casually dressed and sitting on a recent-model small sofa; the prince is scratching the back of a pet dog, who's trying to jump into his lap. The scene now also seems tinged with sadness: three years later, the dauphine was dead.

Louis XIV's insistence on "gaiety" in interior decoration was surely in part an attempt to keep her style alive, first for her orphaned sons and later for their brides, in particular Marie-Adélaïde de Savoie, who in 1697 married his eldest grandson, the fifteen-year-old Duc de Bourgogne, when she was only twelve. Contemporary commentators, and Saint-Simon in particular, were fascinated by the pranks and escapades of an incredible apparition in their midst, a girl so breezy that she could be taken for a modern adolescent. They describe her "jumping" on the Sun King's lap, "throwing" her arms about his neck, "pitching snowballs" at a dragon lady of the court while she was sleeping, and even enlisting her husband (second in line to the throne, mind you) to help her set off firecrackers along this lady's path through the gardens at Versailles. And through it all, everyone absolutely adored her. The king and Maintenon were "charmed" by her, "made a doll of her": "She became the very heart and soul of the court."

The behavior that the dauphine and her son's wife got away with while they were being groomed to become queen of the most powerful nation in Europe took place just when architecture was learning to put intimate space front and center and when comfortable seating was being invented. The fact that the royal family welcomed their behavior rather than frowning upon it proves that the clientele most likely to bankroll the age of comfort was ready to exchange pomp for informality. Things might have changed a good deal sooner had Louis XIV's fabled luck not suddenly run out.

From 1688 to 1697, the monarch embroiled his nation in the ruinously costly decade of military conflict known as the War of the Augsburg League. Then, in the mid-1690s, climate change added to the country's misery: several of the harshest winters in modern memory brought on widespread famine. For the first time, the Sun King was forced to retrench: he closed, for example, the Royal Furniture-Making Manufactory, until then a center for innovative design.

The worst of times always prove highly profitable to some. In the 1690s, military contractors and financiers made fortunes off the war. The newly wealthy spent their riches on fabulous homes and in the process transformed the way the business of architecture was carried out. Until the turn of the eighteenth century, Versailles had been the source of all good taste. Suddenly, questions such as who sets the style or who dictates taste, questions that previously had had only one possible answer—the court and the nobility—could be answered in a new way: anyone with the means to finance a costly project could now become a tastemaker. For the next four decades, the world of style and design was up for grabs. Financiers, actresses, upstarts, wealthy foreigners, all had a chance to set the tone.

This crucial shift in influence was encouraged by urban development that gave the newly wealthy room to show off. In 1697, the Treaty of Ryswick issued in a brief period of peace. During that window, what were destined to be the last great state-sponsored building projects in Paris for decades were completed. In all cases, work had been initiated long before but had been suspended during the financial crisis. Three projects put the talent pool created at Versailles to use in an urban setting and proved crucial to the transformation of Paris into a social melting pot. The synchronization across the fields of architecture, design, and decoration that then took place gave the city a chance to play a role for which time and again it has proved ideally suited: center for avant-garde artistic developments, cultural capital of the Western world.

Today's Place Vendôme—first the Place de Nos Conquêtes, then the Place Louis-le-Grand and the Place de Vendôme—was conceived as Paris's grandest monument to the Sun King. At the war's end, the king wanted to pave over the entire thing but was persuaded to adopt a compromise solution. The result, unveiled in 1699, was a rectangular space, with an imposing equestrian statue in the middle and on three sides glorious façades, but with no homes behind them. It was a gigantic stage set, all show and no substance. Even those grand façades were soon torn down, when it was determined that dwellings up to the architectural standards then being developed could never be made to fit their proportions, more suited to outmoded residential norms.

In time, all ended well. The Crown gave the Place to the city of Paris, which turned it over to a private investment consortium to be headed up by the Place's architect, Mansart. The façades went up again; this time, homes were even built behind them. The second time around, however, the now grand octagonal Place was a monument to the ways in which times were changing in Paris. There was, to begin with, the decidedly modern architecture behind the new façades: a number of homes, notably those designed by Pierre Bullet, quickly became famous for layouts that showcased intimate spaces. (Earlier in the 1690s, Bullet had developed some of the amenities that could justify the existence of new rooms: indoor plumbing and an early flush toilet.)

And then there were its residents. Prior to this, Paris had seen the occasional very wealthy individual of non-noble birth acquire a home literally fit for a king. The square, however, was a turning point so visible that no one could have missed the signal it sent: the most luxurious avant-garde dwellings then known were occupied largely by financiers and investment bankers. For the first time in modern memory, private enterprise was funding cutting-edge architectural projects. Living in number 17, for example, was Antoine Crozat, a financier who had risen from very modest origins to become perhaps the wealthiest man in France, known simply as "Crozat the rich."

Never before had such a visible site been predominantly and ostentatiously in the hands of very, very new wealth. Never before had the new financial elite lived cheek by jowl and in an identical fashion with the first families of the land. The Place turned the French way of life on end, and once it did, things began to happen with lightning speed. In no time at all, the bluest blood in the kingdom was caught up in the melting-pot ambiance created by the Place.

Henri de La Tour d'Auvergne, Comte d'Evreux, like many young men of the day, had expensive tastes and had tired the patience of his creditors. Desperate times call for desperate measures: in the words of the Duc de Saint-Simon, who saw the tale as the beginning of the end for his kind, the count "jumped right into misalliance and, with the king's help, made a princess of the daughter of a former shop clerk, Crozat." There had naturally been misalliances before, but this was the misalliance of the century.

On April 13, 1707, the couple was married from the Crozat mansion at number 17, Place Vendôme; the count made his new father-in-law pay through the nose for the glow of his aristocratic name. The cash-strapped groom received the astronomical sum of one hundred thousand livres *in cash* to pay off his debts. (All Paris joked that the count's mother nicknamed her daughter-in-law "my little bar of gold.") The bride got another fortune in cash for pocket money; Crozat further agreed to pick up the tab for running the newlyweds' household for six years—and even to build their home for them. The count, but of course, got to approve the layout and to furnish it "in a manner befitting his dignity." Later that year, the newlyweds moved into number 19, right next door to Papa, a grand mansion also designed by Bullet. (The Crozat mansion is now part of a modern palace, the Ritz Hotel; the count's home belongs to a bank.) The girl got her prince, but the marriage was no fairy tale: the count treated his bride miserably, chased every skirt in town, and, soon after he had made a killing on the stock market, obtained a legal separation and returned the "little bar of gold" to live with her father.

The Place was inaugurated on the eve of a truly disastrous period for France: from 1701 to 1714, the most ruinous of Louis XIV's campaigns, the War of the Spanish Succession, so exhausted the nation's already depleted resources that Louis XIV was forced to give up what one court insider termed "his last remaining pleasure"—in other words, he could no longer afford even to redecorate existing construction. In the course of the particularly dire year 1708, the king actually tried to back out of the war he had initiated. (By 1709, starving crowds of Parisians were breaking into bakeries to grab every loaf in sight.) Until the spring of 1711, even if international relations were bleak, the future of the monarchy at least seemed rock-solid. Few kings can ever have felt more serene on that score than the Sun King, with three generations of heirs to the throne all present at Versailles.

And then, a true annus horribilis struck. On April 14, 1711, at age fifty, the dauphin died of smallpox. Less than a year later, on February 18, 1712, his thirty-year-old son, the Duc de Bourgogne, died of some form of measles, the disease that only a few days earlier had carried off the light of all their lives, the beloved Duchesse de Bourgogne. When she died, in Saint-Simon's words, "its soul left the court": "No princess has ever been so deeply mourned." And the mourning was not over yet. Less than a month after his father, on March 8, 1712, their eldest son, the Duc de Bretagne, was a victim of the same disease.

In the space of not quite eleven months, France had lost three heirs. The prince next in line, the Duc d'Anjou, was barely two. He had also contracted the disease, but his governess had refused to hand him over to the doctors she believed had killed the rest of his family with excessive bleeding and purges. The child survived and went on to live a long life as Louis XV. The new heir to the throne was the great-grandson of a builder, the grandson of a prince with a passion for interior decoration, and the son of a woman so breezily casual that she once burst into a ball at Versailles in an Indian cotton dressing gown. In time, he was to prove himself a more than worthy heir to all three when he combined their passions to bring the French court back to life. At first, however, a pall fell over Versailles, and its inhabitants began to escape to the more comfortable and casual ways of the city where style and design were being revolutionized.

In the early eighteenth century, modern architecture was beginning to spread its wings in Paris, mainly on or near the Place Vendôme. A brand-new area, called the Faubourg Saint-Honoré, opened up in its immediate vicinity. It became known as the financial district since most of the great homes in it were built by members of the new financial elite such as Antoine Crozat's younger brother, who began construction on one of the capital's most lavish pleasure domes in 1704, the year he became treasurer of France. It's hard to imagine what such ostentatious excess must have looked like as war was bleeding the country dry.

Dubbed "the poor Crozat," since he was less wealthy than Antoine, Pierre Crozat was nonetheless a fabulously rich financier, financial adviser, and adviser to the Crown. This self-made man owned a huge chunk of land in the center of the new financial district that today stretches over *many* city blocks—his gardens alone occupied eight acres. The home he had built on it to house one of the great contemporary art collections—Crozat amassed over nineteen thousand drawings; his more than four hundred paintings were later purchased by Catherine the Great, with Denis Diderot acting as her Parisian agent—was a bucolic haven, a truly suburban urban dwelling. Almost all its rooms had spectacular garden views; the most celebrated spaces, the dining room and the gallery (the setting for famous monthly concerts immortalized by artist Nicolas Lancret), gave the impression of floating in greenery. Crozat never married. He had one ruling passion: art. He collected old masters (Rembrandt, Rubens, van Dyck—he had, for example, two Raphaels in his study), and he was also a major patron to living artists. His dining room, for example, showed off to perfection four overdoors by Antoine Watteau, who lived under Crozat's roof for years.

Savvy architects such as Bullet and Mansart kept Paris's growth going by getting together backers and buying up tracts of land near the square to encourage other financiers to join their friends near the Trump Plaza of the day. Germain Boffrand became a real estate developer: in May 1718, he bought number 22, Place Vendôme, for 28,500 livres; he built a home behind the façade and, less than two years later, sold it with a tidy profit, for 153,000. He then did the same thing next door at number 24. Those who paid top dollar for Boffrand's creations got the latest in architectural innovation. And the energy unleashed in the financial district soon spread across the river, a phase in the reconfiguration of Paris encouraged by the second great urban project of the end of Louis XIV's reign, a new bridge across the Seine.

Until the early seventeenth century, the only bridge close to the Louvre was the Pont Neuf at the tip of the Île de la Cité, home to Notre Dame Cathedral. Then, Louis XIII added a modest wooden affair, painted red and thus called the Pont Rouge, which spanned the river at the level of the Tuileries Gardens. The Red Bridge was destroyed and rebuilt several times. When disaster struck again in 1684, Louis XIV decided to make a proper go of it and build to last: royal architects produced a grand stone bridge that was inaugurated in 1689 and given a properly grand name, Pont Royal.

The Royal Bridge immediately became famous as the first bridge to cross the entire river in a single span; it was also exceptionally wide and featured an "ingenious design" that facilitated access for even the most imposing carriages. All this meant that once the choicest plots in the neighborhood of the moment, the Faubourg Saint-Honoré, had been snapped up by real estate speculators, there was a logical direction in which to look next—straight across the new bridge to the Faubourg Saint-Germain. The icing on that particular cake was provided by the completion in 1690 of the last of Louis XIV's great public projects, the gilded dome of a home for wounded war veterans, the Invalides, a spectacular new focal point on the cityscape and the new area's first great monument.

The fact that Paris's neighborhood of the moment was no longer adjacent to the traditional seat of majesty, the Louvre, but across the river from it was a very visible reminder of the city's new independence from the court. Developers immediately set to buying up land between the bridge and the Invalides. One after another, what remain among the priciest addresses in Paris opened up—the rue de Bourbon (since the Revolution, the rue de Lille), the rue de Verneuil, the rue de l'Université, the rue Saint-Dominique, the rue de Grenelle.

Faubourg Saint-Honoré, Faubourg Saint-Germain: Those names make it clear why the architecture of comfort that flourished in these neighborhoods was able to take on many of the features that make it so modern and also why the residences built there could be so spacious. *Faubourg* means outside of the city; the building boom of the turn of the eighteenth century took place in a sort of no-man's-land situated beyond Paris's traditional limits. In these newly created areas, the first sub-urbs, architects set about reinventing the urban experience by building city dwellings that spread horizontally rather than vertically, each with its own private garden to add the pleasures of the country to those of city life. The original suburbs were an architect's dream. For the first time, Parisian architects were not hemmed in by preexisting construction— even the magnificent dwellings on the Place Vendôme shared party walls rather than being freestanding—but had the room to satisfy their imagination and their clients' whims.

The development on the Seine's Left Bank took place so quickly that cartographers frequently updated their maps to show off the growing cityscape. Jouvin de Rochefort's 1675 map portrays the Faubourg Saint-Germain as virtually virgin territory, a vast tree-covered expanse. By 1710, its development was in full swing: a map by Bullet and Blondel shows an infrastructure and the first new buildings. That same year, when the architect Alexandre Le Blond described one of his own buildings still under construction near the Invalides, he made it plain that all that empty space in the heart of Paris was an ideal testing ground for the new comfort-driven architecture. (This may have been the first time an architect had discussed in print a not yet completed project.)

Modern architects worked so fast that two decades later, significant new territory had become part of the cityscape. The latest maps, such as Turgot's (1734–1739), demonstrate that the area had been almost completely built up. Long-established neighborhoods on the Right Bank such as the Marais looked crowded and dingy in comparison with the rows of gracefully expansive new dwellings surrounded by lush gardens and parks. During the boom years, guidebooks had to be reedited every few years to let visitors know about places that hadn't existed on their last trip to Paris.

And in the first suburbs, comfort continued to spread through society. Thus it was that, in 1720, Charlotte Desmares acquired a plot of land, today number 78 on the rue de Varennes. Desmares was the most celebrated actress of the early eighteenth century, equally at ease in tragedy and comedy. The most celebrated artists of the day—Watteau, Coypel—painted her; she was linked romantically to two of the most important men in France, first Monseigneur and then Philippe d'Orléans, regent during Louis XV's minority. She was also an entirely new kind of client for architecture: both a single woman and a non-aristocrat. Desmares did have, however, the bluest blood in a very modern type of nobility, that of the stage: she belonged to a dynasty, like the Barrymores or the Redgraves. Her maternal great-grandmother, her parents, and her sister were noted actors all: her aunt Marie Champmeslé was the most celebrated tragedienne of the golden age of French tragedy, the favorite actress of Jean Racine, who wrote his finest roles, in particular Phèdre, for her. At the age of eight, Desmares was already a child star, known as Mademoiselle Lolotte. She was sixteen when her aunt died; the actors of Paris's Comédie Française passed on Champmeslé's roles to her and quickly named her a lifetime member of their troupe.

Desmares was an exceptional woman in many ways, first of all because she moved in court circles with an apparent sense of entitlement. When she had a daughter with the regent, for example, he both recognized the child and arranged a marriage for her with an aristocrat, a count no less, the Comte de Ségur. (The Countess de Ségur, among the most famous French children's writers, was the wife of their great-great-grandson.) Desmares was also unusual in that she was very much a woman used to working for a living and to being very well paid for her work. She left the stage (though she continued to receive a handsome pension from the Comédie Française) just after the market boom. In 1721, her personal fortune was evaluated at four hundred thousand livres, a spectacular sum for a single woman of her rank. She was also clearly accustomed to life on a grand scale. She was actively involved in the design of a jewel-box home, whose plan was singled out for praise by the most famous architects of the day; she furnished and decorated it in the latest style, with all the modern comforts and conveniences.

It was also in the Faubourg Saint-Germain that residential architecture was first bankrolled by a previously unheard-of kind of wealth, the profits from a kind of speculation now so familiar that we call it simply . . . the market.

The book is still out on John Law, the Scottish economist and high roller scorned by some as a reckless gambler who nearly ruined France and praised by others as a founder of modern economic theory and the innovator who stabilized the finances of France, which remained in total disarray after the War of the Spanish Succession. This much is certain: Law quickly won the confidence of the Sun King's nephew Philippe d'Orléans, who governed France in the years between Louis XIV's death in 1715 and his great-grandson's formal ascension to the throne in 1723. Law's career was meteoric: he was put in charge of the Mississippi Company and its vast trading operations in 1717, allowed to create first a private bank and in 1718 the Royal Bank, whose notes were guaranteed by the king. (Both were firsts for France.)

In 1719, when the Mississippi Company was given a monopoly on overseas trade, its shares, guaranteed by the Royal Bank, leapt wildly in value; speculation became widespread and feverish. It was a heady moment: all sorts of people were soon indulging in a completely new experience and playing the investment game. Thus, on December 1719, from her box at the opera the wife of a court official spots a woman "fabulously dressed and absolutely covered in diamonds"—and suddenly realizes that it is her cook, Marie! Marie proceeds to stand up and announce to the entire audience that "she has just become rich and can now deck herself out exactly as she pleases." Within months, in fact, the French had learned to speculate on absolutely everything. Silver goes sky-high? Well, why not sell the family plate? Just say, "We'll have more made when the price comes down." The value of the company's shares peaked in early 1720; in the summer of 1720, the original "bubble" burst, probably because of a sudden loss of confidence among investors. Amid rumors of impending disaster, they rushed to withdraw their money. Law fled the country before the end of the year.

Many were ruined by one of the most spectacular boom-and-bust economic cycles ever seen. Many others, however, got out in time and had their fortunes made or remade from their first ever brush with the concept of investment. Already in 1721 a new expression entered the French language, created explicitly to refer to those who had benefited from the market: *nouveaux riches*. Soon, in a now familiar pattern, the very concept of wealth had been inflated. One commentator quipped that it had become old-fashioned to speak in terms of mere thousands (as the speculators on the Place Vendôme had done): "Today everyone talks about millions; you only hear how many millions any project costs." The millionaire had been born.

An impressive number of those made newly rich spent their money on land and spectacular new homes—homes outfitted with everything architects and interior decorators and furniture designers could dream up. In Venice when it was all long over, Law wrote brilliantly of those turbulent times and claimed that it was thanks to his system that Paris had been rebuilt. Many of the greatest architectural achievements of the age of comfort proudly bear out his claim: they are the houses John Law built.

A contemporary commentator, Piganiol de La Force, put it this way: "Never had there been more new construction in Paris" than during the Law epoch; "people were trying to make their new wealth as sound as a dollar." As for Law himself, the minute he got rich off his own system, in May 1718, he grabbed the last remaining lot on the Place Vendôme. And here are but two other examples, one from each of the new faubourgs, of homes that, we can say without a doubt, John Law built.

In 1718, the Comte d'Evreux made a killing in the early speculation generated by Law's bank. (He undoubtedly profited from insider trading information, since in 1717, his father-in-law had given up all his other professional activities and thrown in his lot with Law. From then on, d'Evreux stayed well out of debt: his annual income at the time of his death in 1753 was a handsome eighty thousand livres.) The count was a traditional type of client for architecture; he paid for his suburban castle, however, not with ancestral funds, but in a thoroughly modern way. He instantly invested a vast sum in a spectacular new residence that far outshone that miserable little place on the Place Vendôme: it was designed for him at the outer limit of the Faubourg Saint-Honoré by the architect of the moment, Armand-Claude Mollet. In January 1720, only weeks before the bubble burst, John Law bought the adjacent plot in order to be "comfortably housed" as the next-door neighbor of the financiers' favorite aristocrat.

The second Hôtel d'Evreux (where the count remained after he sent his wife packing in 1720) was everyone's dream house: the regent attended the grand housewarming party on December 14, 1720. It was immediately enshrined as a monument of the new architecture. In 1727, Mariette illustrated three of its rooms in his *Architecture française*; Brice praised the "perfection" of its plan, its abundant new "conveniences," and the fact that furnishings and architecture were "in perfect harmony"; Jacques-François Blondel—architect, founder of the first school of architecture, and the original architectural historian—recommended the study of its interior rooms and their décor as a model for architecture students.

All those features undoubtedly attracted its subsequent owner, someone seen by her contemporaries as an expert in the architecture of comfort, the Marquise de Pompadour. She had it remodeled and redecorated by her favorite architect, Lassurance II, to the tune of one hundred thousand livres. In 1753, when Blondel visited the Hôtel d'Evreux in the process of becoming the Hôtel de Pompadour, he admired in particular the fact that many rooms (bedrooms, a living room, even a bathroom) had garden views and added that its openness to the world outside—it was the only home with direct access to the huge, leafy expanse known as the Elysian Fields, Champs-Élysées, adjacent to its gardens—made one feel as if "you could enjoy the Champs-Élysées as your own private park." (That sylvan setting seems to have awakened the amateur astronomer in d'Evreux, who at the time of his death owned no fewer than six telescopes.) It was, in other words, the ultimate in the new suburban urban architecture. Blondel might have added that the mansion provided in turn quite a nice view for those strolling nearby—a pleasure it still provides today, under its modern incarnation as the Élysée Palace, official residence of the president of the French Republic.

Almost directly across the river stands another of modern France's great public monuments, the Palais Bourbon, today home to the National Assembly. From the start, the palace was recognized by architects as a major breakthrough, the complete realization of comfort-driven interior design—the fulfillment, in other words, of the architectural tradition begun at the Porcelain Trianon and Clagny. And that is just what the women behind its creation had in mind.

Louise-Françoise de Bourbon, known simply as Madame la Duchesse (she was the widow of Louis III, Duc de Bourgogne), was every inch a worthy successor to her mother, the Marquise de Montespan. She was a favorite of Louis XIV and also very close to her half-brother, Monseigneur: architecture and interior decoration were thus second nature to her. To allow her to cut her decorating teeth, in 1696, when she was twenty-three, her father, the Sun King, made her a present of what he considered a "tiny house" on the grounds of his very big house, Versailles: he pronounced the result "very prettily decorated." The woman known as "*toujours la reine des plaisirs*," always the life of the party, was also financially savvy, among those who profited most handsomely from the new art of investing.

From 1720 to 1729, she turned her bundle into a *huge* plot of land at the gateway to the Faubourg Saint-Germain; it stretched from the rue de Bourgogne to the Invalides, from the rue de l'Université to the river. And then she became every architect's worst nightmare. She went through three of them (Giardini, Lassurance, Jean Aubert) on the project until she got just what she wanted: a gorgeous oval reception room with a garden view, more interior rooms than anyone else would have known what to do with, the biggest bathing suite known to man, and a totally impressive flush toilet installation. In Paris following the original stock market boom, in other words, the age of comfort was in full swing and very, very publicly displayed.

Meanwhile, back where it all began, Versailles, a new era was soon to start for the by then dusty monument. The annus horribilis had initiated an endgame for the once fabled court, and after Louis XIV's death on September 1, 1715, the shutters were closed on Versailles. The regent preferred to rule from his home in the Palais Royal (fabulously decorated and furnished, all in the absolute latest fashion); he decided to raise the boy king far from the place where most of his family had died, initially just outside Paris at the palace at Vincennes, then in the Tuileries Palace, a stone's throw from the Place Vendôme and the Pont Royal. Until the king—who was crowned in 1722 and pronounced of legal age in 1723—returned to Versailles, Paris was the only place where everyone who counted wanted to live, and the expression the French court had little meaning.

The young king thus had a ringside seat during that giddy moment of postwar inflation and wild investment. True, he led a sheltered life. True, he was by all accounts an introvert, "taciturn," "secretive." Still, the boy who all his adult life demonstrated a passion for architecture that far surpassed his great-grandfather's can hardly have avoided firsthand knowledge of the new suburban homes taking shape barely a five-minute walk from his residence, particularly when many of them were being built by his closest relatives. (Louis XIV dealt with architecture instinctively, from that inner compass; Louis XV actually worked at it— studying plans for hours a day, discussing them with the architects responsible for them, even drawing his own. The Marquise de Pompadour said of him that he was "most fully alive when he has plans spread out in front of him.")

Thus, when just prior to his coronation he returned to Versailles on a warm day in June 1722, the twelve-year-old king had not only begun to study architecture, but had it in various ways in his blood. On his first day back, he carefully sized up the sights: he toured the gardens for hours and, near the end of the day, stretched out on his back in the Hall of Mirrors to take in the story of Louis XIV's reign as interpreted on its ceiling by Charles Le Brun.

The young Louis XV had learned valuable lessons from France's recent history. During his reign, his country knew long periods with no military conflict; he quickly introduced measures to stabilize its currency, something he achieved in 1726 and that brought immense psychological benefits after the monetary roller coaster of the Law years. The prolonged prosperity that resulted from his policies encouraged his subjects to continue spending on architecture and design as if there were no tomorrow. By the time of his death in 1774, Louis XV was enshrined in French memory as the sovereign who had given France "a previously unheard-of degree of peace, splendor, and opulence."

He was also the perfect ruler for an increasingly intimate, interior age. As the Marquise de Pompadour's lady-in-waiting Madame Campan observed, a split personality—between his public persona as the king of France and the private individual Louis de Bourbon—was basic to his way of life. He used his knowledge of contemporary architecture to find ways of, as Versailles insider Dufort de Cheverny put it, "setting aside his role as king." Thus, Louis XV maintained a double standard with respect to the palace: on the one hand, he restored to their original luster the grand spaces associated with his great-grandfather; on the other, he never stopped adding new rooms behind the façade of the official Versailles, the interior spaces in which he could be Louis de Bourbon.

At first, it seemed as if he sought out architectural intimacy in a way then considered unusual for a king: to enjoy a happy family life. At the time of his marriage in 1725 to Maria Leszczyńska, a Polish princess nearly seven years his elder, he seemed openly in love with both marriage and his bride (see color plates). They immediately started a family; she gave him ten children in quick succession (though only one son). Many explanations have been offered to explain why he turned away from the role of family man. Some blame the queen's rigid Catholicism; others say that no one woman could ever have satisfied a man so sexually (over)active; while still others suggest that it may all have begun with a lack of communication when a miscarriage caused the queen to retreat into her own brand of secrecy.

In the beginning, the king's extramarital escapades were fleeting, over before all but the era's quickest tongues could start wagging. In 1737, the situation began to change: the first royal mistress who had to be taken at all seriously was given a suite at Versailles. And in 1745, the court had its first glimpse of the most serious of them all, a royal mistress of a particular kind (see color plates).

Jeanne Antoinette Poisson d'Étiolles stands out in the roll call of mistresses to the Bourbon kings first of all because of her birth: the king made her a marquise, but no one forgot for a moment that she came from the world of financiers whose wealth had been so ostentatiously visible for a half century. From the start (and the stories about her started right away), her biographers agreed that she set her cap for the king, having been encouraged to believe since childhood that she was somehow destined to become his mistress. (Her will contains a curious, and curiously touching, bequest of six hundred livres to "Madame Lebon for having foretold when she was nine years old that she would one day become the king's mistress.")

Thus it was that while engaged in his favorite outdoor activity, hunting, the king just happened upon a fetchingly attired woman who was by all accounts one of the great beauties of the age. (Court insider Dufort de Cheverny left a particularly detailed description of her charms—her features, her skin, her "well-rounded" curves—that concludes: "Any man would have wanted to have her for his mistress.") Soon, a "very beautiful" woman was spotted in the royal box at the opera. The mysterious blond beauty quickly became less mysterious: she moved into Versailles and was presented at court; she became known publicly as the Marquise de Pompadour and was referred to by insiders as "the officially declared mistress."

The new official mistress maintained her position for nearly twenty years. She was a consummate entertainer: she worked with acting, singing, and dancing coaches and performed for the king, by all accounts with great success, on private stages at Versailles and other châteaux. The roles she studied most closely, however, were those of her two most successful precursors: the Marquise de Montespan and the Marquise de Maintenon. She read everything she could get her hands on about them, including many of the passages from contemporary memoirs that I cite in this chapter. (As soon, for example, as the manuscript of Saint-Simon's memoirs became available, she had the relevant material copied out for her.) And she was once again enormously successful in her reenactments: in Maintenon's role, she was the king's closest adviser; many court insiders claimed that no major decision was ever taken without her consent.

In her role as Montespan, she was the perfect partner for a king who loved to build. After her purchase of the Hôtel d'Evreux, she described herself as "construction mad," and her record bears this out. In 1746, the king and the new Montespan began buying château after château—Crécy, Ménars, Champs, over a dozen in all. Together, they spent a fortune on architecture, furniture, and interior decoration. In every case, magnificence was completely eclipsed by comfort, intimacy, and coziness. Together, they even brought Versailles into the modern age.

Pompadour was the fourth of Louis XV's mistresses to take up residence in the château; she moved into a suite already furnished for her immediate precursor. She was in residence for nearly two decades, until her death in 1764. During that time, she established herself as Montespan's successor: royal mistress as tastemaker. Pompadour quickly set about imposing her personal style on Versailles, adding new furniture, changing the décor, having walls moved in order to improve the layout and to gain space for comfort rooms.

This was, however, not enough for the "building-mad" marquise. In late 1749, she pulled off one of her biggest real estate coups: the king's daughters were after a particularly high-profile suite always previously occupied by members of the royal family; the king caused a scandal when he gave it to his mistress instead. (The king had a gaggle of daughters: in 1749, five of them— ages twelve to twenty-two—were living at court. Pompadour's diplomatic skills were legendary; among her greatest accomplishments was the fact that she for the most part succeeded in maintaining cordial relations with the queen and the royal children.) Everyone from the marquise's most vocal critic to the most vocal spokesman for modern architecture agreed that she turned her new suite into a showroom for comfort-driven architecture.

And a showroom it was. In her role as the king's most trusted adviser, Pompadour received in those newly modern rooms all the most prominent visitors to Versailles. She also, however, carefully controlled access to them, since they were an entrance into the world of Louis de Bourbon and to that second life that Pompadour helped orchestrate. On a typical evening, for example, guests slipped up a back staircase and waited outside his small suite; someone arrived with a list of those to be admitted, and they were called in. Once on the other side and in the king's private world, they found not a majestic ruler, but a genial host: joking with his guests, teasing the hostess (Pompadour), crowding around the table when last minute guests arrived, even heating up and serving his own coffee—and then whispering into Pompadour's ear: "Let's go! Let's go to bed!" As one frequent guest at those little suppers remarked: "How different it all was from the time of Louis XIV."

In one important way, however, this was not the case: it was very much like the life Louis XIV lived with one of Pompadour's role models, Montespan. Since all of the building and renovation projects that Louis XV and Pompadour planned together were paid for from the royal treasury, we know exactly how the state's money was spent. In addition, in the marquise's estate inventory, the detailed listing of her possessions drawn up by notaries after her death, we find listed every piece of furniture, down to the fabric in which it was upholstered, every curtain, and every cushion used in all of her dwellings. These official documents prove that the accoutrements of the comfortable life had come a long way between 1670 and 1764. They also show, however, that the overall effect of what Louis XV and Pompadour created was very reminiscent of the style of interior design introduced at the Porcelain Trianon and Clagny—soft, light, and bright, featuring cotton prints in shades of blue, white, green, jonquil, and violet.

The following chapters are the story of individuals with a taste for comfort and the means to pay for all the inventions that could enhance their comfort. Some of them, in particular those two exceptional royal mistresses, Montespan and Pompadour, were pillars of the court. Many of them, however, were the kinds of clients high-end architecture and furniture had never had before—traditional clients such as Madame la Duchesse and the Comte d'Evreux, who were bankrolling their way of life in a decidedly new way, as well as home owners of very new breeds, the financier Pierre Crozat and the actress Charlotte Desmares. The fact that the homes of such decidedly nonroyal individuals can be reconstructed in detail tells us a great deal about the age of comfort.

The building boom in Paris helped broaden the public for architecture—not only its client base, but the number of people who followed the architectural scene. The enormous number of works of and on architecture then published in France were designed to appeal to very different readers—to professional builders, yes, but to laymen as well. Most are quite readable still; this proves that all sorts of people wanted to learn about the way the home was being redesigned and even to see the plans of new residences.

Some of those crucial to the reshaping of Paris and of the home were also closely aligned with the movement for intellectual and political change known as the Enlightenment that rose to prominence during the very years when comfort was working its way into the fabric of French life. Some of the new way of life's most enthusiastic proponents such as Voltaire were central figures of the Enlightenment. Others, such as the Marquise de Pompadour, also staunchly supported such crucial Enlightenment projects as the *Encyclopédie*. The *Encyclopédie*, in turn, promoted the preeminence of French craftsmen, the very individuals responsible for the age's great design innovations. And while we have little information about the philosophical or political leanings of the age's great architects and artisans, it is evident that many of them understood the role that modern architecture and conveniences could play in helping create a new sense of the individual and in improving the quality of life for all. In many ways, the partisans of the Enlightenment and the inventors of a comfort-driven life shared a common cause.

The *Encyclopédie* and the published work of the finest artisans of the age such as furniture designer Roubo make it clear that the age of comfort may well be the first great age of things. So many new objects for the home were invented; there were so many more things in homes than in the past—and this was true of even modest dwellings. As for grand residences, they were literally full of things as never before. This meant that everyone from painters to authors of guidebooks was eager to show their audiences the new look of Parisian homes. It also meant that more and more individuals had enough possessions of value to be inventoried at the time of their death, an official listing of all their wordly goods drawn up by a notary. In the case of every home owner we'll follow here, both the plans of their residences and the room-by-room inventories of their contents exist, making it possible to take a virtual tour of their homes, to know not only how many bedrooms they had, but exactly how each one was furnished—right down to the fabric on the chairs, the knick-knacks on the mantel, and the color of the bedspread.

The following chapters reconstruct the creation of comfort during the decades from 1670 to the mid–eighteenth century, working from the outside in. We'll begin with architecture, then go inside the walls and follow the invention of conveniences such as the bathtub from the pipes to the fixtures. Next comes the furniture used in the new rooms, followed by the décor that completed the look of comfort. Finally, we'll look at comfort next to the skin: clothing and textiles.

CHAPTER TWO

An Architecture of Comfort

A T THE TURN of the eighteenth century, a new category of writing about the city appeared: Paris guidebooks that featured absolutely contemporary architecture, even buildings still in the process of being built. This new niche in publishing was created in response to the rapid transformation of the cityscape of Paris. As Germain Brice put it in his guide in 1717, if you hadn't been to Paris for a few years, you would no longer recognize the city. Because "people from the business world" are spending "on a previously unheard-of scale" to build "magnificent homes in completely new neighborhoods, you can be absolutely certain that the city is improving every day."

When Jean-Aimar Piganiol de La Force published his guide in 1742, he positively gushed about the way Paris now "spread out in every direction," "the magnificence" of its private homes, the vast number of such dwellings—some of them "seven stories high" (over twenty-three thousand by his tally, which did not include buildings reserved for commercial use). He noted a particularly visible reminder of Paris's new size and complexity: during the first three months of 1728, workers had attached signs to the corner of every one of its more than nine hundred streets, with its name "in big black letters."

The message was clear: The construction boom at the turn of the eighteenth century had made Paris into a vibrant, bustling metropolis and the new world capital for contemporary architecture and design. Never before had privately commissioned residential architecture rather than state-sponsored public projects been commemorated in print. Never before had a city been celebrated not on account of the time-honored splendors of ancient empires, but for the brand-new displays of the quite recent wealth of a very modern kind of mogul.

And the city guides were only the tip of the iceberg. The most noted architects of the day quickly got into the act and began to publish volume after volume—architectural treatises, building manuals, collections of floor plans of noted contemporary homes, compilations of striking examples of current interior decoration, in all a veritable flood of publications. Never before had the architecture and design accomplishments of an era been so thoroughly recorded; never had they been recorded virtually at the moment of their creation. The fact that so many architecture-related works were published and republished indicates that a new readership now existed: a general audience interested in the architectural scene and the way it was changing the home.

In explaining what made each home exceptional, the new city guides focused attention on features that tourists could hardly hope to see even if they did visit Paris, features hidden deep inside the city's new great homes. Some homes were singled out because of their "modern conveniences," others for a particularly original floor plan. In the 1717 edition of his guide, Brice even encouraged "foreign visitors" to see "the fine furnishings and décor" in the newly finished bedroom suite of Marie-Suzanne Guithou on the Place Vendôme—features that the lady of the house, whose husband, the financier Bourvalais, had recently been locked up in the Bastille on apparently trumped-up charges of tax evasion, would hardly have been inclined to show off to random visitors.

Brice was in a sense obliged to lead his readers on in this way in order to convey why the new architecture of Paris was new. For at the same time that Paris became a bustling, public metropolis—and undoubtedly as a direct response to this development—it also became an intensely private city, the place in which the modern concept of privacy first became meaningful. Celebrated architects made the unprecedented move of turning away from the time-honored sign of important architectural projects, their public face or façade. They concentrated instead on the kinds of accomplishments that do not usually guarantee inclusion in the annals of architecture: a particularly imaginative and convenient floor plan, an interesting new shape for a dining room, or even an ingenious way of getting natural light into a windowless room. For a little over a half century, until even some of their own kind began to grumble that it had all gone too far and that the streets of Paris were becoming far too plain, French architects devoted themselves to residential architecture with a single, overarching goal: to make it possible to live daily life more "commodiously"—comfortably and conveniently.

Throughout the first half of the eighteenth century, every work on building and design published in France and even guidebooks included a minihistory of Western architecture, always told in exactly the same way: homage is paid first to the great monuments of antiquity, then to the Gothic cathedrals, and finally to Italian Renaissance architecture. This is always a prelude to an announcement: Italian architecture's moment was officially over, and French architects now reigned supreme. The transfer of power had begun, all commentators agreed, at the turn of the eighteenth century, when French architects decided that all the most celebrated prior dwellings were "virtually uninhabitable." In Pierre Patte's words, until then all "housing was designed only for public display; no one knew how to make homes comfortable; no one thought of the individuals who lived in the house." Natural light had never been a concern; dwellings didn't even contain a good spot for the bed. French architects had therefore become the first of their profession ever motivated by the belief that great buildings should be first and foremost *logeable*, livable. As a result, they "had invented an art completely unknown to the ancients": they called it "distribution," the art of the plan, the design of a home's layout.

For centuries, the basic design for the home remained virtually unchanged. All houses, those of rich and poor alike, followed essentially the same model. They contained relatively few rooms, always of the same, roughly boxlike shape; all rooms were interconnected; all space was thus public or virtually so. Rooms were multifunctional—people might eat, sleep, bathe, and cook in the same room; they usually entertained in the room in which they worked and slept. People slept where the bed was set up, entertained where the chairs were placed. Moreover, since there was very little furniture of any kind and since almost none of it was assigned a permanent place, interior space was largely undetermined.

Only in the sixteenth century did this begin to change in anything like a significant way. The first smaller rooms limited to a single activity were introduced, spaces reserved for work or study. Next came tiny storage/dressing spaces. Large rooms continued to be multifunctional. In winter, for example, people slept where there was a fireplace. Furniture was still moved from place to place as needed, rather than being given a fixed spot. During all this time, in other words, the concept of private or solitary activities could have no real meaning.

In the course of the age of comfort, the aggregate of multifunctional, publicly accessible rooms evolved into the modern home. Key clients and breakthrough projects such as Clagny and the "small suite" at Versailles helped initiate this process; visionary architects jump-started it—this age of great design was possible because it was an age of many great architects. The moment at which the concept of architect-designed residential architecture really took shape was a moment of increased visibility for architecture; it was also a key moment for the profession of architecture.

At least until the mid–eighteenth century, architects were most often members of dynasties: Jacques-François Blondel, for example, who from the late 1720s to the early 1770s chronicled in print all the accomplishments of the age, trained under his uncle Jean-François Blondel. (Pierre Bullet, that most practical of all eighteenth-century architects, trained under still another Blondel, Nicolas-François.) In 1740, Jacques-François (whom I'll refer to simply as "Blondel") established the original modern architecture school, the École des Arts, which was officially approved by the Royal Academy of Architecture in 1743. This marked an important step toward standardized training for architects. Blondel taught architects, French and foreign alike (among his students were the great visionary architects of the late eighteenth century, Boullée and Ledoux)—the foreigners then brought the style of the French school back to their homelands. Blondel thus became the most influential architectural theorist of the age. Craftsmen attended his lectures, as did laypeople. Blondel even showed artisans how to initiate a general audience into the mysteries of their craft—by teaching, for example, engraving to master furniture designer Roubo, who was thus able to produce his series of heavily illustrated design manuals. (Blondel began his career as an architectural engraver.)

The modern home also came into existence as the result of complex interactions between design and behavior. On the one hand, the new designs that resulted from the consultation between architect and client made new behavior possible; on the other, the world of design responded to the manners and customs of the society in which it was operating—what the architect Boffrand referred to as "this century's way of life." At the turn of the eighteenth century, a new way of life required a new context; at the same time, new kinds of homes helped bring order to a society in flux. At that moment, French architects began to reconceive what they called *les dedans*, the insides or the guts of a home, in ways that responded to and encouraged various new concerns, the most obvious of which was the desire for privacy.

The right to and the desire for privacy are concepts whose frontiers are constantly shifting. One generation considers phone conversations so private that individuals in booths shut their doors tightly to close off a space, while the next carries them out in public. At the turn of the eighteenth century, architecture and that part of societal behavior that can be called the desire for privacy interacted in significant ways. From that interaction, something previously unimaginable for any but a handful of the most privileged individuals was created, space in which it was possible to be either alone or in company of one's choosing. The same interaction took place virtually at the same time in different countries. In each case, the need for private space was justified in different, culturally specific terms. In England, private space began to be valued in tandem with the spread of Puritan values: in a room to which access was controlled, women could protect their modesty, and everyone could be safe from prying eyes, separated from the dangers of the world outside.

Nowhere did the desire for a new kind of life have a more dramatic impact on architecture than in France. In France, however, the creation of space to which access could be limited was never justified in terms of hiding or protection from corruption. When turn-of-the-century French architects created rooms in which you could be sure that you would not be disturbed by others, they explained that such space was important because of the new types of intimacy it could foster, because it made it possible to spend what is now called "quality" time with loved ones and to learn to love people one might never have been able to see freely in public rooms. They also valued it in terms of personal luxury: in private space, people could be less formal and therefore feel at ease; private space thus made room for self-indulgence. Finally, these architects created truly private space, the concept of having your own room, space in which you could be totally alone, the kind of space that encouraged self-discovery.

In 1690, the expression *vie privée*, private life, was included for the first time in a dictionary: "the opposite of a public life; someone leads a private life when he . . . has no official position and is not involved in business dealings." One year later, d'Aviler's *Lessons of Architecture* became the earliest professional building manual to proclaim the necessity of devoting space to what d'Aviler calls simply "living." It is thus clear that in 1690, no one was sure just what "living" that new private life might mean. In the course of the half century that followed the original publication of d'Aviler's manual, the interaction between behavior and design would define a set of activities to be included in the domain of private life. In the second half of the eighteenth century, by the time that process was complete and people had had their initial exposure to homes featuring space with controlled access, private life began to be defined as "what takes place in the private rooms of a house." Included in the new domain were the relations between husband and wife, between parents and children, between the house's inhabitants and their close friends.

Eighteenth-century French architects were the first to apply the adjective *private* to space; they often used it as a synonym for the era's buzzword, *commode*, comfortable. Private rooms were thus by definition comfortable. The private spaces they imagined in effect defined the concrete reality of private life for the first generation ever able to use the phrase *vie privée*. The published plans of the most important dwellings of the day are the earliest truly detailed floor plans. Architects began to note as a matter of course the use for which each room was intended. They did so because more and more rooms were now designated for a specific function. From these plans, we can retrace—bathtub by bathtub, nap room by nap room—the creation of a new notion of comfortable privacy. We can learn which clients originally favored each new convenience. (The first lavish bathing facilities, for instance, were built for wealthy women; men fell in love with the original ultraexpensive gadget, the flush toilet.) And the treatises that accompany the plans help us understand the new behavior impacting the world of design, the reasons why both architects and their clients felt that the time had come to reinvent the home.

For the elite in the age of magnificence, the notion of interconnected rooms was ideal, for it turned daily life into a perpetual display of wealth and power. A home's layout centered on one or several long rows of rooms, each with a door leading directly into the next; these were known as *enfilades*. The doors were precisely aligned so that when they were all open, a visitor had a clear view from the first room to the last. Every status symbol—every one of the family's possessions, every proof of the owner's affluence—could thus be taken in at a glance. There was no discretion involved: this was the most frankly ostentatious interior design ever imagined. Traffic flow was likewise brutally direct. The final space in the sequence was the most important one, the room where only the most distinguished visitors were received, and less significant guests were never allowed to venture very far along. However, everyone—owners and servants, residents and visitors alike—had to pass through each and every room in order to progress along the lineup. Thus, all those who lived in these sequences of rooms were on constant, public display.

It was undoubtedly because the Versailles era broke the bank on ostentation that architects and clients revolted against the sequential plan. Architects began to partition residential space in novel ways, each of which proved key to the construction of private life. All the beliefs and principles I'll describe here went into effect in under a half century. The 1710 edition of d'Aviler contains a first, bare glimpse of them; they become more and more visible in Blondel's 1737 and Briseux's 1743 treatises as well as in each successive reedition of d'Aviler, the eighteenth century's most popular building guide; by 1752, when Blondel published his monumental *French Architecture*, they were taken for granted.

The architecture of comfort began with a doubling of interior space. The grand sequence of rooms, the *enfilade*, was officially christened the *parade*, or ceremonial suite. These spaces were reserved for the most official moments in the life of the house; they remained formal and accessible to all and thus a realm in which the notions of comfort and privacy continued to have no meaning. In the late seventeenth century, architects first included as a matter of course rooms reserved for the daily life of the inhabitants of the house, rooms designed *not* to be open to all.

Next, between the 1720s and the 1740s, some architects decided that even this distinction was not enough and introduced still a third type of space, *société*, or societal rooms, space designed with less formal, more intimate entertaining in mind and therefore a kind of semipublic zone. You received the people you most wanted to impress and with whom your relations were status-driven rather than personal (the most important business associates, the most influential people you knew) in the ceremonial rooms, while close friends were allowed access to the social rooms. (Some individuals, perhaps most spectacularly Louis XV, found these degrees of separation insufficient still: the Duc de Croÿ describes the moment in 1747 when he realized that what he had taken for the most restricted space at Versailles was merely the first private zone and that the king had an entire second layer of even more private rooms.)

All this dividing and redividing of interior space produced some consequences that now may seem absurd. The most significant dwellings, for instance, featured two kinds of bedrooms: a grand, showy *parade* bedchamber and a more comfortable one, for actual use. (Louis XV was put to bed in a ritual public ceremony in his state bedchamber; he then proceeded to rejoin the Marquise de Pompadour in her bedroom, where he spent the night.) Other consequences are more familiar to us: there were, for instance, two of the reception rooms then known as *salons* and ever since by a variety of names such as saloon or drawing room. One of them was reserved for the most formal visits, which took place in the morning. The second reception space, located in the society zone, became the place where the family spent time with close friends in the afternoon and evening, where they took coffee after meals or listened to music, or where they just sat around and talked. Homes today tend to have only one room, known since the nineteenth century by a name that would surely have pleased eighteenth-century architects: simply as the living room. Living rooms, however, are often rather schizophrenic spaces torn between display and comfort (the best furniture versus easy chairs); they retain a bit of each of the original salons.

The triple system had, however, notable advantages. It made it possible most obviously to limit access to the private or comfort rooms almost exclusively to the immediate family circle. Blondel categorically pronounced that "outsiders are rarely allowed there." The careful partitioning of space thus helped create the modern concept of a family life.

In French, each suite was called an *appartement*, an apartment—this is the origin of our modern use of the term. Initially, "apartment" designated a group of rooms forming a unit within a home—the master's apartment or suite and so forth. In 1691, when d'Aviler first mentioned the "comfort apartment," the concept of an apartment was still fairly loose. A half century later, apartments were neatly classified: the type of apartment (formal or casual, public or private), the kinds of rooms it contained, and even the order in which those rooms were organized were all prescribed. Most important, the rooms found in a model apartment, which were quite vaguely designated in 1691, had all acquired precise names and therefore precise functions.

During that half century, the rooms now considered essential to an apartment or a home first became a standard option. In almost every case, what had previously been a piece of furniture moved from one space to another as it was needed—a bed, a closestool, a tub—had been turned into a separate room where it was understood that you were not to be disturbed. A proper eighteenth-century private apartment thus contained, as did Françoise de Graffigny's in 1751, a bedroom, a toilet room, and so forth. As soon, in other words, as modern architecture became receptive to the notions of comfort and privacy, residential space was defined in a still familiar way.

For Diderot and d'Alembert's *Encyclopédie*, Blondel illustrated the ground floor of what he called a "grand mansion," a model home that shows off on a truly monumental scale the vision of the comfortable life that French architects had developed by the middle of the eighteenth century (see page 53). Blondel's plan showcases the elasticity of the new architecture, how it allowed for varying degrees of solitude and different combinations of solitude and intimacy.

Across the top of his plan we find the ceremonial suite: note how the doors align and give a clear view from one end to the other. Note also the huge, round salon in the middle—eighteenth-century French architects used rooms with unusual shapes as another way of breaking up the monotony of boxlike spaces—and in the most visible, prominent position, just to the right, the formal bedroom for display purposes only. This is the house's entirely public zone, the realm of formal fabrics and imposing furniture beyond which those not in the family's inner circle never penetrated. The entire left side of the dwelling is devoted to two kinds of "living." The first is semiprivate, the entertaining of close friends and family. These "society" rooms include a small reception room (*salle de compagnie*), the dining room, and adjacent to each of

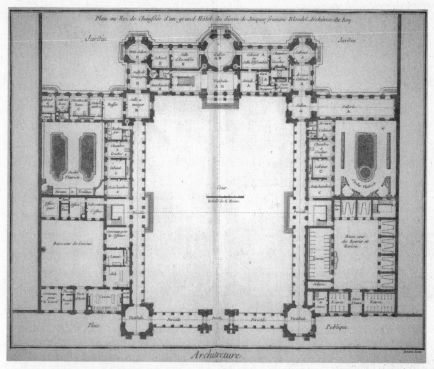

Jacques-François Blondel's plan for a very grand model home highlights the ways in which eighteenth-century French architects subdivided interior space to make possible different kinds and degrees of privacy. Thus, the very large rooms at the top were open to all visitors, while only more intimate relations were allowed into semiprivate rooms such as the smaller reception room on the left, above the dining room. Farther down on the left side were the still more private rooms of the house's female zone; the corresponding spaces on the right made up the master suite. Blondel uses the term "hotel," originally reserved for the home of aristocrats but soon used to designate any grand private residence.

them a kind of room that had gradually come into existence during the first half of the century, a private toilet room. Each toilet room, moreover, features one of the technological innovations of which modern architects were most proud, a flush toilet. (Blondel and other architects frequently reminded clients that toilets should be considered an essential amenity in areas reserved for semiprivate entertaining. They never, ever appeared in public areas. Presumably, only people one knew quite well would ever dare ask to use such a facility.)

The bulk of the property's left side constitutes the truly private domain of the mistress of the house, divided into dual suites. In the age of magnificence, a handful of homes had devoted a room to bathing. Blondel's model home dedicates an entire small wing to personal hygiene. And the bathing suite is linked to a second private set of rooms, for sleeping. (There is much evidence that many eighteenth-century husbands and wives from elite families slept together; they maintained, however, separate sleeping and dressing quarters. More on this in chapter 10.)

The property's right half is also divided between semiprivate and private space. As soon as grand dwellings were built for financiers, domestic architecture began to adapt to the needs of those who did business at home. Aristocrats did not work, so there had been little prior call for this. The second semiprivate zone in Blondel's plan might be termed a business suite. It contains a reception room where the master of the house could entertain clients, offices where he could work, a small *serre-papiers*, or filing room, for business documents. The reception space leads into a gallery or walkway.

If the owner of the house collected art—and many of the financiers responsible for Paris's building boom were major collectors of contemporary art—he could display his collection there and impress his associates with a tour of his latest acquisitions. (This is the origin of the phrase art gallery.) The most-talked-about gallery of the day was found in Pierre Crozat's mansion; it showcased 152 canvases by artists such as Rembrandt, Rubens, and van Dyck and featured a ceiling painted by Charles de La Fosse that depicted the birth of Minerva. The gallery also had a more private function: after a long day, the master of the house could be alone there and, as Blondel put it, "clear his head," "unwind" from the stress of the day. Finally, the business suite leads directly into the greater privacy of the master bedroom suite.

Blondel's model house focuses attention most evidently on newly invented rooms and new ways of organizing them into new kinds of suites, but it also illustrates another, less spectacular use of interior space created by the desire to live in rooms with controlled access. In order to direct traffic through the home—from room to room, from floor to floor—as unobtrusively as possible, and in order to provide and regulate access between different zones, the new residences relied on various circulatory devices known as *dégagements*, removals or separations.

The term originally referred to a spiritual removal, the desire to leave the world and devote oneself to God. Beginning in the 1690s, it became an architectural term used to designate everything from service space to escape hatches, really any way of getting around in a home's private or semiprivate space. Blondel's plan for a model home illustrates two kinds of *dégagements*. The first, visible on the upper right, is a particularly tiny room that provides a private entrance/exit for the business suite. The second, on the upper left, provides circulation between the semiprivate reception rooms and the bathing suite. Related devices, marked passage-way (*passage*), figure in each bedroom suite.

There was a final kind of *dégagement*, *petits escaliers*, small staircases that truly lived up to their name, for they were unbelievably modest in scale. When you see at Versailles, for example, the kind of stairs Louis XV used to move be-tween the public and private parts of his life, it seems inconceivable that the man who mounted the glittering expanses of the palace's formal marble stairs could also have trotted up and down the bare wooden steps of an exceedingly narrow spiral staircase that seems hardly fit for Victorian servants. And that, of course, was just the point. The wealthiest clients in the world had had enough of architecture that forced people to be onstage and were attracted by any use of space that allowed them to keep out of the public eye. Properly crafted *dé-gagements* made it possible to move between zones without fear of being spot-ted. It was said, for example, that "the minute Louis XV crept down a hidden stairway, he was able to set aside the role of king." It was also said that upon the Marquise de Pompadour's death in 1764, he vowed never again to use the most exclusive of all back stairs, those that connected their two suites.

Dégagements also prove that home owners were acquiring a kind of aware-ness of the existence of servants that was impossible during the age of mag-nificence. Because of all the elaborate rites essential to a culture of perpetual display, and because of the very public organization of the home, servants had to be literally everywhere at all times. They therefore became to a great extent invisible, so totally taken for granted that they blended into the décor. To cite a particularly extreme example, many thousands of servants moved about the palace of Versailles; it is clear, however, that to members of the court, it was as if they were not there. One account of particularly grand court festivities in 1674 explained that no one "notices . . . the infinite number of servants; you don't even see them."

By the early eighteenth century, this was clearly no longer the case. Home owners had become aware of servants to the point that they now preferred to be able to choose when they would be present. Architects thus found ways of avoiding what had become an invasion of privacy. They ran a passageway the entire length of the master suite behind its rooms; they camouflaged doors in the walls behind or next to the beds; when it was time to make the bed, the maid did not have to cross a room or rooms but entered right next to the bed, and voilà—the sheets were changed with minimal disturbance.

Virtually as soon as bedrooms were redefined as private space, call bells used to summon servants from a distance were built into the most architecturally adventurous French dwellings. In this illustration from a 1755 novel, we see

This is perhaps the earliest depiction of someone using a
call bell to summon a servant. The scene is set in a small
private bedroom that is furnished with a cozy bed
equipped with multiple mattresses and pillows
and a night table to hold a candle.

a woman in her bedroom pulling the tassel at the end of a long cord that
runs down the wall to summon a servant (see above). Such bells are already
talked about as commonplace in a 1736 novel by Marivaux, nephew of that
technology-mad architect Bullet; in 1746, the actress Charlotte Desmares
had ten of them in her home; by midcentury, the Marquise de Pompadour
had had bells with elegant silk pull cords installed in virtually every room of

her many residences—often several to a room. A point of comparison to show just how far in advance French homes were: call bells began to be seen in English homes only in the 1770s; they were still unknown in German homes in the 1830s.

This was a case of architectural innovations helping to promote interiority. In that 1736 novel, a character pulls the bell to call a maid, who is clearly some distance away; while she's on her way, the three upper-class characters in the room take advantage of their privacy to open their hearts to one another. It's clear that this highly charged scene would not have taken place had the maid been present. Servants' lives also improved as a result of their new autonomy: from the 1720s on, servants' living quarters began to be indicated as a matter of course on architectural plans. The era of their official invisibility was over.

Small stairs, small suites, small rooms—the single most significant difference between the architecture of comfort and that of the previous age may well have been that of scale. Bigger is better governed the age of magnificence. Size was considered an essential proof of rank and status, so supersizing was seen as the surest way to make a room imposing. Then suddenly everything small took the world by storm. With amazing rapidity, the taste of the clientele for whom price was no object changed completely. They wanted nothing more to do with the oversize scale previously de rigueur. By the mid–eighteenth century, big is better was so out that the most read contemporary newspaper, the *Mercure de France*, laid out a new rule of thumb for evaluating status: "The people of the highest rank live in the smallest rooms."

And small really did mean small. In ceremonial suites, ceilings were at least eighteen feet high, most often twenty and often even twenty-two feet high, and rooms were scaled to match that soaring uplift. In the new private sphere, ceilings were no higher than thirteen feet and were more often as low as nine or ten feet. Even the former inner sanctum of magnificence, the salon, or grandest receiving space, came in for serious downsizing.

The salon, imported into France from Italy in the seventeenth century, had at first featured proportions that now seem larger than life. Contemporary dictionaries and architectural treatises all specify that the salon should have "much higher" ceilings than any other room; in most cases, in fact, it was a full two stories high. In the eighteenth century, only residences of members of the royal family still featured salons with that showy, vaulted, two-story-high volume. Other residences had salons on a more human scale, described as "pretty, small salons where people can get together." As the architect Briseux put it: "A small space is much more agreeable when you're entertaining only a few guests." (Artist Jean-François de Troy's scene of friends gathered together to enjoy a good book takes place in just such a salon—see color plates). By the mid–eighteenth century, less is more had so completely conquered the realm of reception space that in his Château de la Chevrette (where Rousseau worked on his *Confessions*), Louis La Live de Bellegarde installed panels that lowered at the flip of a switch and instantly subdivided a salon into two smaller ones.

Some did complain that architects were producing interiors that looked more like "rats' nests"—"fabulously expensive, exceedingly tasteful" rats' nests, but rats' nests all the same—than the residences of important people. Detractors were few and far between, however, and for the most part it seemed as if there were no regrets for the old scale. At Versailles, for example, Louis XV lowered by a full three feet the ceilings on the suite that Louis XIV had considered "small."

Because of the new rule of thumb, individuals of the highest rank aspired only to more private, personalized spaces. When, in the early 1760s, the Comte Dufort de Cheverny and his wife exchanged their city home for the imposing château associated with his title, for instance, he wrote admiringly of her ability to take the sacrifice in stride: while the château "was admittedly superb," behind the grand façade "there was no comfort on the inside," whereas in Paris they had enjoyed all the latest amenities, from a bathing suite to a flush toilet— all in an intimate setting.

And at least one new home owner took the less is more credo quite literally. For her new residence in the Faubourg Saint-Germain, Charlotte Desmares had François Debiais-Aubry build a three-bedroom home, nothing surprising today, but a positively cozy house by the standards of those heady McMansion years, perhaps the only architect-designed residence then built that has the feel of an average home today. (Desmares's little house, considerably aggrandized in 1746 by the Duc de Villeroy, is now home to the French Ministry of Agriculture.) It became by far the smallest building included in Blondel's compendium of great modern architecture. (He said it had "one of the best layouts imaginable.")

The new scale had repercussions that went far beyond the style in which one entertained. In still another highly charged interaction between behavior and design, the preference for small spaces helped along the process as a result of which modern family life—and probably the modern family as well—came into existence. Prior to the development of private space in dwellings, children attracted remarkably little attention on the part of architects. Historians trace the first widespread acceptance both of modern parent-child relations and of the modern concept of childhood to the same period in the eighteenth century that saw the rise of interior architecture. The two contemporary developments intersected in significant ways.

In October 1715, the Princesse Palatine was, as usual, complaining about the new ways: "Nothing is the way it used to be," and the members of the royal family now live like "strangers" under the same roof; they no longer dine together; they no longer see one another on a daily basis in Versailles's "big rooms." "Today, everybody lives separately; my son takes his meals on his own." By 1715, in other words, the proliferation of small suites had redefined the concept of family for the French court. Each single family unit or nuclear family now wanted and was able to live on its own rather than function almost solely as part of the extended royal household.

In 1737, Blondel published plans and commentary on a series of single-family dwellings. (The work is lavishly illustrated and written in a highly accessible style, clearly intended to capture the attention of nonspecialist readers.) Each example shows how a contemporary family could adapt its life to the new architecture and the new architecture to its life. Every house makes ostentatious use of all the bells and whistles, from flush toilets to tubs. The fourth dwelling he describes is also a family residence in a new sense of the term. Blondel describes his client as "someone for whom his family life and the education of his children in particular are so important that he wanted to be able to oversee everything personally." The entire left wing is thus given over to "the children of the house": there is a schoolroom, a library, the children's rooms, lodging for their teacher—and, "since they must have recess after school," even a private garden for the children to play in. It was home schooling de luxe.

It was also a total break with contemporary practice, whereby all who could afford to give their children an education shipped them off to boarding school at a very early age; the children returned home essentially only when the family was ready to ship them off again, this time into married life. Blondel's 1737 home is the earliest recorded instance of rooms designated specifically for the activities of childhood; it marks the moment at which architecture officially began to take family relations into account. Indeed, within a decade or so, architectural plans began to indicate children's bedrooms. And by 1780, Nicolas Le Camus de Mézières gave the first guide to the interior decoration of children's rooms. Children were acquiring an official existence within the home.

The new architecture also gave public recognition to the ways in which culture and the transmission of knowledge were being democratized in eighteenth-century France. In the age of magnificence, reading, too, was a stately activity,

More and more people were reading in the eighteenth century; people owned more and more books. Modern book storage thus became necessary. These elegantly practical cupboards provide ample shelf space and feature sliding doors carved so that they blend into the room's décor.

indulged in by few and confined largely to the ceremonial space of grand libraries. The eighteenth-century home featured a less imposing, more modern type of space devoted to books and reading. In what was now called a "reading room," books were not on formal display in order to impress visitors with their sheer numbers and sumptuous bindings. They were stored instead in built-in cupboards camouflaged behind sliding doors fitted with elegant paneling. These rooms were intended, in Blondel's words, "to induce everyone to come in and start reading," as spaces in which anyone would feel comfortable sliding back those doors and picking out a book. In some bedrooms, the walls on either side of the bed were fitted out with still more bookshelves. People had obviously begun to curl up in bed with a good book.

Reading rooms and the integration of book storage into different rooms of the eighteenth-century home were the new architecture's response to the spread of literacy outside the circles (aristocratic males and scholars) that had traditionally dominated the book-buying public (see above). In the course of the eighteenth century, more and more people could read, were reading, and were reading in new ways. For example, as print runs became larger and books less expensive, people began to own greater numbers of books rather than just a few volumes that they read over and over. They were reading in their spare time and more casually: to inform themselves, to improve their minds, for recreation. Reading rooms—furnished with plump chairs and sofas to put people at ease—were created to encourage this new approach to the world of books.

The earliest private rooms, developed during the Renaissance, were the small studies found in certain elite European dwellings, beautiful little spaces devoted to study and writing. To develop this concept on a larger scale, eighteenth-century architects invented the "writing room." Writing rooms outfitted with desks and all the necessary accessories were part of the society zone and were thus semipublic space. They were ideal for an age during which virtually everyone—men, women, kings, and courtiers alike—was obsessed with another developing form of self-expression: letter writing.

Some correspondence has survived from earlier periods. It is, however, very rarely in any way abundant; even more rarely does it contain letters that are truly personal. In the eighteenth century, on the contrary, seemingly everyone left a correspondence for which the adjective extensive does not begin to do justice. The most personal of all epistolary genres, the love letter, knew its golden age: even the most influential monarch in Europe found time for billets-doux. In July 1745, when Louis XV's long affair with the Marquise de Pompadour was just beginning, the Duc de Luynes reported that "the king writes [the Marquise de Pompadour] at least once and often several times every day. He's already written to her more than eighty times. The letters bear a lovely seal, around which is written: 'Discreet and Faithful.' "

The new architecture facilitated the development of an area of private life that people everywhere still consider somehow particularly French: seduction. Seduction and comfort were mutually dependent. Interior architecture provided visible proof of the desire to have a setting for flirtation, courtship, and sexual life that was cleaner, more refined, more luxurious, and above all more private. Once the French were comfortably set up with their own bedrooms, toilets, and baths, seated on well-padded furniture, and wearing more comfortable clothing, they elaborated for the first time in modern Western history an art of seduction worthy of that name. Eighteenth-century painting and literature—fiction and nonfiction alike—are massively devoted to the portrayal not just of sex, or courtship rituals, or a quick canoodle, or whatever you want to call it, but of an intricate process that involved learning how to be seductive, how to seduce, and even how to be seduced.

The French art of seduction began once beds were no longer all over the house but in the new private bedroom, once many new kinds of lounging furniture had been invented, once the French were sure that servants remained at a safe distance, once they could be sure of being able to devote uninterrupted time to intimacy. Many of the age's most memorable memoirs were authored by men; time and again, they, and many contemporary novels as well, recount a virtually identical scene. (They are, by the way, wonderful moments—vividly recalled, playfully rendered—a generation's often awestruck attempts to chronicle a new type of experience.) Young man, still a bit wet behind the ears in the ways of the world, meets most attractive, at least slightly older woman. Does she come on to him? Does he make a play for her? Is the dance of seduction completely mutual? What is clear from the start is that its key moment will play out only when they can be alone—and not just anywhere.

What sets eighteenth-century scenes of seduction apart from subsequent attempts at re-creating this phenomenon is the starring role they assign to the setting in which amorous adventures take place. Time and again, these seductions are played out in interior rooms made so dazzling by the combined effects of architecture, furniture, and design that when it's all over and the young man has left the charmed space and returned to his senses and the real world, he is left to wonder if it had not all been "just a perfectly beguiling dream." True, the woman's charms are bewitching, but somehow every man seems seduced by the existence of the new private zone and by its trappings of comfort at least as much as by his female companion.

Today, the architecture and interior design of the first half of the eighteenth century are known as rococo, a term unknown at the period and one whose connotations of overly ornamental, lightweight frivolity have surely distracted attention from the significance of the changes brought about by the revolution in architecture that created the modern notions of interior space and comfortable living. When the newly interior architecture was in the process of changing homes and the way people lived in them, however, it had no specific name. In the 1706 edition of his city guide, Brice used the phrase *goût moderne*—in the modern taste or the modern style—to characterize the "incomparably more comfortable" architecture then beginning to become prominent in Paris. In the 1720s, Courtonne spoke of *goût nouveau*, the new taste, and Briseux entitled his volume simply *Modern Architecture*. In 1737, Blondel alternated between "modern taste," "this century's taste," and "the taste of this age." With his 1752 *Architecture française*, he added a final term to the mix and made the new architecture synonymous with French architecture.

Blondel's seminal 1737 work designed to introduce the new architecture to a general audience is now referred to by the title on its official title page, *How to Build and Decorate a Country House*. Its first edition, however, features an unusual pre-title page before the title page, and that one is stamped in letters that are truly boldface: *TREATISE ON ARCHITECTURE IN THE MODERN STYLE*. This was the work that showcased innovations ranging from reading rooms to children's rooms, from flush toilets to bathing suites. That original title page proves that Blondel saw the work less as a building guide than as a manifesto for modern architecture. Modern French architecture was thus defined as the architecture of private life, the architecture that helped create and satisfy the need for all sorts of new creature comforts.

The editors of the *Encyclopédie*, the greatest monument to the age of Enlightenment, Diderot and d'Alembert, asked Blondel to contribute the articles related to architecture and the home. When they featured the plan for Blondel's model home, they broadcast to the enlightened world—the *Encyclopédie* was read by subscribers all over Europe, from Catherine the Great to Frederick the Great—a vision of the way architecture had defined modern life in the country that was setting the standards for the way people in the West wanted to live. Home owners were able to be formal or casual at will. They were able to entertain in various manners: they could make some guests feel important and others feel at home. They could devote time to the life of the family and to the life of the mind. They were able to be alone whenever they wanted or needed to be. And within the newly imagined private sphere, they could perform specific activities that were still in the process of being elevated to the status of needs or necessities—bathing, for instance—not only in private, but in settings so luxurious that they would still be impressive today. (Okay: they didn't have showers.) Every activity had its place, a room specially dedicated to it. They could be convivial, professional, clean, well rested, sensual, sybaritic, and relaxed, all because the modern home was the first one designed no longer only to display the family's wealth and power, but with the goal of being "livable," of bringing comfort into every aspect of its owners' lives.

By the time of the *Encyclopédie*'s publication (1751–1772), the achievements of the age of comfort—from new architecture to new amenities—were already in place, ready to be, as they were, duly celebrated in a number of the vast publication's seventy-two thousand articles. In those pre-Revolutionary decades, it must have seemed to those who favored the Enlightenment's program for intellectual and philosophical progress that their values were indeed transforming society. Modern French architecture offered the perfect residential setting for proponents of this enlightened way of life. It offered the hope of improved living conditions, not only in palatial dwellings, but in general.

Riding thus on the coattails of the Enlightenment, the new French architecture of comfort swept across Europe. It replaced the Italian, Palladian style with a new model based on the values of comfort, convenience, and privacy. The publication of numerous volumes featuring plans of the most visible new buildings in Paris helped establish French architecture as a national school and also helped win international commissions for French architects. Prominent French architects—from Boffrand to Le Blond, from Jean-François Blondel to Robert de Cotte—were soon working far beyond the borders of France, building private homes for wealthy individuals in Geneva as well as palaces for sovereigns in Denmark and Russia. This led another architect, Patte, to proclaim that "France is now supplying the rest of the globe with artists." Soon most of Europe was under the sway of French architecture and its "modern taste." (England, where the influence of classicism remained so powerful that the modern look made few inroads, was the only notable exception. It was only when neoclassicism began to take over from the modern style in the late 1760s that English architecture began to exercise real influence.)

The French, meanwhile, were going wilder and wilder for comfort. Back where "the taste of today" got its start, for instance, on the Place Vendôme, those whose homes had introduced the world to the new comforts that private space made possible soon began to realize that their originally dazzling dwellings had been completely upstaged. Thus, in the mid-1720s, "the rich Crozat," flush with his gains from the Law affair, had the mansion of which he had been so proud in 1704 almost totally redesigned. (He added, for example, a suite to accommodate his daughter, newly returned home after her separation from the Comte d'Evreux.) The new quarters featured smaller rooms, lower ceilings, small back stairs—and two new toilet rooms.

After Crozat's death, his heirs kept his passion for modern architecture alive. In the mid-1740s, they redid the mansion all over again and added *dégagements* of every kind, charming small entertaining spaces, including a tiny "coffee room" off the formal dining room, bigger and better toilet facilities—and lots of additional closet space. They also redid number 19 next door, originally the d'Evreux home, putting in the grandest flush toilet room and bathroom on the square. It was all up to the latest standards and all straight out of the pages of Blondel's 1737 work on modern architecture.

By the time of that second remodel, the desire to enjoy, as the architect Briseux put it in 1728, "all the comfort that money can buy" was spreading beyond the original circle of wealthy financiers and great nobles. We know this because of one of the most enduring legacies of the architecture of comfort, the real estate ad.

The modern marketing of Parisian real estate began in the 1740s, proving that interest in residential housing was already spreading through French society. Those who turned to the papers to find housing were not the beneficiaries, as were the elite, of inherited family homes. When the original ads appeared in the French press, however, they were quite basic: "big house," "beautiful house." For an ad to work its magic, the terms it showcases have to be understood by the newspaper's average readers. The first ads prove that in the 1740s, the general public had not yet experienced the architecture of comfort firsthand.

By the 1750s, however, the moment when novelist Françoise de Graffigny described her experiences "visiting apartments for rent," the latest trends in interior decoration had clearly become sufficiently common for readers to be attracted by ads listing features such as hardwood floors, marble fireplaces, and ample closet space—all features Graffigny was proud to have found in the apartment she chose. Then, by the 1760s and 1770s, readers were familiar enough with new ways of distributing interior space to respond to ads that noted the particular rooms a property contained: dining rooms, small rooms for performing one's toilette, boudoirs. All this time, however, comfort was mentioned only in terms so vague—"every kind of comfort," "all the expected comforts"—that it's impossible to know just what the clientele for high-end real estate understood them to mean.

That situation changed, abruptly and radically, in 1789. In the aftermath of the Revolution, for the first time properties straight out of the pages of the architectural guidebooks began to come on the market. From then on, top-end properties, with interior design "in the new style" and often "freshly painted" as well, were featured regularly in the pages of newspapers. In the summer of 1790, soon after hereditary titles of nobility had been abolished, real estate ads at last began to feature the most expensive innovations of the age of comfort, such as the flush toilet. One particularly well-appointed apartment near Saint-Germain-des-Prés listed in July 1790 had everything: formal dining room, small-scale living room (*salon de compagnie*), boudoir, flush toilet, a floor plan featuring a passage that provided a back way into and out of all rooms, hardwood floors in exotic woods, faux marble painting, lots of closet space—all in "move-in condition."

Ads for guidebook-quality properties became ever more frequent as aristocrats began to flee the country. By the summer of 1792, when the guillotine had begun to create a new kind of spectacle in the streets of Paris, one Sunday paper ran both an account of crowds storming the Tuileries Palace (where the royal family had taken refuge under the protection of the newly formed National Assembly) and an ad for a "big, beautiful house" with no fewer than eleven "complete master suites" and a private theater.

Surely few moments in the history of comfort can have been as fraught with irony. How many clients could, or would, possibly have been looking for a luxurious and expensive property in a city where rioting crowds and fully functional, and functioning, guillotines, rather than architectural monuments such as the Place Vendôme and the Hôtel d'Evreux/de Pompadour, had become the main attraction?

CHAPTER THREE

The Bathroom

PRIOR TO THE eighteenth century, in even the grandest European homes, bathrooms were almost unheard of. The few that did exist, moreover, were largely for show and rarely put to use: bathing was an exceptional event. Then, about 1715, a new kind of bathroom appeared in Parisian mansions, one actually intended for regular use. A mere half century later, the desire for bathing facilities in the home had begun to spread through French society. The modern life of the bathroom, the bathtub, and bathing itself had begun.

Like all facets of the history of private life, bathing has a checkered past. In the Minoan age, a complex system of terra-cotta piping supplied water to the rooms of the Palace of Knossos. Most ancient civilizations developed a culture of the bath as a public experience. Witness the example of the Roman baths, intended less to clean the body, a bath in today's sense of the term, than for an elaborate rejuvenation ritual of steaming, soaping, and plunging into a pool of cold water.

From the Middle Ages to the turn of the eighteenth century, bathing no longer played a central role in daily life. Bathing facilities were extremely rare, which surely explains why we know so little about those that did exist. There was apparently some bathing in private homes; the very few depictions of it indicate that people continued to bathe sitting up and to share a tub with others. Most bathing took place in bathhouses where individuals of both sexes and different backgrounds mingled; several people shared a round tub, in which they sat and steamed. In the late Middle Ages, water was widely feared because it was believed to open up pores and thereby heighten the danger of infection, no small concern at a time when the plague often ravaged Europe. From then to the seventeenth century, people might change linen frequently; they might bathe in a river; they might, à la Louis XIV, rub a damp cloth over their face and hands; but they almost never took a bath.

Some Renaissance palaces had luxurious rooms described as bathrooms; prior to the age of comfort, these were mainly for show—nor were they documented, so we can only guess at what they looked like or how they actually functioned. Elizabeth I, for example, is said to have had servants fill and empty her tub only once a month. The bath itself seems to have been a primitive steam bath: wearing some form of loose garment, people sat on a stool in the middle of a round tub with a canopy over it to hold in the steam; water may have been poured over them from a bucket suspended from the ceiling.

Commentators did occasionally mention most unusual individuals who actually *liked* to bathe. Both of Louis XIV's parents belonged to this exclusive club. His father's childhood doctor recorded the original rubber ducky anecdotes about a boy who loved to play in the tub. His diary entry for Tuesday, July 12, 1611, notes that the future Louis XIII spent an hour in the bath: he asked for his "little boats," "scattered red roses on the water and . . . then loaded the boats with roses and said they were ships returning from the Indies and Goa." (This from someone who later longed to expand the French presence in the Indies.)

His son did not inherit his father's love of water; he did inherit his love for women who liked to bathe. Once again in this respect, no one changed the Sun King's life more than the Marquise de Montespan, perhaps the first person to consider a separate room devoted to bathing essential to every home. She made lavish facilities part of Clagny; Louis XIV had an opulent bathing suite done up for her at Versailles, with huge tubs carved from blocks of marble and marble-tiled walls. While Montespan surely considered these amenities her private space, as far as bathing was concerned, her royal lover was stuck in the age of magnificence. In April 1680, near the end of their long relationship, the king made the most celebrated part of this bathing suite, a charming octagonal room, the setting for an elaborately choreographed sit-down meal for several dozen to welcome his son's new bride into the family. The mistress was on her way out, so there was no point in letting great interior décor go to waste.

When modern architecture began spreading its wings in the new neighborhoods of Paris, the bathroom finally became more than mere decorative opulence. The facilities then built were often showstoppers; sheer magnificence, however, was no longer their raison d'être. In early-eighteenth-century Paris, bathing began to be defined as essential for personal cleanliness, as an activity both pleasurable and to be enjoyed in the privacy of one's home and on a regular basis. For this to happen, new technology—to bring water into the home, to heat it, and so forth—both sophisticated and very, very expensive was required. This technology was developed and used on a notable scale for the first time in the West since antiquity in Paris in the early eighteenth century. In England, in contrast, all this was theoretically possible about 1730; nothing changed, however, until the late eighteenth century. Thus, an English visitor to France in 1787 remarked that the French were "cleaner in their persons." During the decades when the French first bathed in luxury and for pleasure, across the English Channel people limited themselves to cold baths in spartan installations and for reasons of health.

The proponents of the modern style in architecture were eager to encourage the pleasurable bathing experience. In the new private suites, a layout now considered basic, the bath as a necessary complement of the bedroom, was first used in residential architecture (see page 53). Unlike other phenomena of the age of comfort, this did not happen overnight. Le Blond, editor of the 1710 edition of d'Aviler's manual, discussed what he termed a "superb residence" he had recently designed in the Faubourg Saint-Germain and equipped with all the latest conveniences. Unlike the toilet, which Le Blond describes in loving detail, bathing facilities are simply noted on the plan—and only in this one home at that—without a word about what they entailed. Only in the 1738 edition of d'Aviler—all the posthumous updates of this influential building manual had different editors; Mariette the Younger was responsible for this one—did the eighteenth century's standard building guide begin to teach architects the basic facts about bathrooms.

The modern bathroom was thus still another product of the taste for comfort, still another invention of the modern school of architecture. Without, however, the new millionaires created by the original stock market boom, it might never have become a standard option in modern architecture, and bathing would surely never have become a sybaritic experience. Indeed, of all the baths shown and discussed in eighteenth-century architectural treatises, only two of them predate the Law years, and both are relatively modest affairs.

The modern bathroom began in the female zone of the Hôtel d'Humières (1715): both the title and the family fortune that had made that luxurious home possible were controlled by the Duchesse d'Humières. This singular situation had come about when Louis XIV made a most unusual exception to the rule and allowed the Maréchal d'Humières to pass on his title to his "absolutely gorgeous daughter, whom he adored." That "gorgeous daughter" used her father's money to inaugurate a tradition in modern architecture: the original bathrooms were overwhelmingly paid for by female clients. The duchess's new bathroom was small; it was, however, part of the first modern bedroom suite: bedroom, bath, toilet room, as well as the earliest boudoir on record.

The same year, when the government minister, the Marquis de La Vrillière, made bathing facilities part of his new residence, he placed them far from the bedroom. His property was soon acquired by one of the young royals who had made a killing on the market, the Princesse de Conti. The new owner, according to the Duc de Saint-Simon, was "the most meticulous person possible as far as cleanliness was concerned." Elsewhere in the mansion, the princess remodeled with a light touch, but the bath was altogether a different story. She added a substantial addition to the original structure in order to create three spacious rooms, plus a toilet room and a dressing room, all part of her bedroom suite and also close to a second bedroom–toilet room combination. With the first post-market-boom bathroom, the cleanest lady in the land inaugurated both the eighteenth-century French bathing tradition and the modern bathroom: bathing in a space with controlled access, in a space dedicated to bathing, in a bathroom with exquisite decoration and fittings to match. Bathing was the new personal luxury.

At the Palais Bourbon, her half-sister, never one to be outdone and also newly flush from the stock market, made her bathing suite the gateway into her mansion's private zone. On one end, it was just off the imposing formality of the Grand Gallery, while on the other, it was steps away, via a modest passageway, from a private bedroom suite. Both the intimate size of its rooms (three or four of them would fit into one of the public rooms) and their décor (gray-flowered and -checked cotton, wood painted white) prove that, for Madame la Duchesse, bathing was no longer for show, but an everyday pleasure.

In 1721, in his "magnificent home" whose front entrance faced the Seine on the Quai d'Orsay near today's Musée d'Orsay, the Maréchal de Belle-Isle, great military man and diplomatic adviser to both Louis XIV and Louis XV, displayed the considerable fruits of what Saint-Simon called his "unbridled ambition," among them a vast bathing suite whose crowning glory was its view. Its five immense bay windows made for an experience that truly merits the qualifier unique: lazing in the tub and watching the boats drift by along the river. After one of those scenic soaks, however, you had to climb a small staircase up a floor to get to the bedroom.

When Blondel published his manifesto for modern architecture in 1737, there were thus grand bathrooms in Paris, but they were far less common than other new interior rooms such as private bedrooms and toilet rooms. Blondel was the first architect to include the bathroom in an architectural treatise, and he set the bar very high for the modern bathing experience.

The bath as Blondel defined it was to be taken in a metal tub that was filled not by servants who had carried in the water, but by faucets, one for hot water and one for cold, with a stopper at the bottom of the tub that allowed water to flow out. And a single room would no longer do; you had to have a full bathing suite: a room for the water heater, one to dry and to warm up the linen used for drying off (in those pre-terry-cloth days, sheets of linen served as toweling), and still another one to hold the tubs—yes, tubs: Blondel categorically states that "few bathrooms today have only one tub," something for which he offers two explanations. A bather might want to alternate between water at different temperatures, or "two people might enjoy keeping each other company." And there was still more: a room for a nap after a nice hot bath, a room where servants could wait in case they were needed, and, but of course, a room equipped with a flush toilet as well as a "shell-shaped basin to wash your hands."

From then on, the term bathing suite was on all French architects' lips.

*This engraving shows off a luxurious early bathroom as well as
a modern bathing experience. The lady has enjoyed a good soak
in a large tub; she removed her clothing before she did so.*

In 1743, Briseux explained that while those on a budget could simply add a single room near the kitchen, thereby sharing its water supply, if at all possible clients should have a suite. By midcentury, the *Encyclopédie* decreed that "bathrooms in private homes are composed of a multiroom suite," thereby making official to its international audience the arrival of another new component to the French blueprint for modern life. In 1744, this engraving (see page 71) showed that same audience just how luxurious these facilities should be. (Note the big sheets used to dry off.) In the ad for a home for sale on the Champs-Élysées in February 1765 "with all the modern conveniences," the only convenience explicitly named is the *salle de bains*, the term used ever since in French to designate the bathroom. A decade later, a study on water usage in Paris made it official: "When a person of means wants to rent an apartment, he considers a bathroom one of the most essential rooms." Thus, during the half century crucial to the age of comfort, the bathroom had gone from being the last private room on clients' lists to being an indispensable space.

Impressive technological advances made this possible. Everything began with the tub itself. Earlier models had been round and usually made from wood

Baignoire vue en face

*This architect-designed bathtub proves that as bathing became a
more common experience, the tub became a decorative object in its own right,
comfortable furniture for the bathroom.*

and were often set up in the kitchen, since water could be heated there. In the bathing suites of the early eighteenth century, the tub was reinvented and became a piece of modern furniture. The new bathtubs were made from tin-plated copper; though they were up to 6 feet long and 3 to 4 feet wide, the standard model was 4½ feet long, 2½ feet wide, and 26 inches deep. The traditional round tub had thus been replaced by tubs of roughly the shape and size still in use, the first designed so that people could stretch out in them and immerse themselves in water.

Early on—in Madame la Duchesse's mansion, for example—tubs were simply painted on the outside to match the room's décor. By the age of comfort's end, they had become far more decorative. There were even models that were dead ringers for the darling of modern furniture design, the sofa, and that shared the sofa's ideal of wraparound comfort (see page 72).

Even the grandest tub would have been useless without the first water supply piping in modern residential architecture and the first such piping ever to have been fully documented in print (see page 74). The lower half of this 1732 engraving is the earliest diagram of one of the new installations: the two tubs on the bottom right (1)—it's on a scale of six feet, so they are the standard size—are connected via a lead pipe (7) to the cold-water tank (6) and via a second pipe (8) to the hot-water tank (3), which is heated by the furnace surrounding it (2) and the hearth next to it (4). On each tub, faucets for hot and cold water are also indicated. The diagram's upper half illustrates the elegant wall paneling into which the tubs fit and "the thickness of the wall" behind which, as the text explains, the pipes ran.

All this, of course, was merely the tip of the iceberg: the bigger issue was the supply of water to flow through the pipes and faucets and fill those lovely tubs. Initially, getting the volume of water necessary to fill two large tubs would have been so costly that only the very wealthy could have known the experience of running a bath. The 1710 edition of d'Aviler indicates that early-eighteenth-century Parisian residences were often equipped with very large tanks or cisterns to collect rainwater. (There was one, for example, in the courtyard of Pierre Crozat's mansion.) In midcentury, the *Encyclopédie* claimed that when sand was used as a filter, these tanks provided "the best water possible." According to its calculations, an "average home" could collect nearly twenty-two hundred cubic feet of rainwater annually, which would supply eight *pintes*—a *pinte* was a bit less than today's liter—per person per day to a household of twenty-five people, an amount considered "more than sufficient." (Figures for a household included servants, whose personal use of water would have been minimal.) Pumps were installed next to the cisterns; they were elevated

This engraving shows off the elaborate interior decoration—wall paneling, lighting, even paintings—used to increase the impression of luxurious comfort in the original modern bathrooms. It is also the first diagram to illustrate the plumbing required to install a modern bathroom.

above the ground floor to facilitate distribution—d'Aviler's 1755 dictionary provided a table specifying the width of pipes necessary depending on the height of the tank.

By 1779, the estimated daily water use had risen dramatically, from eight to twenty *pintes*. (To put this into perspective, according to U.S. government figures, the average in Washington, D.C., two centuries later, the moment at which water usage peaked, was 677.5 liters; in New York City, it was 757 liters.) All through the eighteenth century, the city of Paris tried desperately to keep up with the demand for water on the part of its some seven hundred thousand inhabitants by relying on such traditional solutions as public fountains (their number was vastly increased but remained woefully inadequate), giant pumps to extract water from the Seine (the Samaritaine near the Louvre, another under the Pont Notre Dame), and three aqueducts, including one that brought water from Arcueil fifteen miles away to a tower near the Luxembourg Gardens that English physician Martin Lister marveled over on his 1698 visit. People increasingly relied on more than one source: a for-sale ad from 1790, for example, describes a tank to collect rainwater into which water also arrived from a municipal pump. None of this, however, was enough.

Since the municipality was not up to the task, private individuals floated schemes. In 1723, the Marquise de Balleroy learned of a plan to build giant pump houses in twelve different neighborhoods so that "all the homes in Paris can be supplied with water from the Seine." In 1778, dreams were becoming reality: three brothers named Périer, the undisputed masters of pump technology, founded the Compagnie des Eaux, the Water Company, taken over by the state a decade later and renamed the Royal Water Company. They built the Chaillot pump to supply Paris's Right Bank and the Gros Caillou for the Left Bank.

By October 13, 1781, the new company was operational, and the Périers were seeking their original clients. Those who signed up at their office on the rue Chaussée d'Antin by February 1, 1782, received a promotional offer: the Périers would pick up the tab for tearing up the sidewalk and running the conduits to connect private homes to the twenty-four thousand yards of municipal piping that carried water under the streets of Paris. They promised to deliver "an uninterrupted supply of water in whatever quantity is desired." The first desire they identified? "To be able to take baths in one's own home without any fuss," just the need already pinpointed in 1765 by another contemporary specialist on water usage. By the end of the age of comfort, the invention of the bathroom had initiated a revolution in both the supply and the demand for water. It was a perfect illustration of the interworkings of the age of comfort and the age of Enlightenment. The technology whose development had been fueled by the fabulous wealth of a few privileged individuals was gradually put at the service of a broader public.

Paris thus became a modern city in still another way: people began to associate comfort and well-being with the ready availability of water. For the poor, this meant more frequent trips to the public fountain or greater reliance on the water carriers who went door-to-door selling it by the bucket. Many others, however, saw the beginning of a sea change in access to water. By the end of the age of comfort, it had begun to be possible to think of water as we still do: simply to take it for granted. The yearly fee advertised by the Périers—fifty livres for a *muid* per day, or twenty *pintes* per person for twenty-five people— would have been within the reach of a broad public. They were right to say that bathing would thus become "inexpensive."

We don't know how many modern bathrooms and tubs resulted from water's easier availability, although in 1782 still another expert did claim that "the public's new predilection for very frequent baths" meant that "every new home now includes a bathroom." At the very highest end of the new bathroom spectrum belong the spaces created for that great bath fanatic the Marquise de Pompadour.

Versailles hadn't waited for the marquise's arrival to embrace this particular form of modern comfort: one of the common bonds between Louis XV and his most powerful mistress was their devotion to cleanliness. Already in 1728, the king had brought the novel experience to Versailles, complete with water tanks and heater; in 1731, the water-supply piping was updated. The marquise had her first bath built there in 1747–1748. It had green and white marble tiles and a single tub, with the tanks and heater on the floor above. On September 11, 1748, a master metalworker named Martin delivered a "faucet shaped like a swan's neck" for the tub. From then on, everywhere she went, Pompadour immediately ripped out the old bath. Thus, when she took over the Hôtel d'Evreux, she moved the bathing suite from its original location near the fabulous garden to a more modern spot, off her bedroom.

It was in the homes Pompadour had built, however, that she was free to develop her personal bathroom style. At Ménars, ormolu faucets added just that touch of glitz to the copper tub. (The room also contained one of the small writing tables that the marquise wanted constantly on hand.) And at Bellevue, she created the bathing suite to end all bathing suites. The upholstery was done in a most unusual cloth with a sort of 3-D effect: a cotton fabric "appliquéd with cutouts" from a piece of the marquise's favorite fabric, the very finest-quality cotton known in French as *perse*, or Persian, even though it in fact was made in India. This was "bordered and edged with braid and chenille," giving it still more depth. Above the doors on either side of the fireplace hung paired paintings by François Boucher, *Venus' Toilette* and *Venus' Bath*. (Today, *Venus' Toilette* is in the Metropolitan Museum in New York, while its companion painting hangs in Washington's National Gallery.)

Pompadour always commissioned paintings with a precise setting in mind. For her, Boucher imagined scenes that capture the spirit of the new bathing experience: the goddess most readily associated with aquatic activities is every inch the ideal eighteenth-century woman—all soft contours and peachy skin, with rosy cheeks and lips, her pale blond hair swept up and fetchingly wayward ringlets tumbling down—very like, in fact, the woman who soaked in the bathroom's tub. In *Venus' Toilette*, the goddess even reclines on what is indisputably a piece of contemporary French furniture, a curvy sofa or daybed.

As the century went on, those who couldn't afford expensive paintings and luxe faucets and even those without running water could still enjoy the new way of bathing. In the 1760s, furniture designer extraordinaire Roubo created bathing chairs (see page 78), which offered the same wraparound, reclining experience as built-in tubs. (The plate also illustrates portable bidets.)

And for those who did have running water but could afford neither an endless supply of it nor the added expense of a water heater, another "new kind of tub" was invented, smaller than the grand models—an article in the contemporary press explained that it thus used nearly 40 percent less water—and with a water-heating device built in. In one model, invented in 1768 by a master boilermaker named Level, a burner using wine spirits fit under the tub to "keep water heated to the desired temperature." Two months later, Level upped the ante by modifying his invention to use coal and thereby further lowered the cost.

That more affordable bathing experience was soon being marketed to a less exclusive clientele. The installation in this 1767 engraving (see page 79) couldn't hold a candle to Pompadour's baths. There is no décor to speak of; the fixtures are merely functional. The tub, while thoroughly modern in shape—it is the new small model: 3½ feet long, 2 feet wide, 21 inches deep—is not a thing of beauty, and the home was not equipped with a water heater. Instead, the strange contraption on the left (I), made of copper and called a "cylinder," was filled with red-hot coals and placed in the center of the tub to heat the water— the pipes (K) allowed vapor to escape.

The image proves that by the end of the age of comfort, bathing was seen as a familiar experience. It was just as clearly also an enjoyable one—a contemporary dictionary explained that people bathed "for pleasure and for cleanliness," in that order. The same dictionary gave as one example of the word's use "to stay in the bath for a long time." Bathing had become a pleasure to be

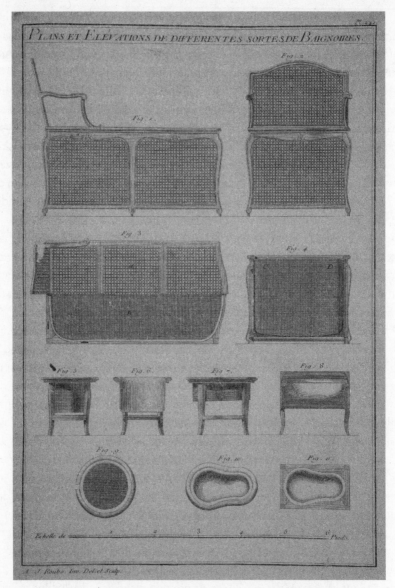

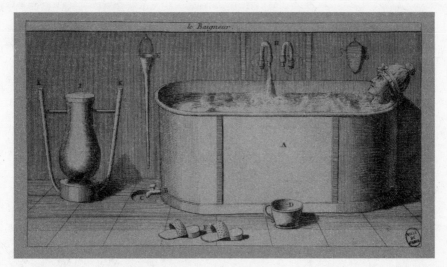

*This may be the original depiction of a modern bather. The man is fully reclined
in a bathtub shaped like those still in use today. He is clearly intending to remain
so for a good while. And he is savoring what is just as clearly a relaxing experience.*

savored, just as the happy bather of 1767 was doing. People were also bathing
just as we still do: the bather is no longer sitting or steaming but is lying down,
immersed in water up to his chin. Finally, he is, in what, as another contemporary dictionary explained, had become "normal" bathing attire, "naked." He even
has refinements such as a cap, clogs, and, at arm's length, a cotton scrubbing
mitt (G). A half century of experimentation had created the modern bath.

During the revolutionary period, many of the finest residences became public buildings in which opulent bathing suites surely seemed ridiculous. The
Napoleonic era glimpsed the return of the grand bathroom, but the revival was
short-lived indeed. From the 1830s on, the idea of bathing as one of life's comfortable pleasures disappeared. Bathrooms were once again extremely scarce;
when they did exist, they were plain and purely functional. And thus another
culture of the bath came to an end.

CHAPTER FOUR

The Flush Toilet

THE HISTORY OF the object now known as "the toilet" is more than usually complicated. Much of the difficulty arises from the fact that people have always daintily refused to say exactly what they had in mind. (Still today, when we want to find a toilet, we usually ask for "the bathroom.") Thus, in the late seventeenth century, a dizzying range of appellations existed. In England, options included the house of office, the closestool, and the privy closet, while across the English Channel one could ask, to name but a few, for the *chaise d'affaires* (the business chair), the *commodités* (the comforts or conveniences), or *le lieu* (the place), aka *les lieux* or *les lieux communs* (the places or the common places).

No other convenience ever inspired anything like this proliferation of names, a proliferation that often makes it difficult to know exactly what was meant by any one of them at any precise moment. Before the eighteenth century, however, the distinctions among different options were not very significant, for this much, at least, is certain: there was precious little privacy in the privy closet, and "the comforts" were decidedly uncomfortable in modern terms.

Beginning in the closing decades of the seventeenth century, a growing mass and no longer the occasional exceptional individual began to demonstrate a desire for increased privacy, cleanliness, and comfort in this "business" of daily life. By the turn of the eighteenth century, a revolutionary object, the flush toilet, had been invented. Unlike the bathroom, which was slow to win over the clients for modern architecture, the flush toilet immediately convinced people that it was worth the expense of its installation. Even prior to the stock market boom, great Parisian mansions began to be equipped with the new convenience. In less than twenty years, personal hygiene was transformed. Before, there was a hard, smelly seat in a place where others could walk in; after, a fixture was available that seems as sophisticated as anything on the market today, a fixture that was housed, moreover, in its own gloriously decorated, gloriously private room.

The toilet may well be the most carefully documented of all contemporary innovations: in greatest detail, in the largest number of sources, in multiple, exquisitely engraved diagrams and illustrations. Clearly, architects and contemporary observers alike could not wait to publicize its arrival in the modern home.

For centuries, waste management was dealt with in primitive fashion; before the eighteenth century, the options were few. The basic installation and the only one available to the less privileged was the latrine (a wooden shelf with a circular cutout placed over a shaft in the wall or directly over some form of cesspool or pit). People of means had closestools, in French *chaises percées*, or pierced chairs, boxlike stools or crudely designed chairs with a cutout ring-shaped seat that might be lightly padded for the most minimal comfort; a pewter pan fit into a compartment below.

As for privacy . . . well, latrines were often lined up several in a row, and closestools were moved around from room to room. Until the turn of the eighteenth century, it seems that most people from all ranks of society expected that others could be present during this part of daily life. Even great nobles did not mind being seen while sitting on a closestool. Louis XIV, for example, made his first move toward privacy, and a minimal one at that, only in 1684, when he decided that a crimson velvet curtain should be placed "in front of his business chair." Prior to this, the Sun King had received visitors and done business while sitting on that business chair. That curtain may have been a concession to his new wife, for the king seems never to have changed his mind on this issue. In 1708, when Montespan's legitimate son the Duc d'Antin asked for a separate building at Marly for one of the new toilet installations, "in order to eliminate filth," Louis XIV wrote in the margin of his request: "Worthless idea; [toilets] are useless and will cost more than you think." At the very end of the seventeenth century, the Duchesse de Bourgogne, wife of Louis XIV's grandson, confided to the Duc de Saint-Simon that "she was never able to talk more openly" than when she chatted with the ladies of the court while sitting on her closestool.

She didn't know that Saint-Simon was busily recording, in volume after volume of devastatingly acute memoirs, how the world around him was changing.

As the age of magnificence drew to a close, the duke is our major source of information on contrasting views of personal hygiene. Saint-Simon makes his point by rubbing our noses in it, as it were, describing in lavish detail a few vignettes from daily life at the turn of the eighteenth century that often feature Louis-Joseph, Duc de Vendôme, war hero and powerful personage at Versailles. One day, for instance, the Bishop of Parma arrived on a diplomatic mission only to find Vendôme on his chair of easement. The prelate was "horrified" when, in the midst of their negotiations, the duke got up and, to quote Saint-Simon, "began to wipe his ass right in front of him." Vendôme had lunch on his closestool; when the pan was full, servants were ordered to carry it out "right under the noses of the assembled company."

There were like-minded ladies of the court as well, notably the Princesse d'Harcourt, who at the end of an overly copious meal would simply slip out of the dining room, "hike up" her voluminous skirts, and "relieve herself" in the hallway. The princess was no longer young, and we witness her behavior through the eyes of those hosting the dinner parties. Members all of the young court, they no longer approved of what had long been standard behavior at Versailles. (To be fair to the princess, what else could one do at a time when the idea of guest facilities did not yet exist? It is said that some of Versailles's gilded corridors, much frequented by ladies in distress, retained a somewhat less than magnificent odor long after the Revolution shut down the court.)

In his clearest illustration of changing behavior, Saint-Simon zeroes in on the moment when Vendôme tried to force the Princesse de Conti, daughter of Louis XIV and Montespan, to admit that "everyone really preferred to act as he did but they weren't honest enough to be open about it." Saint-Simon makes his personal opinion clear: of the princess, he says that she was "known to be the cleanest person in the world," whereas he describes Vendôme as "extremely filthy."

The changed attitude Saint-Simon documents was winning the day just as its advocates had begun commissioning new residences and having them built in what has been ever since the thoroughly modern way: fast and with no expense spared. Small wonder that in a flawless interaction between behavior and design, their architects soon made sanitary facilities a priority. During the first half of the eighteenth century, the flush toilet became an absolute proof of architectural modernity, the first amenity a building had to have to be considered modern. And yes, the Princesse de Conti had one installed.

Three things were necessary to give the young royals the privacy and cleanliness they desired: a separate space to house new facilities, a sequence of waste piping within buildings, and a completely new kind of fixture. In Paris at the turn of the eighteenth century, a coalition of cleanliness fanatics drawn from different backgrounds and ranks of society began to take it for granted that it was worth the vastly increased expense to have these things in their homes; architects responded to this new attitude in record time. We know that it was during the decades 1690–1710 that this type of architectural modernity became possible because the first two editions (1691 and 1710) of d'Aviler's building manual neatly bookend the process of change.

First, the room. Already in 1691, d'Aviler's design for a model home included separate small rooms for its owners, directly accessible from their bedrooms and from adjacent dressing rooms—an arrangement that, in 1751, Françoise de Graffigny called *en suite*. (Servants had only latrines—a men's room and a ladies' room, each with several spots.)

Next the waste piping. Already in 1691, d'Aviler included what is still today the standard double sequence: the first-floor plan specified that there must be "waste piping made from clay or terra-cotta." (The word for waste piping, *boisseau*, was so new in this technical meaning that contemporary dictionaries do not include it.) D'Aviler further specified the need for "ventilation piping," today's vent stack, running up to the roof and with a small lead pipe above the roofline, both to provide air to keep the water flowing and to remove odors. (The name for the mechanism that ventilates waste piping, *ventouse*, first appeared in a dictionary in its technical sense the same year as d'Aviler's treatise.)

Brand-new words for brand-new technology. The facilities all this was designed to make function, however, hardly seem worth the fuss. D'Aviler spoke of a *chaise de commodité*, or comfort chair, without describing the fixture. From the plans, it is clear that what he had in mind was a simple closestool and that it was not hooked up to the plumbing but simply positioned near it.

During the twenty years that separate the first two editions of d'Aviler, creators of modern architecture, notably Pierre Bullet, were on the case. Bullet, too, published a building manual in 1691: he gave detailed specifics regarding waste piping—the best materials (glazed terra-cotta or lead), how to guarantee tight joints—but no information on the fixture it would be hooked up to. Four years later, just before he began a series of residences on the Place Vendôme for the wealthiest clients in Europe, he made public the news that he had invented the missing link that would make the expensive new piping worthwhile. Bullet claimed that the new fixture, for which he had received a royal patent, was both far more comfortable than closestools and a foolproof way to eliminate odor from the home. He refused to divulge its secrets in print but directed readers to the manufacturer on the rue de la Verrerie, Lay, where it was for sale.

By 1710 and Le Blond's revised edition of d'Aviler, the fixture still did not
have a name—Le Blond called it "this kind of place"—but it very definitely
now existed. Le Blond provided an extraordinarily detailed description,
which he justified by saying that it was so new, most people had not yet seen
one.

He began with the new seating experience it provided: with its padded, upholstered seat and back, it could only be compared with the piece of furniture
then setting new standards for comfort, the sofa. Then there was the lid: it
closed tightly and concealed "a porcelain bowl, fitted into a copper surround"
under the seat. You turned a faucet and water "rushed" in from a reservoir positioned on the floor above to wash the bowl out "perfectly." A second faucet
made the toilet into a proto-bidet; when you turned it, you were cleaned by a
"little shower" of water, either warm or cool, "depending on the season."
(The bidet was invented a decade later; this is the first mention of the idea behind it.) A third faucet controlled the water for a basin to wash one's hands.

Le Blond made it seem as if "this kind of place" were already well established
in French buildings by including the plans of a grand mansion in the Faubourg
Saint-Germain and a far more modest Parisian dwelling, both of which were
equipped with them. His message was clear: from now on, those who wanted to
be "comfortably off" would require the new convenience.

This message was repeated by every theoretician of modern French architecture. In 1728, Briseux pronounced the closestool "a thing of the past" and decreed that "modern" people used only the new "easy seats"—he described the
one he had seen functioning at the regent's Château de Saint-Cloud. Blondel's
1737 manifesto for modernism provided the first detailed diagrams to enable
just such "modern" clients to see exactly how the plumbing worked (see page
85). Blondel's figure 1 shows the marble slab (A) into which the wooden seat
cover (E) is set. D = handle for raising the seat cover; F = handle to control the
opening valve; G = handle to control the flushing valve. Figure 2 shows the device's interior and the flushing action. Figure 3, a cross section, shows the fixture's piping. Figure 4 illustrates the functioning of the proto-bidet or water jet
(Q), controlled by the handle (H) in figure 1.

The 1755 updating of d'Aviler's manual explains exactly where each element
in the new system, from tank to waste piping to the piping for the cleansing jets
of water, should be placed, lists Parisian residences where the system was already in use, and concludes that "all modern buildings" in Paris are equipped
with flush toilets. This sweeping proclamation is borne out neither by Blondel's
1752–1756 volumes of the plans of the greatest homes in Paris nor by those
published by Jean-François de Neufforge from 1757 to 1768. Both Blondel's and

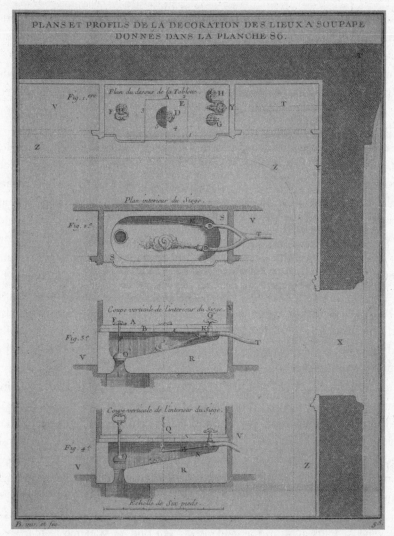

PLANS ET PROFILS DE LA DECORATION DES LIEUX A SOUPAPE
DONNÉS DANS LA PLANCHE 86.

*This 1738 engraving is the earliest diagram to illustrate the plumbing of a
flush toilet. All the innovations are depicted—from the toilet seat
to the handle that activates water flow to a brand-new concept,
the swirling movement of water now called a flush.*

Neufforge's plans do show, however, that whatever type of fixture was used, it
was now housed in its own room. Not a half century later, the victory for privacy that Saint-Simon had hoped for had taken place. The plans also show that
flush toilets, while not in "every" modern home, were indeed found in a great
many of them.

The new fixture initially appeared just where anyone would have expected to find it, in the homes of architecturally forward young royals: the king's son, Monseigneur, had one in his "New Château" at Meudon, which meant that his confidante, Madame la Duchesse, naturally ordered one for the Palais Bourbon.

Financiers loved the flush toilet. Pierre Crozat, for example, had one on the rue de Richelieu. They may have valued it not only in terms of personal comfort, but also as an ultraexpensive gadget sure to impress their business associates. They were thus the first to take up Blondel's suggestion and install toilets not only near master bedrooms, but also where guests could have easy access to them—just off the dining room or near the library or the salon. To have such a convenience available for the first time in homes where one was simply visiting was surely one of those basic life-changing experiences. The hands-down winner in the impress-your-guests use of the new fixture was the home designed in 1726 by Michel Tannevot for an individual at the center of French commerce, the director of the Indies Company, Pierre Castanier. Castanier had amassed a vast fortune through speculation and overseas trade, and he insisted on sanitary installations commensurate with his wealth. All the bedroom suites had toilet rooms; a particularly fine example was accessible from the library and its adjacent studies, where the director would have received clients, for a total of seven toilet rooms in all.

In no time at all, the merely well-to-do became enamored of the new convenience. In 1720, Charlotte Desmares, brilliant and well-paid actress and equally brilliant investor, had one in her bedroom suite. (In midcentury, her toilet room, which by then had been remodeled by a new owner, the Duc de Villeroy, was singled out in the *Encyclopédie* as among the most famous in Paris.) By 1760, even women of very ill repute who wangled only the best from their wealthy admirers demanded a flush toilet as part of the package: Marie-Anne Deschamps—the dancer whose architectural excesses, seen as the ne plus ultra of vulgarity, kept everyone in Paris agog in the late 1750s—got one of Madame la Duchesse's grandsons to pay for hers. By then, people bragged about them as someone today might boast of a painting just acquired at auction for a fabulous sum. Witness the Comte Dufort de Cheverny, who recalled moving in 1760 into the first residence of his married life, near Paris's Place des Victoires: he waxed sentimental about "the superb dining room, the mirror-lined boudoir"—and "the flush toilet." (Dufort de Cheverny, Louis XV's *introducteur des ambassadeurs*, or spokesman to the diplomatic corps, kept diplomats up on all the latest developments in French life and became a particularly acute informant about cutting-edge design and technology.)

In 1738, modernity reached Versailles. Louis XV made his new bedchamber the center of a suite by adding a dressing room and his first flush toilet in its own small room. There was nothing in the least "common" about the "place" he had set up: the fixture was built into a marquetry case in a room tiled with a mosaic of colored marble. During the day, the king had his favorite night table placed next to his latest convenience.

The king's decorators might have been following Blondel's design guidelines (see page 88), published the same year that the walls of Versailles were ripped open to add waste piping. The fixture (B) is recessed; Blondel specified that the seat cover should be of faux marble painted wood to match the room's marble tiles; the seat itself was padded and upholstered in leather. A huge mirror (E) hung above it; Blondel advised using strategically placed mirrors to help light small rooms. On each side, elaborately carved panels (F) disguised built-in storage for anything one might need when using the room, from towels— small cloths appear to have been the original toilet paper—to room-freshening perfume. Blondel added that the fixture "is most often covered with marquetry," just as the king's was.

As always, lavish spending soon got out of hand. By 1749, the French monarchy endured the first ever political toilet scandal. The Marquise de Pompadour had a weakness for sanitary facilities; some said that she owned the most beautiful toilets of her age. In this, she was aided and abetted by her favorite architect, Lassurance II, a great advocate of the new fixtures. In those heady days in 1749 after she moved into that much-coveted suite at Versailles, however, the marquise went too far.

It's easy to understand how it happened. It was difficult to keep adding waste piping at Versailles, and Pompadour simply had to have her comforts. The great furniture designer Pierre II Migeon thus came up with the perfect solution: a corner cupboard that not only was positively gorgeous, but was also fitted with a toilet bowl, a water tank, and a flushing mechanism. Since it was not hooked up to waste piping, it's hard to imagine how well it performed its function. (In the fixtures he created for Pompadour, Migeon did at least use a wood then new to France, mahogany, because of its odor-resistant properties.) The very illusion of hygienic modernity seems to have been enough to satisfy his client: the marquise awarded Migeon a very handsome annual pension. When the news of this was leaked to the public, the ensuing hue and cry was prodigious, as perhaps her bitterest enemy, royal minister the Marquis d'Argenson, gleefully reported. (Pompadour soon got exactly what she wanted: a flush toilet was installed next to her bedroom at Versailles in 1752; the installation was updated in 1756.)

Predictably, the scandal started a craze for the pseudoflush, and soon those

This is the way toilet rooms were decorated at the time Louis XV had his first one added at Versailles in 1738. The new fixture that was the room's centerpiece was covered with marquetry and had a padded seat upholstered in leather. A big mirror was hung above it to brighten the room, and beautifully carved paneling concealed storage space for necessities such as small cloths and room-freshening toilet water.

unable to afford the real thing had options available that allowed them to share the illusion that had delighted the royal mistress. Among the greatest monuments to the eighteenth-century French mastery of furniture design are the four volumes of André Jacob Roubo's *The Furniture Maker's Art*. In the section devoted to "seating of comfort and ease," Roubo explained that people were no longer satisfied with closestools. He realized that not everyone could afford to add waste piping. For the not quite rich who "wish to enjoy all the possible comforts," he therefore announced the invention of a chair with a flushing mechanism, and he provided precise documentation to allow them to have it copied. This engraving (page 90) illustrates the stages in the construction of the chair, the bowl, the tank, the seat, and the flushing mechanism. Figure 16 shows (A) the pipe in the water tank (also visible in his figure 4); (B) the handle that, when turned, initiated the water flow; (C) the pipe that carried water into the toilet bowl.

Roubo specified that the back must be three to four inches thick in order to contain a lead-lined, water-filled tank. He does not, however, enlighten his readers about what seems an evident question: What did a flush toilet mean in a home without indoor plumbing? He specifies that someone has "to fill the tank with water" but gives no hint of what happened after the chair's user had enjoyed the thrill of the flush.

A decade later, Pierre Giraud, the inventor behind the next attempt at providing what he called "portable comforts," finally filled people in on how they worked. His model (page 91) took the form of a very comfortable armchair with a water reservoir added to the back and a large box or vat underneath for waste. In figure I, a = the handle pulled to lift the stopper (b) at the bottom of the tank; c = the pipe that carried water from the tank to the porcelain bowl (d); f = waste piping to the vat (h); g = handle that opens f; n = the vent for the water pipe. Figure II shows the step (i) needed to get up high enough to clear the vat. Figure III illustrates the "accessories": e = cleaning spray or jet; f = compartment that holds a little brush for cleaning the bowl; h = compartment for a sponge.

The tank contained enough water for ten to twelve flushes, Giraud claimed; the front of the box opened to disclose a vat made of wood specially treated with an odor-absorbing substance. According to Giraud, the average-size vat, three cubic feet, "would be sufficient for three months when two people are using the convenience and for two months when three people are involved." The vat could then be slipped out, and two men could carry it down to the basement, where the building's master vat was located.

Giraud's work ends with a series of testimonials from contented customers, surely the first time that private individuals spoke publicly about how their lives had been changed by sanitary facilities. We learn, for example, that for

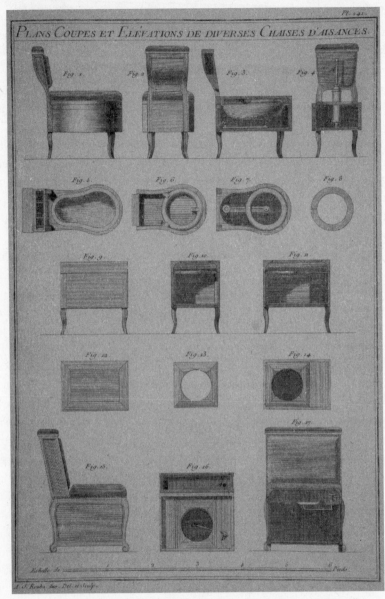

Furniture designer extraordinaire Roubo created flush toilets for those who couldn't afford to add waste piping in their homes. This diagram shows every step in the making of a flushing chair, including the water tank, which was to be filled by hand.

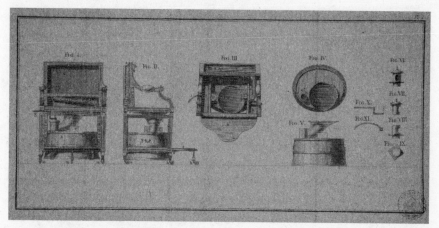

This flushing chair takes Roubo's concept one step further by showing what happened after the flush. A vat was camouflaged under the seat. Made from wood treated to be odor-absorbing, it allegedly could be left in place for months at a time and then carried to the basement, where it was emptied into a master vat.

M. Rousseau, an architect who saw clients in his home and whose comfort room, measuring five feet by three feet, was accessible from his study, his reception room, and his dining room, the best feature of Giraud's invention was the fact that it gave off "no odors," even though it "got a lot of use." M. Tréguguet, an engineering inspector, formally "certifies" that he has been using Giraud's model for six years; he praised its efficiency and added that it gave off no fumes—the elaborate interior decoration, even the gilding, in his comfort room had remained "intact."

Their testimonials prove that less than a century after the clash in practices between the Princesse de Conti and the Duc de Vendôme, the desires for privacy, hygiene, and comfort that had given rise to the creation of a new room with plumbing and a fixture to match were becoming ever more widespread, well beyond elite circles. Already in August 1739, when the city of Paris wanted to throw a giant public celebration, the court-appointed official in charge of maintaining law and order decided that there simply had to be public sanitary facilities. (We are not told which model he chose.) He created two rooms, labeled "ladies' wardrobe" and "gentlemen's wardrobe," with attendants to keep them tidy.

One problem, however, remained: what to call the fixture that had become an integral part of modern architecture and modern interior decoration.

Blondel's suggestion, it must be said, was not catchy: *lieux à soupape*, places with a valve. No one knows why, but people soon began to speak of *lieux à l'anglaise*, English places. Blondel and Roubo railed out. Blondel claimed to have interrogated every English visitor he met and always to have been told that "they were unknown in London," and Roubo backed him up: "They were being used in France long before they were known in England."

It just so happens they were right.

The only flush toilets seen outside of France were put there by French modern architects. In the 1720s, for example, when Jean-François Blondel designed a number of high-profile residences near Geneva, all featured "places with a valve," sometimes more than one per floor. In England by the 1730s, it should have been possible to modernize plumbing, but that did not happen. Yet the English constantly get all the credit for the flush toilet.

Oh, yes, there was Sir John Harrington, godson of Elizabeth I, now enshrined as the fixture's inventor. He is said to have installed one in his home and perhaps a second one for his godmother. In 1596, Harrington published a whimsical volume, *The Metamorphosis of Ajax* (as in "a jakes," or privy), in which he describes and diagrams his creation, which does seem to be a flush toilet, albeit a rather primitive model. Harrington repeatedly insists that this fixture can be built "with little cost," that it is "easy" and "cheap" to duplicate it, but it's difficult to imagine that an efficient model could have been realized on the cheap. While Harrington clearly understood the flush toilet's mechanism, it's also difficult to imagine that all the effort and expense necessary to actualize it would have been expended for a one-off.

Harrington's invention was just that: unique. British patents began in 1617; from then to 1775, no patent mentions a waste-removal fixture of any kind. Finally, in 1775, a patent was issued to Alexander Cummings for . . . a "closet with a valve." (Does that name sound familiar?) The history of the English flush toilet had finally begun. Mass-produced flush toilets began to be manufactured in the 1860s at the Marlboro Works by London plumber Thomas Crapper. As for the French, they reinvented their wheel only in the 1890s, when the Havard brothers began to turn out the (then) latest models.

We should not be surprised that the French were not eager to claim an invention of which their finest modern architects were so justifiably proud. For centuries, the French and the English have played the same game, referring with the enemy's name to things they prefer not to speak of. Thus, in English syphilis became "the French disease," while the French spoke of "the English disease." In the case of the toilet, the game has never stopped. The French replaced "English places" with "water closet" or "WC." "Loo" comes from *lieu*, "commode" from *commode*, and "toilet" from *toilette*.

CHAPTER FIVE

Heating

Everyday life in December 1708 at Versailles, the grandest palace in modern memory: In the bedroom of Louis XIV's second wife, the Marquise de Maintenon, two of the most influential personages in the world have their imposing armchairs pulled up tight by a large fireplace. On the left-hand side, the king is deep in conversation with one of his ministers, while on the right his wife takes her meals on a little table set for one.

Their proximity was companionate. It was also, however, obligatory, for the winter of 1708 was to become legendary. "Never in the memory of man has it ever been so cold," moaned even the king's sturdy German sister-in-law, the Princesse Palatine. By early February, she reported, "in Paris alone," nearly twenty-five thousand had died. One night at Versailles, all the lovely flacons filled with scents that lined every elegant dressing table shattered when the water in them froze. With its immensely high ceilings and vast spaces, Versailles was among the draftiest dwellings imaginable. In one way, at least, the king lived exactly as his subjects did, huddled near a fire to stay warm.

If this were the story of any other convenience from the age of comfort, I would now announce that a mere decade or so later, in the new modern residences of Paris and even at Versailles, it was no longer necessary to suffer this way. This, however, is not like those other stories. Heating was the one convenience that was not modernized during the age of comfort, even though it's hard to see why this did not happen. The technology was invented that would have made it possible—in 1713, just when it should have been. While its implementation would clearly have entailed considerable expense, the same was true for the installation of flush toilets, and people were willing to pay for that.

Everyone knew that the poor heating provided by traditional fireplaces was an immense source of discomfort. Even the most modern architects, however, continued to think of fireplaces largely in terms of their decorative value.

Heating, too, has a checkered past. Ancient sites—the Minoan Palace of Knossos, Pompeian villas—display evidence of heating systems that still seem sophisticated: forced air, warming pipes inside walls and beneath floors. After the fall of Rome, however, heating returned to a primitive state, and it stayed that way virtually until the eighteenth century.

Medieval homes were built around an open central hearth. In the twelfth century, fireplaces were first built into walls, and the chimney fireplace began to replace the open hearth. By the fourteenth, chimney fireplaces were becoming common in bedrooms; thus began the practice of multiplying the number of fireplaces in a home. Until the late sixteenth century, however, even in a major city like Paris many homes still were completely without heat. Then the seventeenth century witnessed a boom in fireplace construction, and by the early eighteenth century in those same Parisian homes, they were found even in servants' rooms. During the final decades of the seventeenth century, the number of fireplaces in French royal palaces more than doubled.

All through this time, however, fireplace design proved remarkably resistant to change. And whenever it did change, improvements were almost solely decorative. Thus, from the fifteenth century on, mantelpieces became increasingly ornamental, and fireplaces therefore became increasingly essential to a room's décor. Guidebooks to Paris in the late seventeenth century included the city's famous fireplaces among must-see sights for foreign visitors.

In the 1690s, architect Robert de Cotte had one of the most influential ideas in the history of interior design. The French mirror-making industry had recently invented the technology that made it possible to produce full-length mirrors: de Cotte began positioning large, elaborately framed mirrors over fireplaces with marble mantelpieces. The combination of marble mantel and huge mirror proved so winning that it issued in the fireplace's golden age, during which its placement became a central focus of each room's layout; it became standard procedure to indicate fireplaces on architectural plans.

The eighteenth century also considered the mantel-mirror duo essential to a room's ability to function successfully as a space for entertaining. In the *Encyclopédie*, for example, we learn that for the design of a reception room in the semiprivate zone, architects should be careful not to make the mantelpiece taller than three feet six inches to three feet eight: those seated around the fire should be able to look into the mirror and check out everything going on in the rest of the room—Had someone new just come in? Was the conversation back in the corner getting interesting?—without leaving their well-padded armchairs. In the room in which the group of friends has gathered in de Troy's *Reading from Molière* (see color plates), everything has been perfectly calibrated so that even from the particularly low armchairs in which they are seated, this is still possible—in fact, the lady in the light dress seems to be glancing up for just that purpose.

Finally, the fireplace became the room's decorative center. Mundane fireplace tools such as andirons became true works of art. The practice of showing off some of one's most treasured objects on the mantel began with the use of big mirrors in the 1690s and soon became all the rage. At first, people displayed porcelain, particularly vases. Small clocks designed expressly for this purpose, called mantelpiece clocks, were introduced about 1750. At the same moment, candlesticks, candelabra, and girandoles were first featured in the place of honor. And to complete the picture, on either side of the mirror were positioned sconces known as *bras de cheminée*, or fireplace arms: when their candles were lit, they were like arms of light extending the fire's brilliance out into the room.

Architects then began to include in their treatises engravings that illustrated the proper way to integrate fireplaces into a room's decorative scheme (see page 96). In a grand eighteenth-century room, the design carved into the mantelpiece matched that used in the frame of the mirror over it and in the frames of paintings, which in turn echoed the design of the wood paneling and of the frames of furniture in the room. Note the large mirror over the fireplace, the fireplace arms on either side. Lovely mantelpieces thus made it possible for the original interior decoration to strut its stuff.

If only they had added comfort to those interiors as well as elegance. However, the fireplaces whose exterior design was so carefully calculated remained absolutely primitive where it really mattered, for on the inside, at the heat source, they used essentially the same crude design already in place for centuries. They thus produced very shallow heat and in addition threw vast quantities of cold air into a room.

They also gave off equally vast quantities of smoke, and this, rather than the question of poor heat, helps explain why, in the early eighteenth century, the fireplace was redesigned. If you stop to add up the number of yards of material on display in rooms such as bedrooms and society rooms—on the furniture, on the walls and at the windows, on the backs of their inhabitants—and think of fabric's astronomical cost, you realize why this would have been the case: all that smoke left a deposit of soot that could quickly dim the beauty of fabulous textiles. People had put up for centuries with burning eyes caused by

This engraving shows the essential role played by fireplaces in the décor of an eighteenth-century room. They brightened rooms: large mirrors hung above them, and sconces (known as "arms of light") hung on either side carried the light they gave off into the room through reverberation. And their carving echoed that of the room's paneling, the frames of mirrors and paintings, even its furniture.

smoke-clogged rooms. Only in the eighteenth century, once architects and decorators had begun to use far more fabric than ever before, once they had begun to favor lighter colors such as white and pale yellow, and once smoke had begun to threaten all this increasingly elaborate décor, did objections to living with smoking fireplaces first appear in print. And it was in France, the nerve center for the comfort-driven life, that these objections initially became numerous enough to attract attention.

The first major salvo in the war against primitive fireplaces came not from an architect, but from a lawyer by profession and a scientist by avocation. Nicolas Gauger, a fanatical defender of modern science, Newtonian physics in particular, had presented to the French Royal Academy of Science his research on topics such as barometers and the refraction of light. His most influential work, the 1713 treatise *La Mécanique du feu, The Mechanics of Fire*, was quickly translated into German and English. Gauger explained that fireplaces had to be radically redesigned both for reasons of health—everyone caught cold because of the uneven heat—and for economic ones as well—all that smoke was ruining fine furniture, fine clothing, even fine coiffures elaborately covered with costly silver powder.

Gauger was in fact the first person completely to rethink the conception of the fireplace. His system would have been enormously expensive to install. He had reconceived not only the fireplace, but also the chimney; his concept required, furthermore, the addition of something never before used in modern architecture, a system of ductwork to bring fresh air into rooms and to circulate warm air within them. What Gauger promised to deliver, however, could have been seen as well worth the expense for the clientele with almost limitless means whose new properties were beginning to transform Parisian architecture at the time his treatise appeared.

Here are some of the ways in which Gauger guaranteed that his new fireplace would improve the quality of life. First, it would maintain even heat throughout a room, so that people would be free to sit anywhere they liked rather than remaining huddled near the fire. Second, the room would be smoke-free, so that windows and doors could be tightly shut without fear of asphyxiation. Third, fresh air would constantly be circulated in the room, making the home both healthier and sweeter smelling. Fourth, heat could be regulated so that the desired temperature could be maintained. Fifth, the fireplace could be adjusted to guarantee that a bedroom stayed warm all through the night even if the fire had been extinguished. During the terrible winter of 1708–1709, bottles shattered not only at Versailles, but all over France when the water in them froze—everywhere, that is, but in Gauger's bedroom, even though he turned off his heat "well before midnight."

Last but surely not least, Gauger imagined various ways in which the fireplace could be made the centerpiece of the original central heating, a system designed to warm more than one room from a single heat source. In the case of large, adjoining rooms, two fireplaces built back-to-back could share the same cavity or air box (the cavity in which air was warmed was one of Gauger's main improvements to traditional fireplace design). A single fireplace could be used to heat a bedroom and an adjacent, smaller room (boudoir, study, dressing room) by means of a system of ductwork and registers. Ducts at the base of the wall would bring cold air from the smaller room to that magic fireplace, and ducts running from the floor to the ceiling and back along the top of the wall would return air that had been warmed. He even imagined a system of ducts within a bedroom so that warm air could be focused directly on the bed to warm the sheets or even right at the feet of a particularly cold-natured person.

Gauger's treatise is a perfect example of the practical science in which the Enlightenment so excelled. He was, for instance, the first to apply a recent discovery, the flue's effects on combustion, to a home heating system. And he wanted his invention to be copied. The treatise contains detailed, beautifully engraved plates that illustrate the exact construction of fireplaces and chimneys, as well as the circulation of hot and cold air (see below). Air from the outside enters the room through D. It then proceeds either through Z into the fireplace to help combustion or through Y into the air box at the rear, where it is warmed before being sent into the room via the cylindrical register on the upper left of the fireplace. Once in the room, warm air displaced cold air, which was removed via the chimney.

And there you have it: a brilliant blueprint for modern heating. Historians contend that Gauger's ideas were the inspiration for many subsequent heating systems and that it was only in the final decades of the nineteenth century

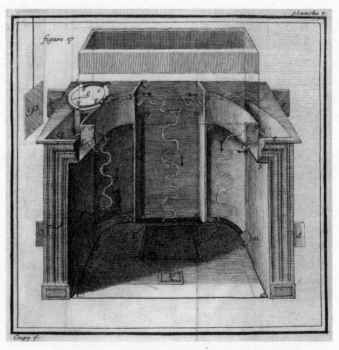

This is a sectional drawing of the improved fireplace design
originally advertised by Nicolas Gauger in 1713. Gauger
was the first to use a system of ductwork to bring fresh
air into rooms and to circulate warm air within them.
The presence of ductwork and registers also meant
that a single fireplace could be used to heat
more than one room. Gauger thus invented
a prototype for central heating.

that systems more advanced than his were invented. Evidence to suggest that Gauger's treatise had any significant impact on the way eighteenth-century homes were built is, however, scant. Only one architect, Briseux, discussed new-style home heating in his publications. In his 1728 *Modern Architecture*, for example, Briseux clearly uses Gauger's findings to modify a traditional fireplace and to add vents to let smoke escape. He went further still in his 1743 work on country homes by suggesting a Gauger-style system of ductwork to use one large fireplace to provide heat to small, adjacent rooms. A second architect, Boffrand, may actually have put Gauger's system into operation in at least one of the legendary residences that brought modern architecture to Nancy in the early decades of the eighteenth century.

A few individuals used Gauger's findings to modify their heating systems. In 1760, for example, the Comte Dufort de Cheverny recounted his visit to a home just off the Champs-Élysées. He rejoined his host in his study, where he positively swooned over the new heating system: "The study stood open to both adjoining rooms, but the registers had been so perfectly positioned that, even though it was quite cold outside, one would have thought we were at the height of summer." A new profession was soon created: *fumiste*—from *fumer*, to smoke—someone who works on fireplaces to prevent them from smoking; so the idea that smoke could be stopped was gaining ground. The word's earliest known appearance is in a 1735 letter from one of comfort's best-known enthusiasts, Voltaire, who requested a copy of Gauger's book in order to learn his "secrets" and thus eliminate smoking fireplaces from his life. And that is it: in an age when so many—architects and clients alike—were in a rush to document the way life was becoming more comfortable, the cozy, smoke-free environment could not have been a high priority, for people were simply not discussing the question.

Gauger's reputation did live on in print. His book inspired a rash of treatises proposing new fireplace models; in all of them, Gauger's work remained the benchmark. None of his successors found a serious flaw in his invention: one after another, they justified their efforts by arguing that Gauger's fireplace was simply too expensive to install and that theirs would prove far more economical. No one made that argument more forcefully than that great apologist for thrifty comfort, the man who brought the fireplace debate to the New World, Benjamin Franklin.

The *Account of the Newly Invented Pennsylvanian Fire-Places* (1744) is vintage Franklin, a muscular sales pitch for what he repeatedly describes as his "invention": how the Pennsylvanian fireplace is made, how it works, and how it will improve "the comfort and conveniency of our lives." Its first page reads "advertisement," printed in enormous letters, and consists of a list of the stores in Philadelphia, New York, and Boston where these "new" fireplaces, "made in the best manner," could be purchased. Franklin dismisses Gauger's design as too "intricate" and too expensive to install, yet the essence of his fireplace is astonishingly close to Gauger's 1713 model. Franklin's model was new mainly because it was designed to be installed inside existing fireplaces, which meant that no additional work was required—no new chimney, no ductwork. This also meant that it would have been far less effective than Gauger's—and also far more removed from the concept of central heating.

Franklin was subsequently treated much as he had dealt with Gauger. In his 1786 treatise, for example, Charles-Louis de Fossé claimed that people in France had tried to install "Pennsylvanian fireplaces" in their homes, but they couldn't be made to work. All the denigration of earlier models found in the work of Gauger's successors is still another mystery. There is absolutely nothing other than vague accusations by competitors to prove that anyone was trying out the different models in order to determine which alleged improvements really worked.

And all the while the smoke kept rushing out of those elegant but old-fashioned fireplaces all over France. In November 1750, to cite but the most celebrated example of the damage it caused, the Marquise de Pompadour threw a housewarming party at the jewel-box château Bellevue, on which she and her favorite architect, Lassurance II, had been lavishing attention—and an amount of money said by many to be wildly excessive—for two years. The party was planned to last for several days, but the first evening sent guests packing in search of more comfortable quarters. To the delight of Pomadour's fiercest enemy, ex–minister of foreign affairs the Marquis d'Argenson, the fabulous fireplaces drew so poorly that "all the new interiors were continuously filled with the smoke that came rushing out." (The enmity between d'Argenson and Pompadour was legendary: he tried to limit the power exercised by a mere mistress, one of low birth to boot; she responded by contriving to force his resignation; he returned to court only after her death.) Small wonder that the marquise ran up a huge bill with her favorite luxury goods merchant, Lazare Duvaux, who regularly sent men all the way from Paris to clean her crystal chandeliers.

And as Gauger—who claimed not to have had a single cold in the eight years since he had installed new fireplaces in his home—well knew, the risks were more than monetary. On January 17, 1709, the Princesse Palatine described the misery of dining at the royal table in the dead of that most dire winter. She had come down with bronchitis because, while the front side of her body facing the monumental fireplace had been broiling, her back had been freezing. This was life in a royal palace before Gauger came on the scene.

In January 1764, a half century after Gauger had made his invention public, little had changed. The Marquise de Pompadour developed pneumonia during another cruel winter. She was residing at the time in Choisy, a château that was a monument of modern architecture, the work of the king's favorite architect, Ange-Jacques Gabriel, who in 1742 had added such features as an elegant bath pavilion. When the marquise fell ill, she moved to the adjacent, more intimate, and even more comfortable small château, renowned for its interior decoration by world-famous architects and painters such as Boucher. It had all the requisite new rooms and amenities, gloriously carved mantelpieces, but . . . not a single new fireplace.

When she died, Louis XV, always careful to keep his emotions hidden, was seen with "huge" tears rolling down his cheeks. Even then, the man who had added plumbing to Versailles did not modernize its fireplaces.

CHAPTER SIX

Easy Seats

I N 1770, JEANNE Genet Campan, a young woman lucky enough to have secured a plush job at the French court as official reader to the daughters of Louis XV, was worried: the youngest, Madame Louise, had run off abruptly to become a Carmelite nun. Would a second daughter, Madame Victoire, decide to follow in the footsteps of her favorite sister? Victoire, however, quickly put her fears to rest. "She said to me as she pointed to the *bergère à ressort* [a heavily padded, luxuriously upholstered armchair] in which she was stretched out: 'Don't worry; I could never be like Louise, because I am far too attached to the comforts of life. This armchair will be the ruin of me.' "

Spoken like a true child of the age of comfort. When it all began, a chair could never have been the ruin of anyone, for there was no such thing as seating comfort. Then, within decades home furnishings went from primitive to sophisticated; the French, and other Europeans after them, became mad for furniture. By 1770, a great many people would have understood why Madame Victoire, "unable to give up the softly rounded curves of her favorite chair," decided to remain at Versailles.

Furniture went modern in close partnership with architecture. New pieces and styles of furniture were originally used in newly invented rooms; often the same architect had designed both the rooms and the furniture; the clients for new furniture were most often also those for new architecture. Between 1675 and 1740, people went from living with only a few stiff chairs with no padding to being literally surrounded by a truly dizzying array of well-stuffed and padded, curvy, and "orthopedically" proportioned seats: from armchairs and sofas to daybeds and chaises longues. And this new seat furniture—the first true designer furniture, the first furniture ever designed with comfort in mind—was abundant, present in all interior rooms (even bathrooms), so that private life could be carried out in perfect ease.

In addition, the original modern seat furniture positively forced people into a new take on life. Stuffy, formal ways were swept away as soon as straight-backed seating was replaced by designs in which it was impossible to sit bolt upright, designs that for the first time ever made more casual posture the norm. Well-padded seats encouraged people to lean back, even to lounge. They forced the French, formerly the most magnificent people in Europe, to learn to relax. The new seat furniture, in short, was responsible for a revolution in style, lifestyle, and consumerism on a scale rarely equaled.

The ancient Greeks were the first to put comfort and seating together: they created chairs whose graceful curves were easy on the body and the eyes. After this, however, any notion of designing chairs for comfort disappeared, to reappear only at the turn of the eighteenth century. The Romans used the chair as a showy status symbol, and with the fall of the empire, the chair virtually vanished in the West. For centuries, most people perched on any available surface. Given the way they lived, complicated furniture was hardly possible.

The French words for furniture say it all: *meuble, mobilier,* from the Latin *mobilis,* mobile, that which can be moved. In the Middle Ages, all great families—and furniture design, like architecture, is naturally dictated by the wealthiest clientele—were regularly on the move, forced from place to place by war, famine, disease. As a result, interior decoration in the medieval castle had to be portable: rich tapestries on the walls, elaborate curtains around the bed. With the exception of the largest piece, the bed, families took their furniture with them. Furniture was thus made to save space during a move, to fold or break down easily. There was no point in making pieces decorative—anyone who's moved a lot knows what that does to furniture.

The effects of a more stable life on furniture first became visible at the end of the fifteenth century. The chair became common again at that time (with three legs rather than four); its frame was sometimes turned; upholstery first began to appear (only a bit of leather or tapestry stretched across the seat of a chair, but still . . .). At least until the middle of the seventeenth century, however, the situation hardly changed. People were no longer constantly on the move, but they had very little furniture: beds, tables, a few stools and basic chairs, some chests. Those who did still move about, royal families in particular, had only one set of furniture, which traveled with them when they changed residence.

The turning point just may have come as the result of events that took place in 1648: the queen mother and the boy king Louis XIV were forced to flee Paris in haste during a budding civil war; when they arrived at the palace at Saint-Germain-en-Laye, it was naturally bare, and most people in the royal entourage were forced to sleep on hastily assembled piles of straw. This was a humiliation too great for the budding Sun King, and like Scarlett O'Hara, he seems to have vowed never to be poor again.

In 1662, one of the major early decisions of his independent reign sounded the death knell for portable furniture: a formerly rather modest tapestry-weaving workshop known as the Gobelins was moved to Paris and elevated to the status of royal tapestry works. The king's painter, Charles Le Brun, was named its director. In 1667, the Gobelins gained still more importance and became the official supplier of the Crown's *meubles*. Many new types of artists and artisans moved into its vastly expanded enclave—various kinds of furniture makers, specialists in bronzework and lacquerwork and the art of marquetry. From then on, the Gobelins had the capacity to produce every kind of decorative object. Le Brun thus became the first architect to design furniture and to oversee every aspect of its production, and the Gobelins began to produce the first furniture taken seriously enough to be documented. The stage was set for the age of architect-designed furniture to begin.

Because of the Gobelins, the original furniture industry was created. Between 1670 and the mid–eighteenth century, French designers and craftsmen invented most of the pieces that are still crucial in homes today. The modern age for furniture began after the young king made a second major decision: he would no longer travel with all his possessions. Henceforth, royal furniture would be immobile, for every royal château was to be kept fully furnished at all times. This gave the newly enlarged Gobelins a gigantic outlet for its production.

The word *meuble* was soon redefined. First, as furniture became less mobile, it was more often used to refer to the furniture made for a particular room: the concept of a matched set of furniture was thus born. Second, the word less often designated the most portable decorative items, tapestries in particular, items we no longer think of as furniture. The realignment of the Gobelins in 1667 initiated, in other words, the process as a result of which tapestry came off the walls and was put onto the chairs. Finally, the word gradually came to refer less to the fabric alone and more to the entire piece, the fabric and the frame combined.

In the early 1670s, when this process began, someone using the word *meuble* in its just emerging meaning of the matching furniture found in a specific room thought little or not at all of the design of that furniture; it was a matched set if all pieces were covered in the same fabric; the value was mostly in the textile. A half century later, the fabric still matched, but so did the design of the pieces: their carving, their shape, and their style. The fabric, moreover, was no longer the only source of value. During that century, the concept of furniture design had been born and become commonly recognized. By the 1720s, people were using the term furniture as we still do.

At the start, Louis XIV's directives did not move furniture in a new direction. The first design studio was initially famous for its great showpieces, the kind produced in Renaissance Italy. In 1673, for example, the Parisian newspaper *Le Mercure galant* announced—and this may be the first time that a newspaper's coverage had extended to furniture—that the Gobelins had just completed "six big *cabinets*." The cabinet—a sort of dresser with doors and compartments— ideally suited the age of magnificence. Itself the height of flashiness—made of exotic woods, inlaid, encrusted with semiprecious stones—it was also a display piece, made to show off its owner's most fabulous collectibles. As for new seating or any furniture designed for comfort . . . well, in all of Versailles when it was unveiled to the public in 1682, there was precious little of that. On his 1687 visit, the foremost Swedish architect of the day, Nicodemus Tessin the Younger, noted in the king's bedchamber only chairs designed as showstoppers: "made of solid silver with a cushion in crimson and gold." The public portion of the age of magnificence unfolded rather like one gigantic cocktail party with people always on their feet.

The Gobelins studio had another outlet for its production: the more intimate châteaux where only the privileged few were invited and protocol was relaxed. There, artists had greater license to innovate. In these places where the age of comfort began, the age of furniture got its start. Only a few decades later, people owned more than just a few pieces of furniture. And once they did, furniture quickly moved beyond the utilitarian and into the realm of style and fashion. In 1769, Roubo felt able to pronounce that "it is disgraceful for one's furniture not to be as up-to-date [*à la mode*] as one's clothing." Furniture also entered the domain of comfort. And as soon as these ideas were in place, artists began to depict a new experience: people in love with their furniture.

The golden age of French furniture was also a golden age for French engraving. An astonishing number of prints are set in the new interior rooms, and they are above all furniture plates, images that show off the latest ways to furnish a room, as well as various kinds of endearing behavior that furniture seemed to inspire in the first people able to enjoy private life in private space. This scene (page 106) features a fashionable woman in her equally fashionable interior. She is looking fondly—not, as one might expect, at the handsomely

*Early-eighteenth-century engravings such as this one are the earliest depictions
of a new phenomenon: house-proud individuals in love with their furniture.*

turned-out suitor seen in the doorway holding out his hands and gazing long-
ingly at her, but . . . at her sofa. Sofas were then still relatively new, and this is
a recent model—one of two that were vying for sofa supremacy—and it clearly
"works" with its surroundings, fitting neatly beneath the mythological scene
on the wall above. She touches her fan to her face in reverie as she gazes at it, as
if lost in her pleasure at the way her interior has turned out.

This print and countless others like it testify to the role that the new conception of furniture played in the age of comfort, a role that became ever more
pronounced as the eighteenth century unfolded. One of the biggest differences
between the daily life of Louis XV and that of Louis XIV involved the presence of furniture. Louis XV was a member of the first generation to grow up
with the modern conception of furniture, and it showed. During his reign,
royal châteaux were stuffed to the gills with furniture, all of it conceived specifically for the room in which it was placed, all of it French made. One category
of furniture had become dominant—seat furniture in a wide range of styles,

not one of which had even been a gleam in a designer's eye in 1675. In the age of magnificence, people lived on their feet; in the age of comfort, they were ensconced in easy seats, armchairs, and sofas—well-cushioned and padded armchairs and sofas. Madame Victoire was every inch her father's daughter.

The revolution in seating naturally began with the chair. Prior to the age of comfort, the chair functioned first and foremost as a status symbol. All chairs were essentially stand-ins for the king's seat, the throne; in every dwelling, the best chair was reserved for the head of the house. This was particularly true of any chair with arms. Larger and more imposing, the armchair was the power seat, the place from which justice was handed down. This explains why there was almost no comfortable seating in Versailles's public rooms: anyone in an armchair in the king's presence could be seen as the king's equal.

During the second half of the seventeenth century, the armchair began its modern life in schizophrenic fashion. On the one hand, armchairs became ever more evidently power seats when they were expanded to previously unheard-of proportions. Their seats became wider and deeper, their backs wider and higher—on average, thirty-two inches high. This was furniture intended expressly to overwhelm everything else in the room. (They were also stiff and rigidly rectilinear—in short, anything but inviting.) Then, soon after the Gobelins received its expanded mission, the armchair moved in another direction: the new chairs were called *fauteuils de commodité*, comfort armchairs. They adopted the oversize proportions of power armchairs, but they added new features, most significantly the earliest use of a device with a big future in the history of seating, wings that projected out from the chair's back. In French, these are called *joues*, cheeks, since one can rest one's cheeks there. Cheeks made the big chairs suddenly cozy and prove that comfort was beginning to steal the scene from power.

At first, many of the new chairs were designed for invalids. These incorporated some sort of contrivance—usually a ratchet system—so that their backs could be adjusted to a variety of angles. For the first time, those confined to a chair could enjoy some ease. The concept of the recliner was an immediate hit—understandably so, since this was the first form of seating ever to allow someone to sit in a manner other than bolt upright—and soon comfort armchairs were no longer just for invalids. The huge armchairs actually provided only minimal comfort—their frames were still rectilinear, their padding slim—but they marked a giant first step toward a completely new life for seat furniture.

As early as 1672, "big comfort armchairs" began to be made for small royal châteaux and the most private rooms in Versailles. A small model was even created for Louis XIV's firstborn, Monseigneur, when he was only eleven, perhaps the first furniture designed for a child's body. (The king's comfort chairs were in crimson velvet, whereas his son's was done up in yellow, which may indicate that Monseigneur always had his own sense of decorating style.) Already in 1673, a Parisian newspaper announced that "fashionable people" had begun to imitate the look Montespan had invented for the Porcelain Trianon. Among the things they were copying was a new armchair, with a much higher back, "elaborate carving on the top of the frame," and a "gilded frame." Thus, a single press release announced three major changes in furniture history: the earliest turning away from brown furniture, the beginning of the frame's importance, and the first evidence of the spread of modern furniture design beyond a royal palace. Within two decades, Parisian merchants were putting big comfort armchairs in their shops to put clients at ease (see page 224). And the idea that a chair should do more than impress, once implanted, inspired the creation of all new forms of seat furniture.

The best introduction to the original modern furniture was composed in 1769. Its author, Roubo, was uniquely poised for the job of furniture historian: he designed and made furniture; he was a protégé of the architect Blondel, who taught him the skills he needed to engrave plates of the age's best designs. For Roubo, the history of modern furniture is the story of the quest for comfortable seating—which he defined as seating that allows the torso and legs to relax—and the history of the modern chair began about 1680, with those comfort armchairs. Roubo's design manual takes readers on a virtual tour of the eighteenth century's easy seats. At the turn of the eighteenth century, the "gigantic back" was lowered. (It came down by a full eight inches, to roughly twenty-four inches high.) Then, the rigid arms were reshaped into various more comfortable forms. Next, about 1715, the armrest was moved back some five to six inches from the front edge of the seat, thus allowing those with less than gigantic stature to take full advantage of its support.

The seat was then completely redesigned. The seventeenth century's square seat became more fluid and gradually relaxed into a continuous curve that could be adapted in various ways to the body's shape and to the way people sit. As Roubo explained it, "When one sits, the thighs naturally take on a bell shape"; furniture designers should use the curved seat so that "the body's weight is distributed more toward the fleshier part, the inner thigh," thereby "making seating more comfortable." And for "those who write" and therefore "spend long periods" leaning forward, he shows how the seat's curves could be adapted to this particular distribution of body weight and thereby help writers "resist fatigue." (I only wish someone would think like this today.)

Finally, about 1740, curving reached the last frontier, the armchair's back, with the invention of what Roubo calls "the most fashionable chair of the day," the *cabriolet* (see below). The name comes from the verb "to caper or frolic about," and the model was indeed sprightly. Prior to this, the backs of armchairs

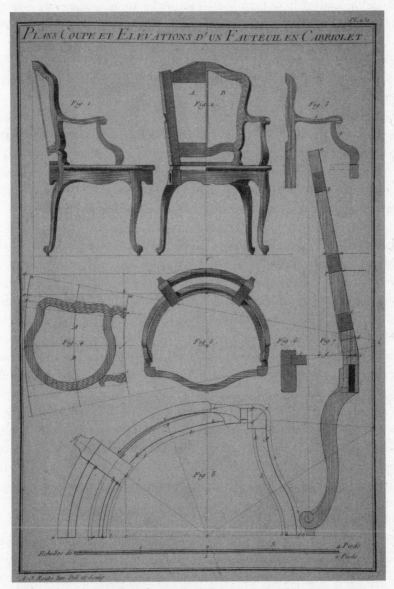

This diagram explains how to make one of the eighteenth century's favorite armchair styles, the cabriolet, *characterized by its flared, circular back.*

had inclined and had curved along the top and sides, but they had remained flat. Once the *cabriolet* came onto the scene, all flat-backed styles became known as *à la reine*, the queenly style, undoubtedly because they forced one to maintain a more regal bearing. Roubo illustrated in detail the making of a *cabriolet*, because, as he admitted, its flared, circular back was "the most difficult for the craftsman to get right." The model's trim proportions—its seat was twenty-two to twenty-six inches wide and eighteen to twenty inches deep, whereas larger armchairs tended to be about twenty-eight inches wide and twenty-two inches deep—and especially the comfortable circularity of "the fit against the back" immediately made the *cabriolet* an essential part of every French furniture maker's repertoire.

Those comfortable curves were the foundation on which a national furniture industry was built. Even though French craftsmen probably produced more of the supersized armchairs than anyone else, that model was not seen as uniquely French. Rounded, curving armchairs, however, soon became known as French chairs; craftsmen elsewhere copied the style, but everyone agreed that the best French chairs were those actually made in France.

In addition, the curves were a visible sign of furniture's participation in the values of the new age. Undulated, curvilinear French chairs signaled not only comfort, but a more casual style. Even gilded and covered in rich fabrics, they were still designed to say: Come sit here and be a part of what's going on in the room. French armchairs were made to work with a room's décor and even with changing styles in fashion (see color plates). In the 1720s and 1730s, a particularly low model (only about eight inches off the ground rather than the standard eleven) with an unusually wide seat shared drawing room space with intimately proportioned mantelpieces, mirrors hung low on the wall, and a softly flowing dress style, the *robe volante*, or flying gown (see color plates), to produce the first interiors designed to be casually inviting rather than imposing.

In barely a half century, the armchair's status changed completely. From a rarely found object and a symbol of majesty and power, it had become the most common form of seating and an invitation to relaxation. The *Encyclopédie* taught its readers that in France, "ordinary chairs" had been relegated to the garden and were "much less used" inside the home, where the armchair had taken over.

Once the basic principles of French armchairs had been established, eighteenth-century craftsmen invented one model after another. Many of these were small, like the rooms in which they were originally used. There were adorable little *fauteuils à coiffer*, hairstyling armchairs, at times with a heart-shaped back whose center dip allowed for the perfect placement of trailing locks. (Some even had a mechanism that made it possible to recline the upper part of the chair, so that the head could be tilted back for washing.) The hairdressing armchair was invented in the 1690s for the court's darling, the Duchesse de Bourgogne.

The most popular seats, however, were among the most capacious armchairs ever imagined. The easiest seats of all began with the *fauteuil en confessional*, the confessional armchair, a wide armchair with wraparound wings said to have been inspired by the chairs favored by priests, who could lean their heads on the wing when hearing confession. In the early 1720s, the confessional's first cousin, Madame Victoire's not-so-little little weakness, the *bergère*, or shepherdess, appeared. The *bergère* had wraparound arms rather than wraparound wings and a seat deep enough so that one could begin to stretch out one's legs. (A *bergère* is depicted on the lower right in the figure on page 123.) Roubo pronounced it the perfect vehicle for a lady of fashion: "Some ladies' ensembles positively demand this model; this is the only way that they can be comfortably seated without wrinkling their outfit."

And indeed, the century's most fashionable women favored the *bergère*. The most celebrated actress of the 1720s, Charlotte Desmares, was an early fan. Her three-bedroom home was tiny by the standards of the age, but she still found room for eleven *bergères*. As for the Marquise de Pompadour, well, she was as much a *bergère* fanatic as her lover's daughter: she had fourteen in the ex–Hôtel d'Evreux in Paris; no fewer than thirty-six in the Château de Ménars in the Loire valley—and three more still on order when she died.

These extrawide, wraparound models could be little worlds unto themselves, where people read and dreamed and spent their most private moments. In 1764, when the Marquise de Pompadour died in her bedroom at Versailles after a long, debilitating illness, she was sitting in her favorite confessional armchair; she had been suffering too much in her last days to lie down on a bed or even to stretch out a bit on a *bergère*.

The scale of fashion's favorites raised a question that gave eighteenth-century furniture mavens pause: When is a chair no longer a chair? Roubo expounded in all seriousness on such fine points of contemporary furniture design as the line separating *bergère* and chaise longue and the difference between a simple chaise longue and another of the era's darlings, the *duchesse* (page 112, top). (Answers: A *bergère* turns into a chaise longue when the seat is 3½ to 5 feet long, long enough to stretch out one's legs completely on it; when the seat is more than 5 feet long and "there is a footboard 12 to 15 inches high rounded and lower than the headboard" at the other end, voilà: you have a *duchesse*.) *Duchesses*, by the way, could also be *brisée*, or broken—that is, divided into two or three sections (page 112, bottom). To outsiders, the new world of the armchair surely

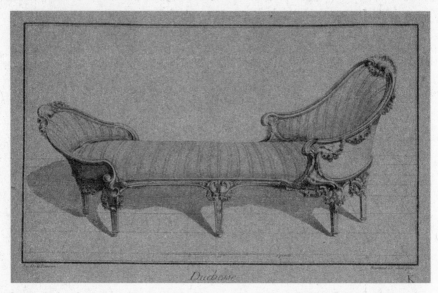

The duchesse *was a sort of cross between an armchair and a daybed on which it was possible to stretch out one's legs fully and still have good support for the back.*

The duchesse *could also be sectional. This made for greater versatility: the sections could be moved around easily; a* duchesse *could provide seating for two if extra guests arrived.*

seemed wildly arcane. In 1755, the most popular paper of the day published a complaint from someone newly arrived in Paris from the provinces: there were so many new words to designate "all the latest fashions in furniture" of which he was ignorant that he felt he no longer knew his own language.

Only a few years after the invention of comfort armchairs, chair makers began to make the chair no longer a chair in a second way: they doubled it up. They thus happened upon one of the great inventions in design history—seating for two, or the sofa. For the first and perhaps only time in the history of furniture, it is possible to follow step by step the creation of an object with an essential place in the modern home. In barely a decade, furniture designers went through four prototypes for the new seating (the two that won out are still with us today) and tried out names for it.

The sofa was the most original product of the burst of creativity generated by the creation of the Gobelins design studio and of the first jewel-box châteaux. Within months of the Porcelain Trianon's completion, on July 20, 1671, a most striking *lit de repos*, or daybed, was ready. Painted in lavender and white, upholstered in lavender, white, and the color of the moment, the golden yellow hue known as *aurore* (dawn), it was obviously tailor-made for the tiny pastel palace. It was also obviously intended for the lady of the house, the *lit de repos* queen, the Marquise de Montespan (see page 25). Finally, it was just as obviously a new departure for the daybed, since it had not the usual one but two headboards. Someone had clearly seen that two could share the daybed's comfort.

Immediately after Louis XIV's remarriage, royal furniture makers took the new design to the next level. In late 1683 and in 1684, they delivered (one was earmarked for the king's private bedroom at Versailles, another for his new wife) three pieces with a strange new name, *lits de repos en canapé*, *canapé*-style daybeds. These had headrests at each end as well as "a tall backrest in the middle." The headrests were no longer in bare wood, as was the case with daybeds, but were upholstered both inside and out with the same crimson velvet used on the removable padding and the mattress and bolsters characteristic of daybeds. These were pieces thus midway between the daybed and the sofa. In 1685, when the design-forward heir to the throne ordered one covered in blue velvet for his private suite at Versailles, the name had been shortened to *canapé*.

Canapé is said to derive from the Latin word for the mosquito netting around a bed; the new term was thus a variant on the *lit à canapé*, a bed draped with curtains as a bed might be draped with mosquito netting. (A bed canopy is depicted on the far left, rear, of the figure on page 123.) (By 1787, someone had come up with the concept of putting a delicacy such as caviar or an anchovy on a bit of bread and decided that the bread resembled a sofa's cushions; those little nibbles passed around ever since at parties were thus called *sur canapé*, on a sofa, or just *canapés*.)

Femme de qualité sur un Canapé

Se Vend A Paris Sur le quay Pelletier a la pomme d'Or au troisieme apartement

This 1686 engraving is the earliest image to depict a new kind of furniture: the sofa. This low-backed model, reminiscent of a bench with padding and upholstery, was highly popular during the first decade or so of the sofa's existence. The engraving also shows off the kind of previously unheard-of behavior that the sofa immediately encouraged: the lady clearly sees its expansive surface as an invitation to stretch out and prop up her legs— and to show off her outfit's expanses of lovely fabric.

By the time the new furniture had been named, it had progressed well beyond the daybed phase (see page 114). This, the earliest surviving image of a *canapé*, depicts the low-backed, benchlike seat that was initially one of the most popular models. Note that this is the original upholstered furniture: every surface is fabric covered. Note in particular the way the lady stretches out a leg and drapes one arm over the back. The original furniture ad campaign was right on the mark: it showed off a phenomenon documented in numerous contemporary correspondences, the *canapé*'s extraordinary ability to encourage those who lived in the age of magnificence to throw off formality and adopt instead carefree, casual poses, posture unheard of before the sofa came on the scene.

A second term, written either *sopha* or *sofa*, from the Arab word for cushion, was in use by 1688. In September of that year, the Prince de Conti ordered one from a craftsman named Grémont, who described himself as "a specialist in armchairs and sophas." The prince was a logical client for innovative comfort furniture. His suite at Versailles was considered particularly "beautiful"; he was "passionately in love" with Madame la Duchesse, already famous for her own furniture, and on the best of terms with his sister-in-law, the Princesse de Conti, she of the great bathrooms to come.

We don't know what the Prince de Conti's sofa looked like; by 1688, two very different models were being referred to by that term. The first is probably best described as a double-wide version of those oversize comfort armchairs (see page 116). (For most of the eighteenth century in England, where it was called "double Windsor chairs without a division," the chair-back model dominated the quite limited sofa production. In France, it soon evolved into the more elegant form of the sofa on page 106.) Like those armchairs, this model is above all large and clumsy. Unlike those armchairs, however, it was never associated with status and magnificence. Instead, once the sofa was invented, it was presented in terms never before associated with comfort: casual is the new sexy. Once she sits on a *canapé*, the images proclaimed, even the grandest lady becomes carefree and at ease. Once she sits on a sofa, the lady becomes, well, just plain easy.

Niece of Louis XIV's mentor and minister, Cardinal Mazarin, the Duchesse de Bouillon was also the mother of the Comte d'Evreux. (At the time of his marriage, she coined the phrase *my little bar of gold* to refer to his bride, Crozat's daughter.) She was a great fashionista; people said that everything she put on looked great on her. And, finally, it was common knowledge that she had had many, many lovers.

It's thus clear why someone trying to market the novel piece of furniture as the trendiest and sexiest seat in town would have picked the duchess as a poster child. In the late seventeenth century, engravers were eager to show off the

Madame la Duchesse de Boüillon
en deshabillé negligé Sur un Sopha.

*This engraving shows off a late-seventeenth-century sofa style
that enjoyed great but short-lived popularity in France—
more a double-wide, extremely high-backed armchair than
what we think of as a sofa.*

way furniture was evolving in Paris: they kept returning to the image of the
sofa as seating so irresistible that it was positively dangerous (see page 117).
Madame de *** clasps her hands in the classic gesture of repentance; she has
cast off her jewels and strewn them carelessly on the floor. Yet she does not
kneel to renounce her past; a very modern Mary Magdalene, she clings still to

Madame de ✳ ✳ ✳ en Magdelaine.

This image of the double armchair–style sofa, also from the late
seventeenth century, is a particularly over-the-top depiction of the
excessive taste for comfort that the sofa allegedly inspired in its
early proponents. The image suggests that sofas are so addictive,
they can be the undoing of any woman.

the comfort of her luxurious sofa. Her appealingly disheveled hair flows over her shoulders; the folds of her glamorous gown fall in studied negligence. Like Madame Victoire, she knows that the sofa has been and will be the ruin of her, and she's still not prepared to give it up.

Madame Victoire was joking, of course, as presumably were the engravers of these over-the-top sofa scenes. (These engravings were not real portraits; engravers simply chose a prominent figure whose reputation fit the bill.) Once invented, however, the off-color image clung to the sofa all through the eighteenth century. Countless French novels featured the sofa rather than the perhaps more obvious candidate, the bed, as the ideal piece of furniture for seduction. Every time you read that a female character is positioned on a sofa, well, you just know that her virtue will be eminently reproachable. Was all this hype grounded in any reality? In correspondences and memoirs from the period, in the commentary of keen-eyed observers of the contemporary scene from Saint-Simon to Dufort de Cheverny, in that of the architects and furniture designers most in touch with their clients' desires, I found not a single remark to back up the sofa's sexy image. There is no evidence to suggest that any real-life woman—from the Duchesse de Bouillon to the Marquise de Pomadour—was sofa-mad because it provided the perfect opportunity to strike a come-hither pose. Some people, however, were obviously taken in by the image.

The English quickly decided that the sofa was a dangerous thing best avoided. In 1745, Horace Walpole joked about the sofa's reputation for being the ruin of all those who gave in to its cushions and curves and characterized sitting on a sofa as "lolling in a *péché-mortel*"—a mortal sin. Walpole's correspondent, Horace Mann, replied that he had "no clear idea" of what such a sinfully luxurious sofa was like and added: "You know we [English] are always some years behindhand"—behindhand in this case because they had steered clear of seating comfort. In 1770, Mrs. Delany—prolific correspondent and chronicler of life in eighteenth-century England—remarked that when an important guest was expected, "all the comfortable sofas . . . were banished for the day, and . . . chairs set in prim form around the room." The mere sight of a well-cushioned sofa could threaten a family's good standing.

Now back to reality, that of the nascent furniture industry. The sofa quickly got itself sorted out; designers created far more sophisticated models. In the late 1680s, furniture makers began experimenting with a new technology that eventually made these new models possible. In 1691, still another prototype was delivered to Versailles for the private suite of the sofa's most loyal backer, Monseigneur. It was described as a *canapé à dossier et bras chantournés*, a sofa with back and armrests that have been *chantournés*. Images soon popped up to

Madame la Princeße de Rohan
Fille de Mons.r le Duc de Ventadour cy devant veusue de M. le Prince de Turenne

*This 1696 engraving may be the earliest image of a sofa that looks
like the models in use ever since. The sofa is cushioned and
upholstered on all surfaces; it features an intricately carved frame.
In a mere decade, the sofa had evolved from a rather primitive
design into a sophisticated piece of furniture.*

show off the sofa's new beginning (see above). The Princesse de Rohan—a
fabulously wealthy heiress who in 1696 was already the widow of one prince
and recently remarried to a second one, none of which had stopped her from
acquiring a string of lovers as long as the Duchesse de Bouillon's—was still

another sexy poster child for the sofa. Her alleged portrait, however, is more concerned with the furniture she's posed on than with her louche life.

With one hand, the princess indicates the model's most remarkable innovation: it has a frame produced not by turning, as had been the case with earlier sofas (see pages 106 and 114), but by carving or sculpting. Like Monseigneur's sofa, it was *chantourné*, a new word meaning scrollwork or fretwork. Sometime around 1680, a curved saw was invented; it then became possible to decorate furniture with the elaborately swirling curves and scallops that would soon be the mark of the modern style, the rococo. The new technology was perhaps the innovation most essential to the modern concept of furniture. From then on, what had been hidden under the fabric could become as important as the fabric itself. Almost as soon as frames began to swirl as they do on the princess's sofa, the grand cabinet and other showstoppers of the age of magnificence disappeared, and the age of seat furniture began.

With her other hand, the princess gestures toward a second innovation: the armrests. Once elaborately carved frames were introduced, serious attention was paid for the first time to another element essential to seating comfort, support for the arms. The modern name, *accotoir*, or armrest, was created just after the word *chantourné*. In just thirteen years, French sofa makers had learned how to make the first piece of furniture worthy of the age of comfort: upholstered all over—front, sides, and back; padded all over; with support in all the right places.

In 1701, as part of the "youthful look" he wanted for the Ménagerie, Louis XIV chose the first sofa in a royal château referred to not as a *lit en canapé* or as a *canapé*, but as a sofa; he chose a sofa that had it all—an elaborately carved frame, a comfortable backrest, armrests. It also featured the most sumptuous fabric on any early sofa: crimson damask whose leaf design was overembroidered with gold thread. That fabric called attention to the last frontier in furniture comfort: upholstery and padding.

From the start, the sofa's many surfaces were covered with fabric, but at first—in those "big comfort armchairs," for example—the stuffing underneath was hardly plush and was attached in primitive fashion. The period during which designers were trying out prototypes for the sofa coincides exactly with the invention of the first sophisticated upholstery techniques. The sofa—by far the largest piece of furniture in the upholsterer's repertory—was the incentive that pushed that craft into the modern age.

Until the seventeenth century, if you wanted to make a seat more comfortable, you simply put a cushion on it. During the sixteenth and seventeenth centuries, upholsterers became less and less concerned with wall hangings and bed

Jean-François de Troy's *The Declaration of Love* shows off a number of the innovations of the age of comfort—from well-designed seating to less constricting dress—as well as showing how such innovations increased comfort and well-being.

Arthur Devis's portrait of an English couple, Mr. and Mrs. Bull, depicts a way of living in the home radically opposed to that being developed in France. Everything from the furniture to the interior decoration to the couple's bearing is stiff and formal; their fine possessions seem merely a proof of their wealth and status rather than conveniences that improve their lives.

This is one in a set of twelve armchairs made in the first decade of the eighteenth century for Pierre Crozat, who had risen from modest origins to become one of the wealthiest men in France. The chair still features its original upholstery in red morocco leather, with strips of leather in a contrasting shade applied to the surface to form a wavy pattern that echoes the soft curves in the intricately carved frame. The armchair is a perfect transition piece between seventeenth- and eighteenth-century seating: its frame retains traces of the earlier period's angularity but is beginning to curve in the style of the new century.

This portrait of Queen Maria Leszczyńska, painted by Louis Toqué in 1740, depicts her in a highly formal context. She stands in a public reception space, wearing the tightly confining court dress that women of the day (the queen among them) found so uncomfortable.

This portrait of the Marquise de Pompadour, painted by François Boucher in 1756, shows her half reclining on well-padded seating, relaxing in the privacy afforded by a small interior room with her favorite books and the kind of tiny writing desk she kept in almost every room in every one of her residences.

This painting by de Troy is often called *Reading in a Salon* or *Reading from Molière*. A group of friends has gathered together in one of the new, more intimate reception spaces. They have arranged their armchairs (a particularly low model fashionable in the 1720s) near the fire to gather around as one of them reads aloud. This is the kind of relaxed sociability that smaller, more private rooms were designed to facilitate.

This is perhaps the earliest surviving French high-fashion dress. The style was known as a flying dress, probably because the loose cut allowed the fabric to move so easily that the dress seemed to float along as women walked. It features the fashionable pagoda sleeves, shorter on the inside and pleated to curve around the elbow. The dress is depicted from the back to show off the pleats that added fullness and helped the fabric "fly."

This *tableau de mode*, or fashion painting, by de Troy, now known as *The Garter*, shows off the harmonious style of décor favored by the original interior decorators, the use of exotic textiles as wall hangings, and the way a well-positioned large mirror added depth to a small room.

This chintz was folk art come to France: Indians with hookahs, humanoid monkeys, wild animals, and mythic beasts all coexist in their own peaceable kingdom.

Many interior rooms at Versailles were covered—furniture, curtains, bedclothes, even the walls—in Indian cotton with a red background.

For the European market, Indian designers played up the exotic touches in their textiles—they even painted the elephants blue.

The multicolored fabric is an Indian textile made for the European market about 1700; the blue-and-white fabric is a French update from about 2000.

Here, Indian designers were trying to blend in, by imitating the lacy motifs and sprigs of flowers found in French silk patterns of the early eighteenth century.

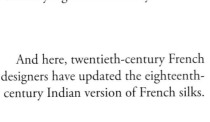

And here, twentieth-century French designers have updated the eighteenth-century Indian version of French silks.

hangings and more concerned with covering furniture. At the same moment, the detachable cushion or mattress was gradually replaced by fabric attached to furniture. Until the very end of the seventeenth century, however, upholstery remained firmly rooted in the age of magnificence. What was then considered a fabulous upholstery job consisted of the most ostentatiously expensive fabric positively loaded down with every kind of lavish trim—fringe (often two kinds—a very wide and a very narrow fringe on the same piece), braid, tassels, the whole nine yards. Yet when it came to padding—well, the upholsterer merely put extremely shallow padding on the seat and nailed a cover over it. Chair backs were simply covered with fabric, since there was no way to hold padding in place.

Prior to 1670, fixed upholstery was exceedingly rare. Then, in a few short decades, every technique on which the upholsterer's craft has since been based was invented by French craftsmen; this was still another area over which the French reigned supreme. (There was one exception: springs were not really used before the nineteenth century. Some experts think that Madame Victoire's *bergère* may have been the earliest sprung chair.) Seat padding was laid on wide webbing like that still seen today; back padding was attached to canvas; down was used for seats, springier horsehair for backs—and more sophisticated stitching techniques kept it all firmly in place.

Just as the sofa came fully into its own, French upholsterers initiated the golden age of padding. They rounded it in all the perfect spots, because this was more comfortable, because this provided additional support, and because this made padding match the new curves then taking over the frames of seat furniture. On seats and backs, stuffing was built up to form a kind of dome. (In England, in contrast, throughout the eighteenth century padding remained firm and so shallow that it was, at most, only very slightly domed. Prior to the nineteenth century, there was very little upholstered furniture of any kind in this country.) French padding was also rounded on all edges to suit the curvilinear furniture. (English stuffing was squared off and seemed to match English furniture's more severe lines.)

Finally, between 1700 and 1715, truly fancy upholstery techniques were imagined. As soon as the armrest received its modern name, new ways of upholstering and padding this tricky spot were devised. And, cleverest of all, a special *châssis*, or stretcher, was invented so that upholstery could be attached no longer to the frame of the chair itself, but to a frame within the frame; it was usually kept in place with turn buttons. The technique was used not only for slip seats, but also for the back and armrests.

The process, known as upholstery *en châssis*, was tailor-made for a society that liked its comfort elegant. Suddenly, upholstery could be changed almost instantly, and seat furniture could keep up with fashion seasons. *Châssis* upholstery came on the scene just as *nouveaux riches* began pouring money into interior decoration. Soon, wealthy Parisian clients had winter upholstery and summer upholstery, all in the latest colors and patterns. A decade later, the practice had become common all over France. In the mid–eighteenth century, at Versailles and in the finest homes, upholstery was changed four times a year. By then, the French silk industry was turning out four collections a year: seat furniture had taken on fashion rhythms; its upholstery could be adjusted to match its owners' latest outfits. (The new practice never really caught on in England.)

Improved covering techniques allowed furniture makers to increase significantly the surface available for carving and make far more elaborate frames. They also funneled vastly increased profits into the textile industry. Those seasonal upholstery changes naturally required many additional yards of expensive material as well as increased labor costs. In 1770, when the master upholsterer Bimont published the original guide to "the art of upholstery," he provided technical tips but above all a great deal of highly detailed information on the prices of various upholstery fabrics and on how much fabric was needed to cover each of the many kinds of chairs and sofas that had by then proliferated in French homes.

As a result of this period of experimentation, and perhaps because of all those highly profitable sales, the upholsterer first gained true professional status, and upholsterers vastly expanded their functions. In the 1692 edition of his insider's guide to Paris, Nicolas de Blégny included for the first time the addresses of the best Parisian *tapissiers* (upholsterers); he described them as selling "the most magnificent furniture": upholsterers had begun to buy furniture from cabinetmakers and sell it to clients, along with the fabric and the cost of their labor (see page 123). This illustration from the *Encyclopédie* showed off the upholsterer's new prominence and the furniture he sold. At the top and the bottom far right, we see the *bergère*, with and without covering. Note the trendy *cabriolet* backs on all chairs, as well as the rounded edges on all upholstery. Note also the nicely domed padding on the sofa.

Perhaps no one had more to gain from the sofa's meteoric rise to prominence than the upholsterer. The two decades following the invention of the *châssis* method witnessed the most spectacular invention of new types of seat furniture of the entire age of comfort. And—surprise, surprise—the models then invented required nearly twice as much fabric as those in existence in 1700. When you factor in changing the upholstery twice and even four times a year, well, you can see why the rush was on to create new kinds of plush seating.

Tapissier, intérieur d'une Boutique, et différens Ouvrages

*In the eighteenth century, upholsterers also sold furniture. This image depicts an
upholsterer's shop. A wide variety of sofas and armchairs is for sale; many
feature the curving,* cabriolet *back that Thomas Jefferson—as well as many
others—found so comfortable. The century's favorite big armchair,
the* bergère, *is prominently displayed.*

Among the biggest fabric guzzlers then imagined are some of the greatest sofas of all time. The two most popular models were created in the first decade of
the nouveau riche decorating boom: the *ottomane* and the *canapé à confidents*, or
confidante. The ottoman was the first of a long line of models with exotic
names—it was followed, among others, by the sultana and the turquoise; by
midcentury, in the Château de Ménars the Marquise de Pompadour had the ultimate in exotic overkill, an *ottomane à la turque*, or Turkish ottoman. Heaven
knows how the word later came to be downgraded to refer to an overgrown
footstool, for the original ottomans were very big affairs indeed: average ones
were 6½ to 7 feet long, and they could extend to 10 feet (see page 124). The
ottoman was distinguished by its rounded ends, upholstered, but of course, on
both sides. The total package, Bimont explained, required roughly twice the
fabric needed to cover a less exotic model.

In the eighteenth century, sofas whose frame was completely rounded,
arms as well as back, were known as ottomanes. *The exotic, Turkish-sounding name*
conjured up an image of exotic comfort. In the nineteenth century,
the ottoman was gradually reincarnated as an oversize footrest.

As for the confidante (also called a *canapé à joue,* or sofa with cheeks), well, the concept that justified its invention (at each end, someone could snuggle up to one of the cheeks and trade secrets with a confidante seated on one of the end seats) masked its other function as a true cash cow for upholsterers: a confidante was like a sofa and two armchairs all rolled into one (see page 125). And on and on it went, as one model after another appeared in those trendy shops. In 1769, Roubo did his best to explain exactly how an ottoman was different from a *veilleuse,* or vigilant sofa, and a Turkish vigilant from a paphose (see page 126), before pronouncing that many models mere marketing devices and railing against "the greed of furniture makers and merchants" for trying to convince clients that they had come up with something really new.

Nothing, however, reined in sofamania, which by Roubo's day was already nearly a century old. In May 1690, less than two years after the sofa hit Paris, the Marquise de Sévigné's daughter had managed to have one delivered to her home in the far reaches of Provence. Her proud mother exclaimed that it was "a piece of furniture worthy of Versailles!" "Sofa" was first mentioned in a dictionary in 1691, and the following year the word was featured in a spoof of

Canapé à Joué dans le goût Pictoresque

This 1768 engraving introduced a kind of sofa that soon became hugely popular.
It featured joues *(literally "cheeks"), wings at each end that turned it into a*
combination of a sofa and a pair of armchairs. It became known as a confidante,
since two people could draw in close to the wings and share secrets.

the French love of all things luxe and trendy, *Des Mots à la mode* (*Fashionable Words*). When the Maréchal d'Humières died in 1694—after he had managed to pass on the family name and fortune to the beloved daughter, who used her new wealth to build, for instance, the original modern bathroom—he passed on to her as well one of the earliest sofas; it was ornately carved in walnut.

In 1695, the sofa craze had spread beyond French borders. Daniel Cronström, posted to the Swedish embassy in Paris as a sort of cultural attaché, reported to Stockholm all the latest sofa news from Paris. Ready-made ones were already for sale; the new furniture was so hot, however, that he couldn't lay his hands on two matching sofas. The French had gone sofa-mad, and "there's hardly a room in Paris without one." Six months later, Cronström's self-described "sofa campaign" had paid off, and he announced proudly that he was shipping off to Stockholm a matched pair "in a most singular design."

Throughout the eighteenth century, the passion for a well-cushioned life continued unchecked. The first pieces designed by the royal furniture makers for the future Louis XV, in 1718 when he was only eight, included two sofas covered in a yellow damask with a leaf design overembroidered with silver thread. In 1725, Charlotte Desmares had seven sofas, two of which were

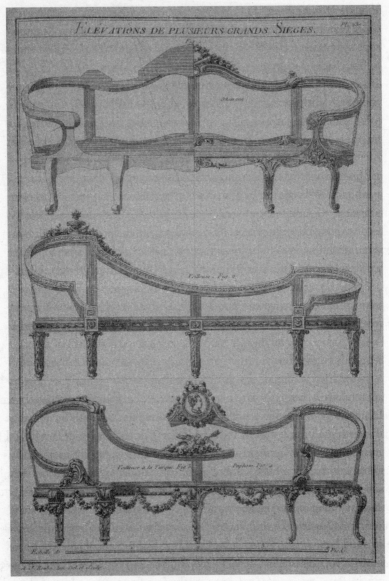

Master furniture designer Roubo used this engraving to show potential clients the distinguishing features of several popular kinds of sofas—the veilleuse, for example, was rounded like the ottomane, but higher on one end. (Its frame often featured a carved representation of a flame, since the word veilleuse also designated a night-light.)

described as big, in her small home. Madame la Duchesse, an early champion of the sofa, understood its potential to make even the grandest space cozier and more inviting. Many of the Palais Bourbon's signature rooms featured rounded corners—its salon, its formal bedroom, its gallery, even the rooms in its bathing suite. All through her very big house, the woman described as "always the life of the party" helped transform those rooms into settings for intimate entertaining by positioning sofas—a total of thirty-six, in fact—whose curves complemented those of her curvilinear rooms. And when she redid the Hôtel d'Evreux, the Marquise de Pompadour put in six sofas, five ottomans, two chaises longues, and one small ottoman.

Sofas were indeed found, as the Swedish envoy remarked, "in every room of the house." Their function, however, changed with the type of room. Those *canapés* lined up (sometimes three in a row) in great public spaces such as salons were proof of the home owner's casual good taste, but it's not clear that they were very much used. Sofas in dining rooms were probably above all decorative. Madame la Duchesse had one, covered in jonquil velvet, made to fill one wall of hers; it was "cornered" for an exact fit. (If the two sides of the corner were not identical, the sofa was cut asymmetrically.) In Blondel's vision, the perfect, two-tubbed bathroom was equipped with a pair of sofas.

Elsewhere, sofas were used to help promote interior life. For reading rooms and the smallest of all small rooms, designed by Blondel and christened "sofa," Roubo championed models with rounded ends such as the ottoman and the *veilleuse* for "reading comfortably in front of a fire." He also suggested positioning a pair opposite each other for companionate reading or relaxed conversation.

The sofa thus came to be seen as indispensable to any dwelling in which reading and the life of the mind played a key role. Imagine Françoise de Graffigny's surprise when she visited Cirey, home to Voltaire and Emilie du Châtelet. She was astonished to find no sofas and not even "a single really comfortable armchair. I mean, they have perfectly good chairs, but they are merely fabric-covered and not at all padded." She concluded that as far as Voltaire was concerned, "apparently the body's well-being is just not his kind of voluptuousness." (Voltaire did have one of those minimally padded, by then quite old-fashioned big comfort armchairs—his was functional, with a sliding shelf added as a writing surface. He was sitting in it when he died in 1778.)

The revolution in seating of which the sofa was the centerpiece had numerous long-lasting consequences. It inaugurated the marketing of furniture and the practice of buying furniture as we now know it: those upholstery shops were the first modern furniture stores. In addition, it created the bond between

furniture and design that we now take for granted. No prior age had ac-
corded furniture anything like the degree of importance it acquired in the age
of comfort. Beginning at the turn of the eighteenth century, architects such as
Mansart and Blondel not only designed furniture, they considered it essential
that an architect take the placement of furniture into account when drawing up
a plan, and they indicated the principal pieces on theirs. In still another interaction between behavior and design, the great furniture makers knew full well that
the role furniture played in people's lives was changing dramatically and that
with their designs, they were shaping the way people lived. Roubo explained
that new kinds of furniture were being created every day "in an attempt to respond to all the new needs that seem to pop up as soon as [furniture makers]
are able to satisfy them."

The combination of many new types of furniture, an explosion in the amount
of furniture found in individual residences, and the new importance given to
its placement produced a radically new look for the home. As their inhabitants
were well aware, eighteenth-century French homes were completely unlike the
sparsely furnished interiors decorated essentially with the occasional flashy
showpiece that had previously been the norm (see color plates). One Frenchman remarked in 1755, "Our home furnishings look nothing like those of our
fathers." Thanks to the changes sparked by the revolution in seat furniture,
homes looked for the first time by our standards truly furnished.

The new emphasis on furniture and the fact that people were investing
more of their wealth in furniture created another new type of tourism, furniture tourism, also with its guidebooks for foreign visitors. In 1749, for example, Dezallier d'Argenville singled out the Hôtel d'Evreux as a "must-see"
because of "its refined and luxurious furniture." The Comte d'Evreux had
certainly gone to great lengths to garner that mention in the *Architectural Di-
gest* of the day: at the time of his death, more than half of his fortune was
tied up in furniture. Like mother, like son.

Among the first homes promoted as a stop on the furniture tour was that of
Pierre Crozat. Crozat's fabled gallery displayed the masterpieces of his art collection; it also showcased the first truly great furniture ever designed for an individual not to the manner born: "twelve armchairs, two sofas, two benches, four
stools, upholstered in red morocco leather," according to the inventory drawn
up after Crozat's death (see color plates). Many of those pieces designed in the
first decade of the eighteenth century still survive. Three centuries after they
were made, half of them stand proudly as the centerpiece of a room in a palatial
building a stone's throw away from the site of the Crozat mansion, the Louvre

museum. The first time I visited it, I literally sank to the floor in admiration: this
is no ordinary seat furniture.

The armchairs have grand proportions, suited both to the gallery's dimen-
sions and to the aspirations of a commoner who lived on a truly regal scale. No
one, however, would confuse them with the hulking big comfort armchairs of
the age of magnificence. All the aspects of the evolution that Roubo saw as essential to armchair modernity are in process in them. Their backs are much
lower and less rectilinear; their frames have soft, relaxed curves. The backs and
sides are nicely domed with padding; the gently inclined armrests are cushioned as well. These are not yet fully eighteenth-century armchairs, but they
are fully on the cusp. When visitors to Crozat's gallery at the turn of the eighteenth century encountered these easy seats, one look would have told them
that a new age for seating was dawning. This furniture was clearly not simply
made—it was designed. There's just the right tilt to the backs, just the right
slope to the arms, just the right amount of padding. They were clearly intended to be comfortable—and to provide proper back support.

Those who enjoyed these plush seats also found themselves in the lap of
design luxury. The furniture's intricate motifs were sculpted, using the *chantourné* saw, on every surface—front, sides, back, and even inside the legs—the
carving is of extraordinarily high quality, and the gilding shows that off. These
pieces offer definitive proof that furniture was no longer just about the fabric.
And as for the morocco leather upholstery, still miraculously the original upholstery from the turn of the eighteenth century—it is almost inconceivably
luxe: it is actually of two distinct shades of reddish brown, with, as the crowning touch, strips of leather edged with silk ribbon to hide the stitching applied
to the surface; these were shaped to form a swirling pattern that echoes motifs
in the sculpted frames. The leather upholstery seems perfect for a bachelor's
home—in his gallery on the Place Vendôme, Crozat's elder, married brother
had blue velvet with a floral pattern—and also gives the furniture a sporty
flair.

Furniture design books and engravings of individual pieces, notably those
by J. C. Delafosse that illustrate this chapter, quickly publicized the latest looks
from Paris. The new way of furnishing an interior being developed in Paris
thus came to be seen as an integral part of the French art of living in elegant
comfort. By 1776, the Neapolitan ambassador to Versailles, the Marquis de Caraccioli, proclaimed that France had "furnished" all of Europe and "had done so
admirably." As a result, he added, you could now go into the innermost rooms
of homes all over Europe and inspect their furnishings; you would find that

everywhere "pomp" had been banished; in its place, "comfort reigns." (He had not traveled to England.)

And last, but surely not least, upholstered furniture and easy seats had become essential to private life as the age of comfort had defined it—to family life, to companionate moments, to the life of the mind. Think of the image of the woman in love with one of the original sofas (page 106): as she gazes at the sofa, she's holding a letter in her hand; her desk is set up for writing, and sheets are scattered all over its surface. Her beloved sofa is part of an interior designed to favor the development of an interior life, as were the rooms with paired sofas favored by Blondel and Roubo. In the eighteenth century, the interior furniture of the home and the mind's interior furnishings were thought to be interdependent.

CHAPTER SEVEN

Convenience Furniture

EIGHTEENTH-CENTURY FRENCH FURNITURE makers never forgot that the era's buzzword, *commodité*, had a double meaning: comfort and well-being, yes, but also convenience. They thus imagined one piece of furniture after another designed to facilitate activities such as letter writing or clothes storage that first attracted attention after modern French architecture had redesigned the home. The pieces then invented provide still another example of the phenomenon Roubo described: the furniture makers of the eighteenth century were endlessly inventive, able to come up with innovative designs as soon as a need became visible—and perhaps even able to anticipate desires and create objects before people knew they needed them.

Virtually as soon as oversize armchairs were described as *commode*, the adjective was also used by designers at the Gobelins studio to inaugurate the furniture of convenience. They created the kind of piece that was conceivable only once sleeping and dressing were taking place in specifically designated spaces: the chest of drawers.

Prior to the seventeenth century, there was really only one storage device: the trunk. Today's all-purpose storage space, the drawer, was first widely used in the Renaissance, when small drawers were added to desks and other kinds of furniture. Before the late seventeenth century, however, drawers were not used to store clothing. This began to change in May 1692, when four pieces of a brand-new kind were delivered to Versailles: the original chests of drawers. They were soon known as *commodes*, which in this case I'd translate as "conveniences," because they certainly were that. For the first time, rather than taking everything out (and later putting it all back), if what you were looking for happened to be at the very bottom of a trunk, the *commode* made it possible to organize things into categories and assign each a separate drawer.

The *commode* was the first piece of furniture ever composed solely of drawers, the beginning of modern storage furniture—and the beginning of the end for the trunk. At the turn of the eighteenth century in low- to moderate-income Parisian households, the trunk was still the all-purpose bedroom furniture, used for both storage and seating. By 1740, the trunk was rapidly disappearing; by 1760, it was gone. That's how quickly the desire for comfort and convenience changed the furnishing of Parisian households. The trunk was replaced by the more compartmentalized storage of the chest of drawers, which knew its golden age during Louis XV's reign. Designers soon imagined other kinds of drawer-based storage, such as the *chiffonier* and the adorable tiny *chiffonière* (usually only eighteen inches high and a foot wide), in which women could organize their sewing materials. (Their names come from *chiffon*, a rag, which can also mean clothing, just as we say the rag trade.)

One influential group, however, was opposed to drawer-based storage: architects. In his 1710 edition of d'Aviler's manual, Le Blond explained why small rooms dedicated to a single activity would be convenient: *chaque chose se trouve à sa place*—everything will be in the right place. Yet neither Le Blond nor any subsequent proponent of modern French architecture advocated the use of storage furniture to help home owners achieve this sense of perfect organization; they complained that it cluttered up a room with its bulk. Architects championed instead what they saw as a more elegant solution: built-in shelf-based storage.

The basic tool in eighteenth-century architects' struggle to keep interiors clean-lined was the *armoire*. The word already designated storage devices, most often large, freestanding wooden pieces designed for books or china. Its dominant meaning changed when the *commode* became the architect's bête noire. Modern architects promoted an altogether different kind of *armoire*, recessed storage, what we know as built-in closets, cabinets, and cupboards.

The new reading rooms thus featured recessed book-storage cupboards (see page 60) while the new toilet rooms contained built-in cabinets for towels and toilet water. For dining rooms, there was the buffet, discreetly elegant storage for china and table linen (see page 133). The most elaborate designs built in two different kinds of buffet, a center sideboard for serving, flanked by two storage cabinets. And bedrooms got the first ever clothes closets. The one in the Marquise de Maintenon's suite at Versailles, for example, was nearly twelve feet high, five feet wide, and over three feet deep. A half century later, in her suite at Versailles the Marquise de Pompadour had six enormous closets, an entire

Elevations d'un Buffet à vaisselle.

This engraving illustrates one of the first forms of recessed storage promoted by eighteenth-century French architects and popular with home owners: buffets built into the walls of dining rooms to hold tableware and linen.

corridor, in fact, lined on one side with closets. (This was, of course, shelf-based storage; suspended storage became the norm only after the clothes hanger was invented at the turn of the twentieth century.) The new *armoires* were neatly camouflaged behind paneled doors. Blondel considered such elegantly invisible convenience among modern architecture's great achievements.

Designers put built-in storage at the service of another new need: privacy. The desire for furniture that could protect one's secrets—already evident with the 1686 piece designed for Monseigneur with locking drawers that faced the wall—spread rapidly through society once people had access to private space. By midcentury, there were secret drawers within secret drawers, locking mechanisms so sophisticated that owners knew upon returning if someone had tried to gain access to their secrets in their absence. Locks on doors and closets were common from the 1730s on. And the original safes appeared, secret compartments built in wherever architects could use an empty space (under floorboards, in window frames).

Built-ins were the invisible side of convenience, which had another very, very visible face: occasional furniture, pieces—for the most part small and often very small tables—designed specifically for particular activities. Occasional furniture was the final stage in the furnishing of the modern home. Designers would never have turned their attention to small tables before the major pieces were in place. Indeed, there were virtually no small tables in the sixteenth century and very few prior to the seventeenth century's final decades; tiny pieces would have been swallowed up in the vastness of the age of magnificence.

Small tables came into use as soon as people began to spend a lot of time sitting down. The experience of well-being in one's favorite armchair or sofa was more satisfying still with a little table by its side to hold a drink or a favorite book. Once there were private rooms with smaller proportions, and once those rooms had been filled with upholstered furniture, small tables appeared on the scene. From then on, small tables changed the way people structured and perceived space; they were used to give shape to groupings of furniture, and they even helped draw people together.

Unlike seat furniture, which from the beginning had almost more names than models, no one seems to have given much thought to what to call the new designer accessories of the furniture world. In 1751, Françoise de Graffigny proudly described her new *table courante*, or running table. Then, at the end of the eighteenth century, after the Revolution had swept away the world task tables had helped enable, small tables were officially named *tables volantes*, or flying tables. Both adjectives highlighted the fact that they were not kept in a designated spot but moved around as needed.

The adjective *volant* was first used in the language of furniture to designate the *machine en fauteuil*, mechanical armchair, or *chaise volante*, flying chair, the proto-elevator installed at Versailles in the late 1740s to help Pompadour avoid too frequent trips on the treacherous spiral staircase that connected her private rooms and the king's small suite. The chair "flew" up and down stairs thanks to a system of pulleys and counterweights—and to the efforts of the men who operated it. It seated two people on the comfort of a well-upholstered banquette.

"Flying" next appeared in the 1750s to characterize a new kind of dining table, one that gave Louis XV a measure of the privacy he so craved by allowing him to dine in his small suite at Versailles without having servants present. His dining room floor would open and the *table volante* "flew" down; the floor then closed up again. Moments later, the floor reopened and the table reappeared with fresh china and the next course. By 1769, the concept was ready to be marketed. Its designer, M. Loriot, received extensive press coverage describing how his model worked; you could choose between a table for eight and one for sixteen. Loriot had also invented the original dumbwaiter, called a *servante* (a female servant): small tables slightly higher than the main table flew up at the same time, one between each pair of diners, so that they could help themselves to extra plates. One reporter described the dining experience as "magical."

Most flying tables, however, were small. The earliest ones on record are the tiny gaming tables, each with a different shape (triangular, octagonal) and designed to meet the specifics of a particular card game, placed in Versailles's Hall of Mirrors in the 1680s on evenings when gaming was allowed there. Configuring small tables to fit specific tasks or functions was one of the brilliantly simple concepts on which the original furniture industry was founded. In 1684, six small tables in walnut were delivered to Marly—"for eating in bed." In the late seventeenth century, the Marquise de Maintenon had a number of tables about two feet long in her private suite.

By the boom years of the 1720s, the design and marketing of small tables was in full swing. Whatever the special interests or needs of any individual, a model could be adapted to suit: it was behavior and design in perfect alignment. From then on, each bed simply had to have its night table, each comfortable chair its little writing table or sewing table, and so forth. There were in fact so many models that in the 1720s, Charlotte Desmares became one of the first individuals ever able to be mad for tables—night tables, dressing tables, some of the earliest very small tables, well before the craze for such models several decades later—she used nearly thirty small tables in all. She had immediately grasped their ability to be eminently convenient, as well as their ability to bring together both other furniture and the people in a room, to make space convivial. By midcentury, the Marquise de Pompadour was as wild about them as for easy seats: she had over twenty in her suite at Versailles alone. Her passion was so well-known that in 1750, the Parisian merchant Lazare Duvaux was advertising new models by calling them "Pompadour tables." (This was still another area where French and English taste diverged: the English dismissed small tables as not "substantial" enough. In 1792, John Byng waxed lyrical about his "firmly fixed," "immoveable" tables and railed against "little skuttling tables.")

The night table was the original task table and the table with perhaps the biggest impact on daily life. In the seventeenth century, the need for a new piece of furniture was evident. People had begun to pull up a chair next to the bed—putting a candlestick and perhaps something to drink on it. Only about 1720, however, did designers make the breakthrough: a very small table—normally twenty inches wide and from twenty-three to thirty-six inches high—with two shelves, usually of marble, open in the front, and often with little openings on each side (see page 137). (The marble and the openings were added to help fight odor buildup, a perennial problem, since the lower shelf often held a chamber pot.) The fanciest models also had a small drawer, just big enough for a few basic items. The night table thus also spoke to the desire for independence from servants in one's private life.

The new design was at home in the most modern contemporary residences. Charlotte Desmares owned a very early night table made of rosewood with gilded legs; she placed a more modest one in walnut in a guest room. From 1747 on, the Marquise de Pompadour preferred tables inlaid with odor-resistant mahogany. On a single day in 1750, she ordered six of the finest night tables from Duvaux. One of the most luxurious of all, delivered for her bedroom in her Château Bellevue in 1751 and with its inventory number still visible on the underside of its tiny drawer, is now on display in the Metropolitan Museum of Art: veneered with tulipwood and kingwood, with very discreet gilt bronze mounts, it makes convenience into a masterpiece of the modern style, all gentle curves and not a straight line in sight.

Designers soon customized the tiny piece in various ways. There was the *en cas*, or just in case, a model with a special shelf designed to hold a midnight snack rather than a chamber pot. There were multifunctional night tables; some, intended for those who loved to read in the middle of the night, had a stand that pulled up to hold a book. For those who wanted to be ready in case inspiration struck, others were equipped with a writing slide, an adjustable sloping panel for writing. (The English once again were reluctant to embrace a new convenience: night tables were virtually unknown in England before the 1760s.)

No night table, however, ever matched the intricacy of another of the age's great convenience pieces, the *table de toilette*, or dressing table, invented along with the private bedroom suite. It helped transform the process of getting dressed in the morning. Before the age of comfort, the process had no designated

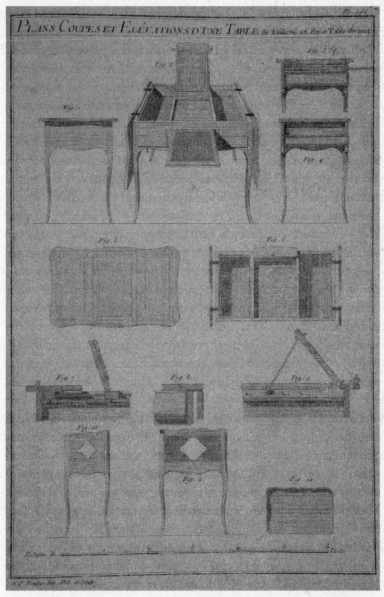

Here, Roubo diagrams the construction of two of the eighteenth century's favorite pieces of convenience furniture: *a* table de toilette, *or dressing table, and a night table.*

space: a piece of fabric (*toile* = cloth, *toilette* = a little cloth) was spread out on an ordinary table in any room, and grooming accessories were arranged on it. Then, in the late seventeenth century, a small room began to be earmarked for grooming: *cabinets de toilette*, dressing rooms. They appear frequently on plans by the 1730s; the name was often shortened to *toilette*.

Next, in the early eighteenth century, a piece of furniture, the *table de toilette* (sometimes also shortened to *toilette*), or dressing table, was invented; beauty aids—from perfume bottles to combs—no longer had to be put away after every day's toilette. The most intricate models had compartments to keep everything, from powder box to creams, "in the right place," just as modern architects preferred. In his design manual, Roubo illustrated a model with a built-in, slide-up mirror, even one with a tiny writing slide (see page 137). Charlotte Desmares put on her face seated at a *toilette* with a lace skirt and a big mirror; it was equipped with lots of crystal flacons, little Chinese lacquer boxes, and even its own cups and saucers, presumably for her morning coffee. Later, a fetching garment, known as a *peignoir*, became de rigueur for ladies sitting in their new *cabinets de toilette* in front of their *tables de toilette*. Getting ready for the day had become a ritual, also known as *la toilette*.

One activity, however, generated by far the greatest volume of convenience furniture: letter writing. It will come as no surprise to anyone who has ever read the kind of eighteenth-century novel in which characters seem to spend their days writing letters to learn that those who had a sudden urge to compose a letter never had far to go to find a surface on which to write: there were small writing tables and tiny desks in virtually every room of the eighteenth-century French home. Furniture makers continued to turn out the kind of huge desk that was a showstopper of the age of magnificence—the one produced for Louis XV, now on display at Versailles, was the most expensive piece of eighteenth-century furniture—but these were eclipsed by another new piece of furniture, the *secrétaire*, or small desk.

The writing furniture of the age of comfort might seem underwhelming in comparison with those majestic big desks: small desks were the ultimate flying tables, built to be moved easily wherever they were needed. Roubo explained that portable writing tables should be two feet wide, *secrétaires* three feet wide *at most*; neither should be more than fifteen to eighteen inches deep. Furniture makers, however, packed a huge amount of decorating punch into those tiny frames. The best pieces were crafted in the rarest exotic woods; they were veneered and inlaid with delicate patterns that were repeated in their gilt-bronze mounts. They are the quintessential pieces of the age, the perfect union of form and function, as elegantly graceful as they are useful.

The Marquise de Pompadour posed for many portraits during her long reign. The most famous, and the only one that was exhibited in public in her lifetime, was painted by François Boucher in 1756 (see color plate). It's a carefully orchestrated scene, Pompadour's way of proving to the king's subjects that she knew her place at Versailles. She is sitting in one of those small, interior rooms with controlled access. Everything on display—her fabulous outfit, the furniture and decorative objects, the many yards of luminous silk that envelop her person and the entire room—is a paean to the artistry of French craftsmen. Her pose could be an ad for the way of life made possible by the combined forces of French architects and furniture makers. Half-reclined on the curves of a very easy seat, her arm supported on a plump cushion, she reads in a very casual and modern way: she holds the well-thumbed copy of a favorite book, using her fingers to mark several passages.

To complete the picture of casual well-being, the woman who loved fine furniture as much as anyone in the eighteenth century singled out one piece of convenience furniture, an exquisite tiny writing table. (It's identical to a model by Bernard II Vanrisamburgh now in the Metropolitan Museum, nearly identical to one in the National Gallery of Art.) On top, we see a candle, sealing wax, and an envelope waiting to be closed up. A small drawer on one end is open, displaying writing implements ready at hand; a quill is poised in the inkwell. The table is the perfect piece for this overwhelmingly floral décor: both its veneer and its gilt-bronze mounts depict sprays of flowers. The portrait could thus also be seen as a tribute in particular to the contemporary furniture designers who had added beautiful convenience to private life.

CHAPTER EIGHT

1735: Architect-Designed Seating Begins

IN 1735, A sofa became the first piece of furniture ever to attain instant celebrity status, to be immediately covered by the contemporary press and quickly illustrated in a design manual. It was even put on public display and won rave reviews. Thus, unlike earlier particularly fine pieces such as Crozat's chairs and sofas, which were viewed only by the chosen few allowed admittance to royal residences and the finest homes, this sofa was brought to the attention of the broadest possible audience. The sofa's story proves that by 1735, those who did not live in palaces were developing a taste for fine furniture and wanted to follow contemporary trends in design.

In addition, the 1735 sofa's fame indicates that furniture design had become essential to the age of comfort. Indeed, in France the design and making of fine furniture was acquiring the status of a decorative art, and the concept of signed furniture was providing official recognition of furniture's new status. The practice of stamping or signing fine furniture became common only in the late 1720s. (This explains why we can't identify the maker of Crozat's ensemble.) In 1737, the guild of Parisian furniture makers began to require new master craftsmen to register their names and the date of their appointment with guild authorities; from then on, we know who was making fine furniture at any given date. Then, in 1743, new guild rules, finalized in 1751, required all members to stamp their works. Furniture was now being treated like painting and sculpture.

The decade during which furniture was attaining for the first time anywhere this new status was a heady moment for the fledgling French furniture industry. Its national reputation newly solidified, it began to go international. New furniture designs, the sofa in particular, were first featured in architectural treatises and architectural and interior decoration design books in the 1730s; potential foreign clients thus had their first glimpses of models newly available in Paris.

Then, about this time, furniture tourism began. Foreign visitors started to come to the French capital when they wanted to be sure of having the finest furniture and the latest styles in their homes. Among the original furniture tourists was the grand marshal of the Polish Crown, Count Franciszek Bieliński. In addition to his official functions—he was head of the royal police— Bieliński found time for his personal passion: natural history. When he arrived in Paris early in the 1730s, eager to turn his home into the showplace of War- saw, one man was thus the obvious choice to make this happen: Juste Aurèle Meissonnier. Since Meissonnier wore many hats—architect, decorator, de- signer, silversmith—he could do a full-service job. Meissonnier was, in addi- tion, the most visible creator of the modern style that was taking the Parisian decorating and design worlds by storm. The rococo was a stylistic match made in heaven for a naturalist such as Bieliński: its sinuous, asymmetrical lines and elaborately carved surfaces were inspired by the curves and crevices of such natural phenomena as shells and rocks.

By the time Bieliński sought him out, Meissonnier was design's darling of the moment, already established in the reverse of a pattern familiar to us today, whereby architects become celebrated for their daring buildings and only then create useful objects for the home. Meissonnier's architectural output was not vast; he produced instead quantities of everyday items that, when touched with his whimsical decorative verve, became magical rather than quotidian. He de- signed fabulous scissors with a case both handy and gorgeous. He designed what could be the most imaginative soup tureen of all time. If he designed great can- dlesticks, he did a great snuffer as well. For Louis XV, Meissonnier imagined a *nef* truly fit for a king. (This was a boat-shaped object designed specifically to hold the king's napkin on the royal dining table.) This one is a swirling mass of cherubs and fleurs-de-lis; like all Meissonnier's work, it is playful and fanciful, the product of an imagination gone nearly wild, to the edge of zaniness, à la Gaudi or Hector Guimard. In his hands, salt cellars became shells, while can- dlesticks morphed into palm trees.

We know so much about Meissonnier's designs because, like Thomas Chip- pendale after him, his reputation rests mainly on his published rather than on his surviving work. Well over a hundred plates were engraved and sold, indi- vidually or a few at a time, between 1734 and 1750, when all were gathered to- gether in a complete edition. This practice guaranteed that Meissonnier's best designs were quickly and widely known and that designers all over Europe would be influenced by his ideas.

But for Bieliński, a copy was not enough; he wanted the real thing, and a full measure of it at that. He commissioned from Meissonnier a complete room—naturally not any generic room, but a *cabinet*, the kind of intimate space promoted by modern architects. Every aspect of the space—architecture, painting, sculpture—and every single element—from the paneling to the mantelpiece, from the ceiling decoration to the sconces—was designed and carried out by Meissonnier or under his supervision. When it was ready, in 1735, the room was both the most complete and the most unified decorative statement yet produced by the man who was setting the realm of style on end.

There was only one problem: the prize package was scheduled for immediate and definitive removal from French soil.

The design world quickly mobilized, and a solution was found so that this definitive expression of the new French style would not disappear without a trace. That solution was an unprecedented event, the first ever public design show. Bieliński's room—dismantled and ready for shipment to Warsaw—was reassembled, down to the last touch, *inside* one of the rooms in Paris's Tuileries Palace, conveniently but a stone's throw from the city's newest neighborhoods. There, it became quite literally a showroom for furniture and interior decoration: Parisians and foreign visitors of 1735 flocked to the Tuileries to study Meissonnier's masterpiece, just as their contemporaries attended the yearly display of current French painting known as the *salon* and just as people now take in the latest blockbuster exhibit.

The most important paper of the day, the *Mercure de France*, described the "great satisfaction" expressed by viewers and provided a detailed account of all there was to admire. There was, to begin with, the room's paneling: Meissonnier's take on a then fashionable motif of garlands of flowers mixed media—the garlands were partly painted and partly carved—and this caused, the press claimed, "quite a stir." There was also the spectacular "sea green marble" used for the mantelpiece and the console table.

And then there was the pièce de résistance, the original celebrity sofa (see page 143). This was the first time Meissonnier had turned his attention to furniture; in his entire career, he designed very little furniture and never again produced a sofa. Prior to this time, there had been very little architect-designed furniture, and what little there was never left royal residences. Meissonier's sofa began the public life of architect-designed furniture. The contemporary press said the sofa was "absolutely unlike anything ever seen before," and Meissonnier's engraving makes it clear that only a radically new design could have worked in

Canapé exécuté pour M.^r le Comte de Bielowski Grand M.^{al} de la Couronne de Pologne, en 1735.

In 1735, this sofa designed for a Polish nobleman by the most influential decorator of the day, Juste Aurèle Meissonnier, was the most famous piece of furniture in Europe. It was put on display in the Tuileries Palace in Paris in the first ever public design show.

the room he had imagined for Bieliński. The sofa's wildly swerving curves and its resolutely asymmetrical swirls hold their own next to his breakthrough concept for wall paneling: the sofa served as particularly eye-catching proof that furniture was no longer primarily about the fabric. And even the fabric, which features a swirling, asymmetrical design, combines richly with the sculpture of both the sofa and the paneling.

The reporter for the *Mercure de France* concluded that the Bieliński ensemble "will bring to Poland a most favorable idea of the progress of the fine arts in France." He might have added that the mixed-media installation, in which painting, sculpture, architecture, and furniture design were given equal weight, would help demonstrate to a new audience a fact of which Parisians were already well aware: by 1735, interior decoration was poised to become a force to be reckoned with; it was beginning to take on an identity independent from architecture and was about to become what we call a field.

CHAPTER NINE

The Original Interior Decorators and the Comfortable Room

IN NOVEMBER 1698, two Swedes who followed the European architectural scene avidly, Nicodemus Tessin the Younger and Daniel Cronström, decided that the state of contemporary architecture was absolutely clear. If you were for some reason interested in grand façades (for them, an outdated concern), you still had to look to Renaissance Italy, for even the finest contemporary accomplishments—they cited Versailles's main façade—were hardly noteworthy. If you were, on the other hand, up-to-date, then you were looking to the French and to what the Swedes considered a new frontier for architecture. They referred to it with a brand-new phrase: *décoration intérieure*, interior decoration. (The appearance in their correspondence may be the first use of the phrase.) In this area, the "genius" of French architects was unsurpassed and indeed "becoming more refined every day."

Tessin and Cronström's correspondence was uncannily prescient. At the turn of the eighteenth century, French architects created new floor plans and new spaces and thus a new blueprint for private life. In the 1730s, it was as if those same architects suddenly realized that they had been doing all along something else as well, something that must have had a name, since Tessin and Cronström already knew what to call it in 1698, but that no one had as yet named in print, something whose potential finally dawned on the creators of the new architecture: they had been inventing interior decoration. The new field was a match made in heaven for the archetypal house-proud age.

Interior decoration thus came into existence as a subset of the new architecture of private life. For this reason, its discovery marked the origin of a concept that has had currency ever since: the domestic interior could and should be the expression of its owner's personal taste; it should be styled to complement the owner's life and with his or her comfort in mind. From then on, "taste" became a buzzword in interior design, particularly in the phrase "French taste"—for in the eighteenth century, this was still another domain in which, as trendsetters all over Europe were well aware, the French had no rivals. With the clever use of all the design elements that together added up to an image of "French taste"— from the first ever window treatments to the first ever windows deserving of treatment—the original interior decorators reinvented the room. They made it a space designed no longer strictly to impress others, but above all with the well-being of its occupants in mind.

Prior to the seventeenth century's final decades, there was no need for the phrase interior decoration, for the concept of decoration barely existed. During all the centuries when households were often on the move, a room's ornamentation was limited to fireplaces, wall hangings, and ceiling decoration. In the late Middle Ages and the Renaissance, Italy ruled supreme over the world of style, and French monarchs brought artists from Italy to ornament the interiors of their residences. Frescoes then became a standard option and ceilings more elaborate; a sense of an overall decorative plan emerged. The Italian model—which remained the dominant mode all through the age of magnificence—made statements that were colorful, splashy, larger than life. A room showcased a few gorgeous objects designed to stop viewers in their tracks; decoration was above all an overt demonstration of wealth and power. In February 1751, Françoise de Graffigny described her visit to a Parisian home in which the interior hadn't been touched since the 1680s. "It's embellished just as they did in those days . . . : nothing adds to one's well-being."

When, beginning in the 1670s, baroque megalomania began to be replaced by coziness, French architects rejected the Italian model and replaced it with their own vision for domestic style. When this process began, only a few residences, and only the grandest, had anything that could be called a style. However, the notion that one's domestic interior should be decorated, not simply cobbled together, spread so quickly through French society that barely a century later, Beaumarchais's friend and editor, Gudin de La Brenellerie, declared: "Today, the most modest shopkeeper would turn up his nose at an apartment without interior decoration."

Belief in the importance of interior design spread not only through the social ranks, but also far and wide. Home owners from Sweden to Poland would do anything to be certain that their interiors replicated French taste. In this, Tessin and Cronström were trailblazers: their letters document "the incredible lengths" to which they were prepared to go in their attempts "to lure away" the finest craftsmen so that the look of Paris would be copied exactly in Stockholm.

By 1740, Tessin's son Carl, court official and statesman and every inch his father's child, wrote from Paris to ask Carl Hårleman, his architect in Sweden, for the "exact measurements of the places in my new home that might be appropriate to display decorations. . . . Please give me the measurements for upholstery materials and include the width and height of walls." He then proceeded to buy up the wherewithal—from overmantels to overdoors, from corner cupboards to new-style beds—necessary to create a true interior in the modern style, joining thereby the ranks of foreigners coming to Paris to acquire French decorative arts by the containerload. Indeed, by midcentury, the *Encyclopédie* rated interior decoration right after modern architecture among the achievements "that conferred the most honor upon the French nation."

By the mid–eighteenth century, in other words, interior decoration had become what we think of as a field. For the first time, objects were valued not as dazzling showstoppers, but for their ability to work in a context and thereby to make a room into both a personal statement and a place that enhanced and facilitated daily life. For the first time, there were individuals whose business it was to help others choose their decoration, to have objects made to fit their clients' interiors, and to arrange them in their homes. For the first time, the world of style opened up to design in a new sense of the word, one that included the arts of design, those based on the union between form and function. The new field also gave official recognition to the fact that French craftsmen and designers were establishing the first industry of the decorative arts.

You did not, moreover, have to be a globe-trotter to keep up with the latest decorating trends from Paris. The French turned interior decoration into a field by following the example of architecture: they recorded all their neatest innovations and accomplishments in print, in richly illustrated books. With a veritable flood of publications, an audience both socially and geographically diverse gained access for the first time to the world of decoration. The French thus came to dominate the very influential and very lucrative world of design for the better part of a century. The English and the Dutch contributed goods but few new ideas, at the same time that French concepts and designs redefined daily life all over Europe.

Their takeover began with pattern books compiled at the turn of the eighteenth century by architects such as Robert de Cotte, Pierre Le Pautre, and Jean-Baptiste Le Roux. These compilations of designs for fireplaces and wall treatments showed how mirrors and a few well-chosen objects could be used to create a total look for a small part of a room (one wall, a single fireplace). Each style was given a name—"royal" (*à la royale*), "in the latest style" (*à la mode*), "French" (*à la française*), or simply "new"—and on occasion the space for which it had been created was specified ("this new design was used in the private apartments of the Trianon Palace" and so forth). At the origin of interior design, we thus find a practice that is still the bread and butter of decorating magazines, an attempt to give outsiders a feel for how the rich and famous live in their domestic interiors.

This idea was fully developed in the Paris guides of Germain Brice and especially of Piganiol de La Force, who took his readers on room-by-room virtual tours of the most notable French residences, such as the Marquise de Pompadour's château, Bellevue: "When you go up to the second floor, in the first room on the left, look for the overdoors by . . . Next you enter a lovely boudoir with furniture upholstered in . . . ," and so forth. (This, by the way, is an overdoor [see page 148], a spot to which no one had paid attention before but one that eighteenth-century decorators made an essential decorating space.)

The new "taste" in décor was also publicized in unexpected ways. Many eighteenth-century book illustrations, for example, rather than featuring a scene from the fiction's plot, showed off rooms decorated in the latest style, thereby introducing all those who read French novels to the French look for the home (see pages 56 and 106). Beginning in the 1720s, a new type of painting was first seen in Paris. Best exemplified by the canvases of Jean-François de Troy, three of which illustrate this book, these are scenes that focus above all on the decoration of interior rooms.

When de Troy's paintings were publicly exhibited in Paris, first in June 1724 and the following year in the *salon* at the Louvre, their innovativeness was immediately recognized. The art connoisseur Pierre-Jean Mariette referred to them as *tableaux de mode*, paintings about style or paintings about fashion; the contemporary press enumerated the points about the new French style or taste that de Troy was making—the fact that the couple was seated on a sofa, for example, the types and quality of the fabrics depicted, the fact that the space was "very successfully decorated." Such scenes of interior decoration were particularly popular with the same clientele that sought out the latest French designs for their homes. In the early 1740s, for example, when Carl Tessin was frantically matching up his new home and new objects from Paris, he also ordered several such interior scenes from the artist of the moment, Boucher. Another foreigner enamored of the French decorative arts, Frederick the Great of Prussia, acquired no fewer than ten of de Troy's "style paintings" to complement the heavily French décor in his residences.

The breakthrough that made interior decoration into a publicly recognized

Decoration du haut d'une porte et de son couronnement

Eighteenth-century interior decoration featured overdoors,
small paintings positioned above every door in a room.

field was the brainchild of architects Blondel and Mariette. In 1738, Mariette
published the final volume of his *Architecture française* (its plates were largely
engraved by Blondel), and Blondel published the second volume of his manifesto for modern architecture. Both works took the unprecedented step of including, in addition to plans of the most famous contemporary residences, the
first plates ever to depict in complete detail the interior decoration, often including furniture, of entire rooms. They thereby finally made official an idea

that had been germinating for thirty years: there was a new field, and it was called interior decoration.

Blondel devoted his work's entire second volume to the field he was thereby establishing. This is in fact the earliest comprehensive work published on interior decoration. He featured lots of lovingly detailed engravings; he supplemented them with commentary, so that decorator wannabes could follow the process step by step, in word and in image, and understand exactly how to get the latest look just right (see below). Blondel spelled it all out—from wall color to wall treatments (by the way, those are very big mirrors above the sofas), from furniture to lighting. He indicated the scale (the serving table is six feet wide) and put letters next to the essential components so that he could make clear anything that didn't come across in black and white (those frolicking children holding candles are made of bronze; the overdoors should be *camaïeux*, or monochromatic; while the central painting should be in full color).

And, in case all this wasn't enough, in the accompanying text, Blondel walked would-be decorators through every room he depicts, adding further details such as how many sofas each room requires (he was crazy about sofas, for they allowed home owners to entertain a big group without crowding a room with

*The architects who created the field of interior decoration also invented
this kind of illustration, a step-by-step guide to putting a room together.
In this dining room view, for example, Blondel spells out everything from the
color of the overdoors to that of the walls.*

lots of ill-matched chairs dragged in from all over the house) and the kind of
room in which only a seascape will do. In true dictatorial decorator fashion, he
prescribed the types of knickknacks suitable for display on various surfaces.
Blondel even attempted to win permanent control over great interiors: he claimed,
for example, that architect-designed sofas and armchairs should never be removed from the rooms for which they had been conceived; if an "architecturally modern home" was sold, the owners had no right to take the furniture
with them.

The timing of this initiative was hardly accidental. By 1738, one thing was
absolutely clear: the building boom that had reconfigured the cityscape of
Paris was over. If French architecture was to remain prominent, a new direction had to be found. Interior decoration was thus brought to the rescue to
teach people that even if they had a new home, they could not simply rest on
their laurels: its interior style had to be kept up-to-date.

Mariette repeated this message in still another 1738 publication, a new edition
of d'Aviler's manual. In 1710, Le Blond had increased the manual's coverage
of distribution and interior space; Mariette added a section on interior decoration: "Interior decoration has been revolutionized; the décors being designed
today are so different from those used a few years ago that we decided to illustrate them." From then on, publication after publication—Briseux in 1743,
Boffrand in 1745—repeated in print what Tessin and Cronström knew in 1698:
a phrase had been coined to designate a new subset of architecture. The same
architects who had proclaimed the revolution in modern architecture now announced the birth of interior design—and they added images to make their
message loud and clear.

In 1738, the interiors of the Palais Bourbon were still intact, and Mariette included seven plates to show readers exactly what they looked like. Those images guaranteed the palace's status as the original monument in the history of
interior decoration. From then on, all agreed that Madame la Duchesse's home
was the new field's first great achievement. Pierre Patte—Blondel collaborator
and the first architect to produce a city map with cross sections to show practical aspects of urban planning such as sewer systems—praised the Palais Bourbon's style as delicate and airy rather than monumental, as bright and luminous
rather than dark. He saw its rooms as exemplars of "informality" rather than
"gravitas."

His description highlights Madame la Duchesse's debt to the intimate palaces
at Versailles where she had cut her decorating teeth. Those who invented interior decoration were obliged to discuss the daughter's work rather than that of
her interior decoration–obsessed parents, Montespan and Louis XIV, for by

the 1730s, the place where interior decoration had really come of age, the tiny, fairy-tale palace the Porcelain Trianon, had long since been destroyed.

This explains why we have no images of the very first modern interiors. We do at least have contemporary press coverage from late 1673. The editor of a newspaper with a pan-European readership, the *Mercure galant*, invited three "fashionable women" to give their views on a subject never before discussed in print, "ways of decorating the interiors of residences." Their conversation touched on every element that, decades later, at the time when interior decoration was officially invented, everyone still considered essential to the perfect French look and essential to comfortable, casual living.

The *Mercure*'s coverage of the Trianon was a watershed in the democratization of taste. For the first time, you didn't have to travel to a faraway place or win access to the most exclusive properties in the world to get basic decorating ideas; for the first time, that kind of information was made public in a widely accessible medium. The article even makes this point clear, when the ladies note that, while the richest people in France were building their own little "jewel-box" replicas of the Trianon, "all the ideas created for it were being copied by private individuals of all kinds." They might have added that this was possible because the Trianon was itself a milestone, the first setting fit for a king in which interior decoration did not break the bank. All its innovations were thus eminently copyable—in fact, we're still copying most of them today.

The first one mentioned (and, tellingly, this was still the first thing Patte stressed in his eulogy of the Palais Bourbon) was the way its ceilings were decorated—or, in this case, not decorated. Apparently for the first time ever, ceilings were not covered with elaborate paintings or coffered beams, styles so costly that they were beyond all but princely budgets. Instead, the Trianon featured ceilings that instantly became the fable of Europe because they were . . . well, just plain white. As the *Mercure*'s decorating experts put it, "Absolutely no one today would dream of spending a lot of money on a fancy ceiling." So there it was, in 1673, the beginning of the end for one of the oldest, most basic components of the look of magnificence. And thus, with the invention of simplicity, modern interior style began.

The rise of what eventually came to be known as a "modern-style ceiling" (*plafond dans le goût moderne*) was unstoppable. By the key year for interior decoration, 1738, Mariette heaped scorn on old-style ceilings—"spider's nests" good only for collecting dust, "ponderous" by day, "impossible to light" at night—and spelled out what the modern look entailed: "a simple plaster ceiling, whose whiteness makes an apartment brighter," with at most a curved molding between the ceiling and the wall or a delicate stuccowork border. In the decorating section of its February 1755 issue, the *Mercure de France* named these borders "lacework" and pronounced anything "more magnificent" "completely out of style." In 1771, Blondel illustrated a modern ceiling: white with simple lacework. By then, Parisians from all income brackets had followed suit and thrown off the older fashion for exposed beams decorated or not. The brightness and casual simplicity of the white ceiling had completely won the day.

After the ceiling, the decorating mavens of 1673 tackled wall colors: both plain white with perhaps a touch of gilding, or "the Trianon style," blue and white, were à la mode. Once again, the ladies, like the Trianon itself, were on the cutting edge. Earlier in the seventeenth century, walls, done in strong colors—red, green, yellow—dominated a room. During the reign of Louis XIII, red became the official color of the kings of France, and the walls of staterooms were covered in crimson damask and velvet. At first, his son was faithful to his father's taste, and at Versailles he remained so to the end. In the mid-1680s, however, royal suppliers began to deliver textiles for more intimate palaces such as the Ménagerie in the lighter palette introduced at the Porcelain Trianon: soft blues, greens, and yellows, and just plain white. These were hues intended to blend into an ensemble rather than to set the tone.

When the Parisian building boom began, the palette of Versailles's intimate palaces became synonymous with French taste or the modern style. Already in the original 1691 edition of his manual, d'Aviler called white "the most beautiful color because it adds light and lifts our spirits." At the same moment, Le Roux declared that "white makes rooms brighter, cleaner and fresher." And so it went—from the Place Vendôme to the urban suburban mansions of the 1720s—it was white, white, and white on white. There were even all-white salons—Madame la Duchesse had one—in which all the upholstery was white and gold frames provided the only contrast. White had become for the first time a color, the dominant color in modern homes.

In 1693, that décor watchdog Tessin confirmed that "paneling, ceilings, doors are all now painted white, with or without a touch of gilding." Gilding—in which gold was beaten into extremely thin sheets and then applied to stucco with an adhesive—was rediscovered in France in the late seventeenth century as another way of brightening rooms. During the ruinous turn-of-the-century wars, the process was officially banned to save the gold, but some, notably the rich Crozat, went ahead and gilded anyway. Bullet gave this rule of thumb: Add the gold if you can afford it, but plain white is just fine.

Furniture was soon swept up in the craze for a brighter look, never more spectacularly than in the Porcelain Cabinet. The Cabinet was designed in 1686 to show off Monseigneur's collection of 169 Chinese porcelains, almost all decorated in blue and white. The seats (including one of the original sofas) on which visitors could perch while they admired his treasures were covered with fabric embroidered with—what else?—Chinese vases in silver and blue. And their wood frames were painted, also silver with blue highlights. Thus, the increased presence of furniture in royal residences and the increased amount of exposed frame did not mean that when you walked into a room, you were faced with a lot of brown furniture.

In the mid-1760s, Horace Walpole grumbled that so much whiteness was just plain boring: "I have seen but one idea in all the houses here; the rooms are white and gold, or white. . . . I could not perceive any difference, but in the more or less gold." And signs of the same discontent had been evident in the design world for some time. Briseux claimed that already around 1725, people decided that white got dirty too easily—given the reality of those smoking fireplaces, this is all too believable. Briseux was also the first, in 1743, to point out something that dogs decorators to this day: It's notoriously difficult to get exactly the right shade of white.

White would never have been able to sweep the original interior decorators off their feet if the concept of wall treatment had not been revolutionized. Until the late seventeenth century, in all fine residences walls were, as Patte put it, "all covered up"—with tapestries, or heavy fabric, or frescoes. Then, in 1691, d'Aviler formulated what became the party line of modern architecture: paneling kept rooms "dryer and warmer"; it did not retain odors as tapestry did. Now, wall paneling had existed for centuries. Prior to the late seventeenth century, however, it usually stopped at the height of very tall chimneys and had very rarely been floor to ceiling; never had it been integrated into a room's décor. Fine eighteenth-century French wall paneling was altogether a different thing. It was expertly carved by master craftsmen, who executed the plans of great designers such as Meissonnier (see page 154). Each panel showed off the delicate, asymmetrical scrolls typical of the modern style; the ensemble was considered an integral part of a room's décor.

Rooms were also decorated and brightened by the large mirrors that, from the 1690s on, were placed strategically in interior rooms. In 1697, Tessin announced that the use of mirrors over fireplaces had become de rigueur: "*c'est le goût qui règne*" (it's the reigning style). In fact, Louis XIV had just ordered that the "reigning style" be adopted for every room in his apartments at Versailles and Marly. Mirrors also added depth and a sense of context to intimate spaces. In de Troy's *The Garter* (see color plates), we get a glimpse of the architecture

Panneaux de Menuiserie   Planche 89

*Instead of the frescoes and tapestries favored in earlier periods,
many eighteenth-century interiors featured floor-to-ceiling
wall paneling intricately carved to echo the pattern of the
room's other essential design elements.*

beyond the small room in the mirror over the console table. In de Troy's painting of a group of friends gathered in a small reception room (see color plates),
the mirror amplifies space, patterns, and objects, to make those in the cozy nest
feel they had still more of everything that made them comfortable.

Interiors were brightened in still another way: by the *bras de lumière* positioned on either side of large mirrors. Tessin explained that when the placement
was just right, "the reverberation makes a room lit by only two to four candles

seem brighter and more cheerful than one with a dozen tapers." Boffrand dictated that they should be placed *exactly* six feet off the ground, for "if they are one bit higher, they will make people's eyes seem baggy and deep-set, and ladies will find this unforgivable."

An age so obsessed with a brighter interior style faced one hard fact, however. Before the technology that made it possible to pour large panes of glass was invented in France in the late seventeenth century, very little natural light entered interiors. Until the late Middle Ages, windows were made largely of squares of oilcloth, canvas, or even oiled paper—glass was very rarely used outside of churches and ecclesiastical buildings. In France, glass came into wider use only in the Renaissance. By the mid–seventeenth century, glass windows had become the norm in France, though they were a far cry from what we know now: many very tiny squares of glass were set into lead frames. The year of the Porcelain Trianon's construction, 1673, was a milestone in the history of domestic architecture in still another way: it marked the beginning of the end for tiny windows. When the French Royal Academy of Architecture met on July 26, 1673, its members criticized Palladio for having used windows that were "far too small and narrow to suit us today, when everyone is trying to get as much light into rooms as possible."

Soon after, design caught up with the new desire. When large panes of poured glass became available, the modern window was created. To some, this development was as dazzling as Versailles's still fabled expanses of mirrored glass. In 1687, Tessin toured Versailles. When he visited one of the palace's great sights, the king's staterooms, his attention was drawn first not to the glories one might expect—the famous paintings, the solid silver furniture—but to the windows. He exclaimed in amazement that "throughout these rooms, the windows rise up from the hardwood floor all the way to the ceiling." Tessin lingered over every detail concerning those magical windows—their intricate ironwork closing system, the gilding on the wood between the panes—and got around to the paintings only later, almost as an afterthought. His logic is easy to understand. The world had seen lots of old master canvases, but those huge windows—today known appropriately as French windows or French doors—were a real revelation.

French windows immediately won over all the architects instrumental in the age of comfort. Already in the 1690s, Pierre Bullet, architect of the Crozat and d'Evreux mansions on the Place Vendôme, had begun to insist on precise kinds and sizes of glass for all his projects. And in 1703, Cronström wrote Tessin that "tiny, square windows" were now a thing of the past, since architects could no longer understand how "anyone could continue to follow the Italian style."

In a matter of decades, because of the newly rich able to afford amenities previously found only in royal palaces, a completely modern window had arrived on the scene. By the turn of the eighteenth century, all the technology—a system making it possible to open or close a big window in a single gesture, for example (the *Mercure galant* reported on that, too)—in use until the late nineteenth century had been invented. And whereas in the mid–seventeenth century a "large" pane of glass was five to six inches square, by the end of the century these were referred to as "small" panes, and all fans of the comfortable life wanted only large panes. Look at the image of a trendy Parisian shop in the 1690s (page 224). The shopkeeper uses big comfort armchairs and big windows to give his clients a luxurious experience.

By 1720, panes of glass sixteen inches square were available—Madame la Duchesse was among the first to have them installed—and by roughly mid-century, panes nineteen by twenty inches or even twenty by twenty-three were being used. In 1738, Mariette promoted the ultimate ostentatious display of big glass, already featured in Pierre Crozat's gallery, big mirrors positioned opposite large-paned windows or French doors. And by 1752, Françoise de Graffigny positively crowed over "the panes in my windows [that are] as big as mirrors." When you see old- and new-style windows side by side, it's easy to understand why she would have been so proud, why, as Blondel put it, large-paned windows had "taken over," and why, when they redid their homes, most people had their windows changed (see page 157).

Good lighting soon came to be seen as an essential component of the comfortable life. And no one proved more resourceful in introducing the world to the well-lit home than Blondel, the first architect to be concerned with lighting in residential architecture. He was endlessly creative in his attempts to get as much natural daylight as possible into small interior rooms and hidden passageways, many of which were windowless. He praised the way Pierre Crozat's architect, Jean-Sylvain Cartaud, had used a small inner courtyard to bring light to windowless toilet rooms. He also praised the use in the Palais Bourbon of clever *jours*, lights or proto-skylights, to brighten a tricky back passageway. (There were even openings in the floor to let light through to the floor below.) And when any kind of direct opening was impossible, Blondel suggested placing in a room next to a small room with no windows a large mirror above a door, so that daylight would be reflected into the small room.

As soon as windows started to change, modern window treatments began. They were now essential to protect privacy, for large-paned windows and higher-quality glass also made it much easier to see what was happening inside a room. That same 1673 discussion on domestic design included a news flash:

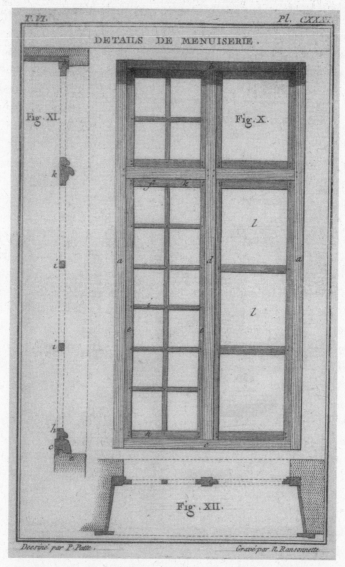

This engraving demonstrates the superiority of the large-pane
windows that were introduced in the late seventeenth century and
had come into widespread use by the mid—eighteenth century.

"Even the curtains placed in front of windows are subject to fashion's capri-
ciousness; now they are being divided down the middle and, rather than drawing them only to one side, now they are drawn to both sides. This style was
invented because it was both more convenient and more decorative." Thus

was announced the creation of something we still see around us every day: the modern curtain.

Until the 1670s, curtains had not been much used. Then, the Trianon style jump-started the quest for bigger, better windows, and curtains became an essential component of a room's decoration. Initially, grand fabrics called attention to the novelty item: the original curtains in Versailles's Hall of Mirrors were white taffeta with gold fringe. Soon, however, window treatments moved with the times and became casual: simple cotton curtains, often in plain white, were a big part of the young look devised for the tiny royal châteaux. By the 1720s, curtains were part of every room in a wealthy family's home and were widely used in modest residences. In her small home on the rue de Varennes, Charlotte Desmares sometimes chose formal fabrics such as yellow damask, but she also had lots of cotton curtains.

Next came a subset of the curtain, the blind. These were usually raised and lowered with cords; however, in one of that window treatment's inaugural appearances, in Monseigneur's Porcelain Cabinet, the blinds—designed to cover not only the windows, but every wall—were mechanized: a system of springs had been devised to roll and unroll them automatically. They were made of moiré silk with a design of blue branches. When they were lowered, the room's décor was unified, and visitors could concentrate on the Chinese vases. When they were raised, the paintings on the walls—by Raphael, Titian, and Giorgione—might well have held their attention.

Blinds helped make evident the need for valances to conceal the fittings of all window treatments; fabric was also draped to hide curtain rods. Ads in the contemporary press prove that craftsmen were constantly coming up with new systems, each said to be "more convenient and more elegant." In June 1755, the Marquise de Pompadour had installed in her boudoir at Bellevue the blind to end all blinds: "a blind in Italian taffeta painted with translucent bouquets and garlands, the blind in its matching box, supports and hooks in polished copper, the cord in silk and gold, with a pear-shaped tassel ornamented with spinach seeds, jasmine flowers, and sequins."

One final component became synonymous with the modern French look in interior decoration: hardwood floors that were easy to keep up and as streamlined as built-in storage. Until the seventeenth century, wood was an infrequent option for flooring, except in modest homes, where fairly primitive plank floors were found. People of means used stone and terra-cotta tiles; in the sixteenth century, marble tiles became common.

In 1664, when floors described as "oak parquet" were laid at the château of

Fontainbleau, the tide began to change. These were no ordinary planked floors, mind you, but a new kind, the patterned hardwood floors still known as parquet. The word—literally, "a little park"—originally referred to a fenced enclosure for sheep and later came to designate both the part of a courtroom fenced off for the judges and lawyers (like the railing we call "the bar") and the part of a room where the throne or chair of state was placed. Wood was often used in these official areas to set them off visually from the rest of the room; "parquet" was thus a logical choice for the new kind of flooring. Soon after Henrietta Maria returned to England after years in France, she copied the new French look for floors, and in 1664, John Evelyn taught the English its name: "The French call it parquetage." (The Princesse Palatine complained in 1710: "There's still no word in German for parquet.") In 1673, the *Mercure galant* made readers aware of the change: "Important people have gotten rid of the rugs in their bedrooms since they do nothing but collect dust; they have replaced them with parquet, even using different colors of wood in the patterns." And in 1684, the death knell sounded for marble tiles. When Versailles's architects decided that all the water used to wash them down was rotting out joists and causing leaks in the ceilings below, marble was ripped out all over the palace and replaced with parquet.

In January 1700, the Royal Academy of Architecture made it official: "In the 22nd chapter of Palladio's first book of architecture, he says marble should be used in bedrooms. We do things differently in France; in bedrooms and all the rooms in which we spend the most time, we use parquet." Parquet had thus been decreed the official floor covering of the new interior rooms. Modern architects had not waited for that green light. In 1691, Bullet (dreaming of those upcoming luxury residences on the Place Vendôme) discussed the different styles and pronounced the new *losange*, or diamond pattern, the way of the future. The first editions of d'Aviler mention only terra-cotta and marble, but in the 1738 decorating edition, Mariette declared that parquet had taken over the home: "No one uses any other type of flooring anymore."

The diamond pattern—large (about three feet) squares set on the diagonal—is what is now known as "parquet de Versailles," Versailles-style parquet, and with good reason, for it was soon found all over the palace (see page 160). In March 1679, payment was made by the royal treasury to the craftsmen (Falaise and Associates) who had laid the parquet in the apartment destined for the lady of the Porcelain Trianon, the Marquise de Montespan. In 1682, the trendiest young royal, Monseigneur, one-upped the woman whose style had set the tone for a decade when he had a parquet created for his rooms whose intricacy went far, far

*This diamond pattern, in which three-foot squares were
set on the diagonal, became known as Versailles-style
parquet because it was used all over the palace.
It was the most fashionable flooring in fine
eighteenth-century homes.*

beyond the diamond pattern. The design still exists, so we can see why, during
his visit to Versailles in 1687, Tessin raved about it ("very fine, exceptionally
well-executed: they say it all should be attributed to Monseigneur's genius").

From then on, everyone wanted to give their floors the Versailles look, for
parquet had quickly come to be seen as essential for comfortable interior settings.
(The pattern is shown in de Troy's *Declaration of Love*; in Devis's portrait, the
Bulls have covered up much of their rather less sophisticated hardwood floor

with a dust-trapping rug.) In the 1692 edition of Blégny's guide to the best addresses in Paris, he added a new category: craftsmen who installed parquet,
along with their rates. And by May 1693, Tessin ordered a square of Versailles
parquet for the Swedes to replicate.

Put all these components together, as French architects and their clients were
doing in the 1720s and 1730s, and you had the "French look," the rococo, that
combination of seductive curviness and whimsical asymmetry evident in Meissonnier's celebrity sofa and just beginning to emerge in Crozat's furniture.
These were the first interiors ever to be styled or decorated with the goal of
putting people at ease rather than on display. For Blondel and Mariette and
their generation, the new French style just simply *was* interior decoration, the
art of making interiors elegantly convenient and comfortable.

For Blondel, interior decoration had two cardinal rules. First, there was simplicity: "Simplicity is my sole objective. . . . I never praise décor that over-
whelms us with its splendor. I will only discuss interior decoration that wins
accolades for the beauty of its lines and the variety of its contours." Then there
was harmony, the master plan that "coordinates" the beautiful lines and contours of different objects and decorative elements so that they work together to
create "*un beau tout*," a beautiful ensemble.

To achieve harmony, everything, absolutely everything, had to share the
same lines, even the rooms themselves. In the age of magnificence, all rooms
were rectangles or squares, and ceiling height was uniform. All the grand sequences of rooms in palaces were thus sequences of virtually identical units.
Fabulous boxes they may have been, but they were boxes still. Then, architects
such as Bullet began to include as a matter of course rooms that curved; both
the Crozat and the d'Evreux mansions on the Place Vendôme had rooms with
rounded corners. The boxy look was on its way out as soon as comfort became
a value for architecture. The masterpieces of the new architecture showcased
the rounded corner and curving rooms—round rooms, ovals, ellipses, rooms
rounded at one end—all of which, as Blondel pointed out, was ideal from the
standpoint of interior decoration, since the room's design scheme could continue all around the space without interruption.

Truly harmonious simplicity did not come easily, and it certainly did not
come cheap. We see Tessin, for example, ready to spend a fortune in order to
obtain just that one special door lock. He not only allowed but positively
begged the master locksmith to set his terms: Would he come to Sweden?
Would he make molds and send them instead? Tessin knew well that "everything had to be up to the same standard of taste": the perfect room positively
demanded a lock worthy of "a beautiful ensemble." He also felt the excitement

of knowing that this kind of lock was as innovative as the new wall treatments. Until the 1690s, even the grandest locks made for "royal residences," as Blondel would explain to his readers, had been as "square" as those boxlike rooms; now, for the first time ever, locks were "sculpted" so that their shapes (even the form of the knobs) would "be coordinated" with "the varied contours of the wood-work."

Furniture, too, was subject to the rule of harmony, and even a master crafts-man such as Roubo understood that since furniture "was part of interior deco-ration, its design has to function in relation to the contours of the walls of the room." This meant that the sofa's lines followed those set by the paneling and the frame of the painting hung above it; it also meant that Blondel designed his sofas so that their "scrollwork" would echo the "curves" of the wall and would "nestle" under the frame of a very large mirror. Each individual element was supposed to be gorgeous in and of itself, but there was not a showstopper in the lot—that's why Monseigneur had blinds made to cover his Raphaels: they were too magnificent for comfort. The overall equilibrium among all elements was the ruling factor that made a room harmonious, a place where people felt at ease.

Harmonious interior decoration came of age along with the interior rooms that, as d'Aviler said in 1691, were "less grand and more used." It was thus dé-cor at the service of daily life, functioning in tandem with easy seats and mod-ern conveniences for the comfort of the inhabitants of those rooms. Letters and memoirs make it clear that individuals from Françoise de Graffigny to Du-fort de Cheverny believed that modern life was best lived in settings in which all design elements worked in concert, for such harmonious surroundings were comfortable surroundings. This was décor that, or so the same individuals tell us, facilitated intimacy, from companionate sociability to new love, as de Troy illustrates in his *tableaux de mode*. Settings that were light and airy, that put dust-free Versailles parquet underfoot and harmonious frames on everything from sofas to locks, made it possible for their inhabitants to feel at home.

That desire for tasteful comfort was the springboard that gave rise to the new profession. In the case of the great homes built in Paris's new neighborhoods, for the first time we know the names of those responsible for the interior deco-ration of private residences: Gilles-Marie Oppenord, for example, designed doors and paneling considered among the finest ever produced when he styled Crozat's fabled gallery. (Charlotte Desmares copied Oppenord's designs for her salon.) Meissonnier's interior decoration for Bieliński became the talk of Europe.

The original interior decorators were all architects, usually the same architect responsible for the building itself. Then, just as interior decoration gained independence from architecture, so a new professional gradually appeared on the scene: the decorator. "Decorator" originally designated those responsible for set design in the theater. Blondel sometimes spoke of the person responsible for interior decoration as a decorator, but he meant the architect. In 1773, however, the article "décorateur" in Jaubert's dictionary of arts and crafts officially proclaimed that the decorator was an independent professional. Many decorators were still architects—in 1768, prolific furniture designer Delafosse used the title "architect-decorator"—but this was changing. Jaubert admitted that the profession was just getting started and had become necessary because the new "opulence" everywhere visible in Paris had brought about such a proliferation of luxury goods, beautiful objects, and master craftsmen that the need had become apparent for someone to oversee every aspect of the ever more complicated world of interior decoration. Jaubert anointed the decorator "as the only person who knows how to arrange the products of genius of different craftsmen, how to position furniture . . . how to give a home that uniquely striking look."

Probably no one did more to broaden the parameters of interior decoration than the age's most fanatical advocate of the new field, the Marquise de Pompadour, the original brand name in the history of interior decoration. She was the first individual ever whose name was used to characterize colors, textiles, types of furniture, and even a style in general. Her best-known portrait, by Boucher (see color plates), in which the décor is truly an extension of her person, a person obsessed with interior decoration, makes it easy to see how all this began. There were Pompadour tables; there was Pompadour pink (a deep, reddish pink) and Pompadour blue, Pompadour cloth (featuring sprigs of flowers in which pink and blue dominated). All the naming began not only during her own lifetime, but virtually as soon as she became seriously involved with decoration. The practice is attested in France by 1750; already in 1752, it had spread outside French borders, and the English were speaking of Pompadour this and Pompadour that. By the early nineteenth century, people had even begun to say of a look, "That's *so* Pompadour" (*Cela est pompadour*). Finally, "the Pompadour style" (*le goût Pompadour*) became a synonym for the rococo soon after that term was coined.

The marquise was taken seriously by the man who put interior decoration on the map. Blondel recommended that students who studied architecture with him visit her personal rooms in the former Hôtel d'Evreux: "These rooms will make them understand what interior decoration is all about." Yet the marquise was hardly the kind of purist one might have expected Blondel to champion.

For her renovation of the Hôtel d'Evreux, Pompadour's architect, Lassurance II, is credited with its décor. Pompadour, however, did not espouse the
conviction shared by Blondel and Briseux and Mariette that the building's architect should retain absolute control over every aspect of its decoration, from
the design of the furniture to its placement in the room. Lassurance did not design everything in her famous rooms; he was far from the only person whose
advice mattered to the marquise. Luxury goods dealer Lazare Duvaux, for example, did a great deal to shape the look of her interiors, a role dealers such as
Duvaux played for many by the mid–eighteenth century.

And the real competition was yet to come. In 1780, Le Camus de Mézières
still insisted that the architect should make all decisions concerning "the entire
decorative ensemble." (He was, after all, an architect.) He was well aware,
however, that those days were either gone or fast disappearing: "It happens all
too often that the upholsterer makes all the decisions concerning furniture and
decoration." There it was; someone had said the word: the upholsterer, the new
power in interior decoration. Remember the image of an upholsterer's shop
(page 123), well stocked with furniture of all kinds and with upholstery fabrics
as well? By the last decades of the century, in most cases upholsterers were
calling all the shots. By then, as Gudin de La Brenellerie pointed out, even shop-
keepers wanted the look of interior decoration for their homes. Upholsterers
could get the job done for less; they could open the world of interior decoration's magic to those whose homes were not architect designed.

Thus began the period in the nineteenth century during which, according to
architects, at least, upholsterers used their influence to guarantee that rooms
were overdraped and oversheathed and positively enfolded in vast expanses of
textile, jam-packed with great plush cushions and overpadded seat furniture.
(Le Camus de Mézières warned ominously that "upholsterers don't care about
the principles of interior decoration" and want only to sell stuff of all kinds.)
What now seems the stuffed-to-the-gills, bloated look of many nineteenth-
century interiors is a direct result of what has been called "the reign of the upholsterer." It was interior decoration at the service of an entirely new definition
of comfort, no longer orthopedically sound, no longer clean-lined, no longer
seductively harmonious.

CHAPTER TEN

The Bedroom

No room was more changed by the age of comfort than the bedroom. In the 1670s, the sleeping area was essentially a public space, open to all in the household. By the 1720s, a new room, the bedroom, had become the center of a residence's private zone, and everything about it—from its layout to its interior decoration, from the activities that took place in it to the design of the bed itself—had been transformed. In less than a half century, the bedroom had acquired its modern identity as the essence of intimacy and comfort.

In antiquity, neither beds nor bedrooms were complicated affairs. Sometimes beds were in a fixed place within the house; often they were moved about, and the bed was simply curtained off from surrounding space. The Egyptians used headrests made of wood or ivory; Greeks and Romans had bolsters (one on each end for those who liked to sleep with their feet on pillows). Day couches—for reading and dining—and night beds were nearly identical (and people often fell asleep on the couch after eating). Beds tended to be single rather than double. Comfort was conceived in terms very different from ours; the mattress, for example, became common only late in the Roman Empire.

All through the Middle Ages and the Renaissance and until the late seventeenth century, most beds were moved around in the home rather than left in a designated room. During this period, the bed was the most expensive item in the home; textiles were costly, and beds were composed largely of fabric. In the fourteenth century, the tester bed was developed, not as a thing of beauty, but as a prop for curtains to increase privacy and warmth. And even once beds had a significant frame, it was almost worthless next to the bedclothes.

Bedding gradually became plusher: straw mattresses were replaced by feather; bolsters were introduced. Once those hangings or curtains were closed off, a four-poster didn't have to be as big as the biggest and most famous of them all, the late-sixteenth-century Great Bed of Ware (nearly eleven feet wide, over eleven feet deep, and originally nearly that high—it was probably made for an inn and supersized as a curiosity to attract customers), to give those inside the sensation of being in their own cosseted space. Even though the big four-posters are the first beds that seem recognizably modern, we would not recognize the ways in which people used them. In those virtually chair-free days, the bed literally *was* the room, in fact a bed-sitting room all in one, and its surface was used for all types of social interaction.

Then, beginning in the final decades of the seventeenth century, after centuries of no change or very slow change, it was one quick shift after another. Sleeping arrangements went through more transformations than they had in over a millennium. Within decades, it was generally accepted for the first time that a home should contain rooms reserved for sleeping.

The original grand bed frames were created in the early 1670s for—where else?—the Porcelain Trianon. Fit for a love nest, closer to Las Vegas than the Louvre, these were affairs so extravagant that they stopped that decorating maven, the Swedish architect Tessin, in his tracks. He sent sketches back to Stockholm, showing testers festooned with garlands of tassels and fabric swags and topped with bouquets of plumes; in what Tessin realized was a major innovation, curtains had been replaced by the grandest of canopies. Most amazing of all, however, is the fact that the frame was no longer merely an invisible support for all this textile overkill. The Trianon's beds called attention to the frame by, for example, setting mirrors into the headboards. The headboard in the Chambre des Amours, or Love Bedroom, also featured full-size cupids holding ribbons in place.

In the years to come, the same carving techniques that produced the original sofas and modern armchairs were applied to the bed. The frame became more and more apparent, more and more an object of value in its own right. And sure enough, it was soon referred to no longer as a *châssis*, or invisible frame, but as a *bois de lit*, a bedstead: the bed had gained independence from the bedclothes and had become a true piece of furniture.

During the same period, the use of comfortable seating became increasingly widespread, and the bed lost its role as the home's principal entertainment center. It then became fixed rather than mobile and the centerpiece of a new private space in the home. Words—*chambre* and *chambre à coucher* in French, bedchamber and bedroom in English—then came into general use to designate the new space, a room reserved specifically for sleep.

Nowhere else in the home was the new distinction between public, ceremonial space and private, comfort space more clearly visible. For several decades, all architect-designed residences featured two bedchambers: a ceremonial one and a private one. This made it possible to divvy up all the activities that had previously been centered around the bed. By the mid–eighteenth century, the formal bedchamber had become an architectural dinosaur, and home owners increasingly had or used only the informal bedroom. The formal, public life of the bed was over, and the modern bedroom had become a fact of architectural life.

The public bedroom, known as the parade bedroom, was a ceremonial space, a throwback to the age of magnificence. These rooms featured beds that were as gigantic as they were grandiose; increasingly, however, they no longer functioned as bed-sitting rooms. Antoine Courtin made this official in his 1671 guide to "the new rules of etiquette now practiced in France" when he announced that "it is indecent to sit down on a bed, especially on a lady's bed." Instead, the lady of the house stretched out on the bed for the great ceremonial functions of her life: newlyweds accepted compliments, and after childbirth, women saw visitors propped up on bolsters on their formal bed; after a death in the family, it was there that condolences were received.

Parade bedrooms conveyed above all a sense of unapproachability. The bed itself was set in an alcove often—as in the Comte d'Evreux's mansion, for example (see page 168)—framed with columns. The alcove was in turn separated from the rest of the room by a balustrade, as though the bed were a stage cordoned off from a separate viewing area.

In the course of the eighteenth century, the public bedroom gradually became a vestigial space, a highly visible reminder of the fact that times had changed and people were no longer willing to act out the most significant rites of their family life in the public eye. Those who wrote memoirs of their years at Versailles and chronicled relentlessly every shift in court etiquette noted each step in the parade bedroom's disappearance. The Duc de Luynes, for example, recalled how, at the time of their wedding in 1710, he and his wife had endured all the then accepted public rituals lying on their formal bed; by 1738, however, people were opting out of these performances. In his report on the marriage of Louis XV's son in 1747, the Duc de Croÿ pronounced such rituals "highly embarrassing" and said that they were proof that a king's life was "most uncomfortable." And when in 1762 de Croÿ's own daughter was married,

*This depiction of the parade bedroom in the Comte d'Evreux's grand home
just off the Champs-Élysées proves how off-putting and formal the traditional
bedroom was intended to be. The bed is framed with columns and positioned in an
alcove separated from the rest of the room by a balustrade.*

"there were no such ceremonies." By 1780, it was all over: Le Camus de Mézières pronounced the formal bedroom "too big" for anyone to be able to sleep well and declared that they were no longer used. Rather than comparing the two types of bedroom, as earlier treatises do, he discussed only "the bedroom," by which he meant the private bedroom.

The public bedroom's demise is still another proof of comfort's triumph. In the place of off-putting theatricality, people had acquired a brand-new conception of the bedroom: a space intended to be cozy, intimate, and private and also—something that seems obvious today but that had never before been articulated—a room designed to promote a good night's sleep. The room created as the alternative to the parade bedroom, the *palais du sommeil*, or temple of sleep, as Le Camus de Mézières proudly christened it, was the original modern bedroom.

The private bedroom acquired its distinctive personality between 1710 and

This interior decoration plate by Blondel illustrates the décor appropriate for the new private bedrooms introduced at the turn of the eighteenth century as an alternative to the formality of the parade bedroom. Private bedrooms were far smaller; they were intended to be intimate, even cozy, rather than grand and imposing.

1730. Gone were the balustrades and columns. As visible proof of the room's new mission, the bed was tucked away in a cozy niche or nook (literally a recessed portion of the room)—hence the new room's name: a *chambre en niche*, or niche bedroom (see above). The niche bed was placed sideways in the niche rather than facing out into the room and was thus protected from drafts, thereby eliminating the need for heavy curtains. The niche bedroom incarnated all the new architecture's values of cozy intimacy. Le Camus de Mézières called it "a place that so nicely enveloped you that you could just be alone with yourself." It protected the privacy of the room's inhabitants: doors camouflaged in the wall on either side of the bed opened onto a corridor behind it. Françoise de Graffigny was pleased with this arrangement because it would allow a visitor to reach her bedroom without being seen. Those doors also made it possible for someone to make the bed without disturbing the room's occupant. Wheels were installed so that the bed could be pivoted easily, and the process became even simpler.

And as soon as there was a new-style bedroom, there were new-style beds. In fact, within decades, designers had made available more models than in the entire prior history of the bed. There were two basic designs, one with one headboard (for the parade bedroom, where the bed faced out into the room) and one with two (for the niche room, where it was positioned sideways). Variants were then spun off for each of them. The first ones—less extravagant than their prototypes, those over-the-top creations for the Porcelain Trianon— were described in the press in 1673: angel beds (*lits d'ange*), beds without a footboard and with only short posts at the foot end, but with a very tall headboard to support the tester, which was said to "fly" because it was attached to the wall rather than resting on posts. These became the rage along with everything else about the Trianon look; the *Mercure galant* reported that "no one

The duchess bed had a very tall headboard that served as a support for the canopy or tester. The tester was said to "fly" because it was attached to the wall rather than resting on posts.

wants any other kind." They were so hot, in fact, that if you wanted yours designed by *the* specialists, the Bon brothers, you had to wait a full year.

The newspaper reported that there were "a hundred different kinds of angel
beds." In the original 1696 version of "Sleeping Beauty," by Charles Perrault,
the Princess slept off the long wait for her Prince Charming on one model. By
the turn of the eighteenth century, the very latest style was the "duchess bed"
(*à la duchesse*) (see page 170). Duchess beds were part of the "young look"
Louis XIV was seeking at the Ménagerie. Beds with headboards came in three
sizes: the average model was 4 feet wide; the next, which Roubo called "beds for
those who want to be more at ease," was 4½ to 5 feet wide. The original king-
size beds, known as "beds for great lords," were 7 feet wide. (In his typically

The niche bed, which had a low headboard and bolsters,
came into fashion in the early eighteenth century as
the bed of choice for the new private bedroom. Niche
beds were positioned sideways in a recessed space
rather than facing out into the room.

practical fashion, Roubo commented that "this isn't because [great lords] need all this room, since they are normally neither bigger nor fatter than other men.")

In the niche bedroom, people used beds with a low headboard and bolsters (see page 171). (Thomas Jefferson was so taken with this design that he added nine bed niches when he remodeled Monticello upon his return from France.) And whereas single-headboard beds were called French beds, niche beds were often christened with foreign names—for example, the Marquise de Pompadour's favorite, the very sofalike Turkish bed. The latest trends in bed design were thus clearly intended to give anyone tucked away in a cozy nook the illusion of spending the night in a land of exotic warmth and indolence. They may have dreamed of sunny skies, but they were also in all likelihood spending

The Turkish bed was a particularly sofalike variation on the niche bed. This was the Marquise de Pompadour's favorite kind of bed; she chose Turkish beds for the private bedrooms in most of her homes.

the night alone. As Roubo pointed out, if two people tried to share a niche bed, one of them would be trapped next to the wall and would have to climb over the other "if they needed to get up during the night."

Smaller bedrooms reserved for sleep became the center of a bedroom suite, and other rooms, each devoted to a related activity, were grouped around it. There was the *garderobe* (literally "protect dresses"), or wardrobe. The word originally referred to a trunk big enough to hold dresses without folding them. It changed meaning at the turn of the eighteenth century; in 1710, Le Blond included a "big wardrobe" next to the bedroom. The equivalent of modern walk-in closets, it included lots of storage space; it also functioned as a dressing room.

In those big wardrobes, closets entered the modern age. Le Camus de Mézières said they should be floor to ceiling, that the closet room should have a northern exposure, so that textiles and furs would be protected from harsh light—and there should be no fireplace that could deposit soot. In those new closets, a first baby step was made toward hanging storage for clothing: the 1694 edition of the Académie Française dictionary included a new word, *portemanteau*, literally a "coat holder" or hanger, a kind of wooden hook installed inside closets.

By the end of the age of comfort, everyone understood the makeup of a perfect bedroom suite: a room for sleeping, a clothes storage space, a *toilette* or separate dressing room, a toilet room. The male zone of the house also contained an office, while the female zone had a room reserved for "gathering one's thoughts" (*recueillement*), called by some architects a boudoir and by others a nap room. The bathing suite was adjacent to the female zone.

At a time when aristocratic marriage was a contract between two great families, it was not considered part of the bargain that husbands and wives should love each other or want to spend more time together than was necessary to produce heirs. During the age of comfort, however, aristocratic marriage was increasingly affected by the new concept of falling in love; we know this because more and more couples decided to share a bed.

That avid chronicler of changing times, the Duc de Saint-Simon, was fascinated by the ultimate power couple of the early eighteenth century, the Comte de Pontchartrain, chancellor of France (head of the judicial system) and its chief finance minister, and his wife, Marie de Maupeou, known as Madame la Chancelière. The chancellor was the most influential man in France after the king; his wife was a friend and confidante to the young royals, especially that free spirit the Duchesse de Bourgogne, for whom she organized in 1700 a party so extravagant that newspapers couldn't stop talking about it. During the terrible winter of 1708–1709, when the War of the Spanish Succession was bleeding

France dry, Saint-Simon told how Madame la Chancelière created a new image for the society wife: she ran a soup kitchen out of her own home. "All day long," every day for seven months, volunteers gave out bread and soup and even meat until supplies ran out, feeding more than three thousand starving Parisians a day. The chancellor was "thrilled" with her work.

For Saint-Simon, that soup kitchen was no more incredible than the couple's take on marriage: "They shared the same friends, the same relations, the same company. In every matter, they were as one. They were separated only if absolutely necessary, and everywhere they went they slept in the same bed."

To accommodate such modern couples, architects conceived of a number of carefully managed crossings between the male and female zones of the home. The simplest solution, adopted by Boffrand, among others, was to add "a corridor linking" the two master bedrooms. And no architect paid more attention to this change in the way people wanted to live their lives than Briseux. By comparing the treatment of sleeping arrangements for spouses in his two major works (1728, 1743), we can see just how quickly the new sharing that so shocked Saint-Simon at the turn of the century became an accepted way of life.

In 1728, Briseux favored a novel layout: two matching suites with a common entertaining room. He also included plans for modest homes not large enough to have suites; some of these feature two adjoining bedrooms with a common study and dressing room or a niche bedroom with twin beds placed side by side in the niche. In 1743, Briseux made further suggestions for facilitating various degrees of nighttime intimacy. In one home with matching suites sharing a salon, each bedroom has twin beds. In another, the woman's suite has the larger bedroom, with two beds (this time full-size ones), while the man's much smaller one has only one bed. In addition, Briseux was the first to make the trend official by declaring that the male zone and the female zone must be "next to each other" and "there has to be direct access between the two bedroom suites." In the space of just fifteen years, the closeness between husband and wife had become an accepted fact of architectural life.

Before the age of comfort, architects identified rooms simply as "bedrooms" without designating their occupants. They first indicated shared sleeping arrangements for husbands and wives; they next started to designate guest quarters. By 1780, Le Camus de Mézières took it for granted that there would also be children's rooms, in fact, a suite reserved for the children of the house. By the end of the age of comfort, an architect-designed home was thus intended to accommodate all the members of a family and for entertaining on an intimate scale.

New kinds of beds, new kinds of bedrooms, one bed or two—all that choice meant that bedroom looks tended to be highly individualized. Here are the options elected by key figures of the age of comfort: two bedrooms decorated by men, two decorated by women, the same bedroom as it was decorated by two successive inhabitants of the same home, as well as the bedroom of one person at two different moments (1725 and 1746). The various decorating schemes give a sense of the evolution of both personal and collective taste during the decades (1725–1765) when comfort ruled the world of interior decoration.

There was, to begin with, Charlotte Desmares, free spirit and woman of means. In 1725, she had just furnished her tiny gem of modern architecture. She had a parade bedroom, but a very informal one. The bed was not set off by a balustrade and columns; she chose blue damask to complement her collection of porcelain and lined it with cotton to offset the room's rather formal furniture: a richly carved and gilded bed, sofa, and six armchairs.

This single woman turned her small home's entire first floor into an entertaining suite; the old-style bedroom thus makes sense. Visitors stepped from the garden into a room with a harpsichord, then into the living room, and finally into the formal bedroom. On either side of the bed was a door opening into a passageway that gave onto a smaller room in which she kept a fourteen-cup porcelain coffee service (and undoubtedly some of her eight dozen cotton "coffee napkins"). There were also back stairs leading up to her private bedroom suite decorated with her best paintings (hunting scenes by Desportes, two Nattiers), where she slept in a less elaborate bed decked out in crimson damask.

Two decades later, Desmares's sleeping arrangements were completely different. Gone were the gilded furniture and the display of porcelain. She had a single bedroom and a niche bed with four mattresses for maximum comfort: the bottom one of springy horsehair (metal springs were introduced only in the nineteenth century), two wool mattresses, and a feather bed to top it all off. (When beds were so high off the ground, a footstool was used to climb in.) She still loved crimson, but by 1746, textile formality had disappeared; everything was in cotton.

The bedroom in which Pierre Crozat died in 1740 was quite similar to the one decorated by Desmares in 1725. Like hers, it was accessible from the living room. Like hers, it was a study in blue and white to match the porcelain shown off on a marble-topped console table. By 1740, however, the niche bed had won the day. This single man slept in a Roman bed (a precursor of the Turkish model), with bedclothes all in blue damask, trimmed, like the curtains, with gold braid. (Crozat used a lone mattress over a horsehair base.) He had six armchairs covered with petit point tapestry (a flowered pattern on a white background), a "confessional" armchair, no fewer than forty-five paintings on the walls by everyone from

Dürer to Veronese—and a little house for his dog. In the adjacent dressing room, his wig sat on a stand and his dressing gown of taffeta lined with silk hung on a peg in the built-in closet. It all seems very much the orderly world of someone obsessed with his art collection—and hardly typically masculine.

And then there was the Comte d'Evreux. Even though he lived until 1753 and inhabited one of the great masterpieces of modern architecture, he resisted the way the world was moving in one key manner: his sleeping arrangements prove that he was unwilling to sacrifice a most visible proof of aristocratic rank. The count, who never remarried, continued to use his formal bedroom, even when it had become hopelessly out-of-date, a shrine to a bygone era, the turn-of-the-century years of his misspent youth. Only one recent invention was present in the count's bedroom: furniture that locked. All over his mansion, in fact, closets, chests of drawers, cupboards, desks, and cabinets had locks—even his servants had locks on the closets in their bedrooms. The count was clearly obsessed with privacy. He did not, however, make a single step in the direction of informality: his bed (see page 168), all its trimmings, and the room's curtains were in crimson damask, already rejected as too formal by Desmares in 1746. There was no décor to speak of—merely the odd bit of porcelain and the occasional painting, mainly unsigned family portraits. Seating was decades behind the times, for like Voltaire, the count was still using the original comfort armchairs.

A decade later, the Marquise de Pompadour died at Versailles. Her apartment there was quickly stripped of her possessions, which were taken to the former Hôtel d'Evreux, which the marquise had snapped up the minute the count died and had proceeded to modernize. There, a team of notaries worked for a full week to draw up a list of everything she owned. Now it is foolish, of course, to speak of choice in relation to someone like the marquise; she had so many bedrooms that she was able to try out every decorating option available. She had kept, for example, the count's formal bedroom, columns and all, undoubtedly as a highly visible reminder of her status at the French court. The marquise, however, had brought the vestigial space as fully as possible into the new age. Her bed, its frame lavishly sculpted and gilded, was swathed with expanses of embroidered white satin, giving the room a lighter feel. There was lots of plush seating—one of her favorite confessional armchairs, four *cabriolet* armchairs—upholstered to match. (In summer, she switched the upholstery to the casual luxury of an Eastern look, red *pékin*, hand-painted Chinese silk.) And in an absolute break with tradition, the bed had two headboards, like a niche bed. But for the columns, the room could have been taken for a new-style bedroom.

The niche bed was clearly Pompadour's signature touch in bedroom style;

even the most elaborate of her beds, such as the one at Versailles with a "tall back, richly sculpted," had two headboards. (There was also an *ottomane* sofa in the room.) Some were Turkish; some were tucked into niches; every one was in the sofa style. To complement the niche bed's coziness, the marquise made lavish use of cotton. For Versailles, she chose cotton curtains and cotton upholstery "in several different colors." In the restyled Hôtel d'Evreux, one niche was lined with checked cotton, and the bed's duvet was covered with red-striped cotton, while the bedroom in her opulent bathing suite featured an *ottomane* sofa, an armchair, and a niche bed, all upholstered in a red cotton floral print.

As the range of options found in the sleeping quarters of these four individuals indicates, the bedroom inspired people to express their personal taste and to indulge in whatever they saw as essential for comfort—they might pile on four or more mattresses, or they might, as Pompadour did, use lots of "feather pillows" (others favored bolsters); they could keep their treasured possessions under lock and key. They could even have fabulous paintings all to themselves.

CHAPTER ELEVEN

The Boudoir

Soon after architects began subdividing homes into zones—public and private, male and female—a discrepancy became apparent. An essential component of the business suite was a small room where the master of the house could enjoy absolute privacy in order to collect his thoughts and meditate on important professional dealings. The female zone contained a number of specialized rooms considered particularly important to a woman's life—a *garderobe* for clothes storage and so forth. Initially, however, no one thought of giving women a space devoted to the life of the mind. That's where the boudoir came in. It was invented as the archetypal room of one's own, a place where women could have the same kind of privacy as men, also in order to collect their thoughts, to meditate, to read and write. There, they could be casual and relaxed in the way possible only when one is sure of being alone. There they could devote uninterrupted time to their personal intellectual pleasures. The Marquise de Pompadour's most famous portrait may well show her in one of her famous boudoirs (see color plates): the small room is equipped for reading and writing, just the activities for which women used the original boudoirs. The boudoir was thus in a sense the ultimate interior room, a place where architecture, furniture, and interior decoration made absolute privacy absolutely comfortable.

The boudoir was part of the last wave of "tiny spaces" to which, according to Briseux, the clients for modern architecture fled to escape the burdens of public life. First there were private bedrooms; then there were those products of the technology of comfort, bathrooms and toilet rooms; finally there were the more specialized kinds of personal space, the filing room for important papers, for example, or the boudoir.

Initially, the boudoir was called a *méridienne*. (The name refers to the idea of taking a siesta at the hottest time of the day; the boudoir was also the original nap room.) The *méridienne*, as its advocates such as Blondel made plain, was conceived as the most private of all private rooms, reserved for absolute solitude and *recueillement*. *Recueillement* originally meant to free oneself from worldly thoughts in order to think only of God. When the new architecture began, the word was losing its religious connotations and taking on its modern, secular meaning of getting away from the outside world in order to concentrate on one's inner life. The *méridienne* was thus designed to be the ne plus ultra in interior space, the ultimate proof of the interworking of modern architecture and the life of the mind.

Soon, the new room received a second name: boudoir. Boudoir, everyone now says, came from *bouder*, to pout: the boudoir thus allegedly made room for a decidedly unappealing by-product of the new private life, the desire to sulk and be a spoiled brat in solitude. It was only in the mid–eighteenth century, however, at a moment when French novels featured characters both male and female who were positively addicted to pouting, that anyone came up with this explanation for the boudoir's existence. Initially, the boudoir, like the *méridienne* before it, was promoted to clients as a room reserved for the inner life.

The concept quickly caught on. The new room first showed up on an architectural plan in 1715, in the Hôtel d'Humières, in the original bedroom suite with both a bathroom and a toilet room. The boudoir was thus still another innovation that resulted from Louis XIV's decision to allow the Maréchal d'Humières to pass his name and his fortune directly to his beloved daughter. The boudoir initially appeared in an architectural treatise in 1741 when Briseux mentioned that if you had a large bedroom suite, a nice option would be "a small room with a daybed in it, known as a boudoir." By that time, Emilie du Châtelet had added near her niche bedroom in the château she shared with Voltaire a "small boudoir" so overwhelmingly adorable that, as Françoise de Graffigny remarked in 1738, "you're ready to fall to your knees when you walk in." (By 1751, Graffigny was marveling over her very own "delicious" boudoir.) The queen had one at Versailles, as did Madame la Duchesse in her Parisian palace. The Marquise de Pompadour was, predictably, a boudoir fanatic: she added one to the Hôtel d'Evreux (that phenomenal window shade was designed for it) and outfitted Bellevue with the boudoir to end all boudoirs.

The architectural record also shows that the room reserved for interior life was placed in various locations. Blondel often made a *méridienne* part of the entertainment suite; he specified that it should contain a niche daybed so that a guest could have time out from socializing. Pompadour put a boudoir in her bathing suite in the Hôtel d'Evreux; at Versailles, she had a *méridienne* in her bathing suite and a boudoir in her bedroom suite. The Hôtel d'Evreux's boudoir contained a writing desk, writing implements, and a small armchair. At Versailles, the marquise received top-level diplomatic briefings in her boudoir. (Rumor had it that it was within its red-lacquered walls that she hammered out the terms for the Franco-Austrian alliance with the ambassador to Versailles, Wenzel Anton, Count of Kaunitz.)

The boudoir may be the ultimate proof that the need for privacy and ease quickly became as addictive as the need for stress seems to be today. The *méridienne* was more relaxed and private than other rooms, the place where you went to get away from everything—even the already intimate and stress-free socializing in private and semiprivate rooms. The boudoir spread through Europe along with the French style of residential architecture. The plan for a fairly modest German home from the late eighteenth century, for example, is divided into male and female zones; the wife's apartment ends in a tiny boudoir—it's the only word in French on the plan. The boudoir's success is among the clearest indications of the key role played by women in the spread of the new values.

Early boudoirs featured décor as casual as it was understated (see page 181). Madame la Duchesse, for example, chose simple flowered cotton. And Emilie du Châtelet's was a cozy "little nest" in pastel shades, the ideal retreat for one of the great female intellectuals of the age. Then came boudoirs far less restrained: the Marquise de Pompadour's, for example, showcased the kind of pseudo-Eastern look that mid-eighteenth-century Europeans found particularly compatible with notions of comfort and informality.

Take the example of Pompadour's most famous boudoir, at Bellevue (1748–1750). The marquise decided on a Chinese style—or at least what passed for such in mid-eighteenth-century France. Its walls were covered with gleaming lacquer with touches of gilding; Chinese wallpaper added to the mural décor, which was completed by the use of Indian cotton embroidered with gold thread. Pompadour's favorite painter, Boucher, contributed a series of canvases depicting pseudo-Chinese scenes. A final stylistic dollop was provided by very French lighting fixtures: bunches of lifelike porcelain flowers made by the new manufactory at Vincennes, which the king and the marquise were wild over.

Today, the mix sounds both incongruous and over-the-top. In the mid-eighteenth century, however, this exotic patchwork, as well as its association

Decoration de lambris avec un renfoncement en Niche pour un Boudoir

This engraving shows off the understated décor preferred in the original boudoirs.

with a royal mistress, may just have been the beginning of a completely new life for the boudoir. Pompadour created her boudoirs at the moment when interior decoration's star was on the rise. In addition, the marquise was perhaps the most celebrated of the new field's early patrons: all eyes were on her every decorating move. The Pompadour style taught would-be decorators that in the boudoir, the focus was on the periphery: the walls, the ceiling, the floors. In the late 1750s, this concept became the foundation for the boudoir's reincarnation. Suddenly and virtually out of nowhere, the boudoir was reinvented. The room conceived as a solitary, serious spot began a second life as the sexiest room in town, a place where the only thoughts collected were on subjects no weightier than the arrangement of a fetching décolletage and the best way to show off a trim ankle, as a place where women used their personal charms, as well as those of their décor and furniture, solely for seduction. The blame for this remake should be laid at the feet of the original decorators. In their hands, the boudoir became the prototype for all subsequent attempts—from brothels to fleshpots and bachelor pads—to imagine a décor that instantly and unequivocally said, This room is reserved for sex.

The boudoir where the room took on its new identity was completed in November 1757. It was, hardly surprisingly, part of a grand Parisian mansion. Almost everything else about the project, however, fails to conform to the patterns on which the age of comfort was founded. To begin with, the mansion had not been built for the boudoir's mistress; she was merely renting an apartment in it, a set of ten rooms. The new tenant was a single woman unlike all prior female clients for modern architecture: she was neither independently wealthy nor a great aristocrat nor a celebrated artist.

Marie-Anne Deschamps was instead a kept woman who had once worked in brothels and more recently as the period's equivalent of a chorus girl. She was very, very minimally a dancer; at the Paris Opera and Comic Opera, she stood around looking pretty whenever a work called for a large cast of extras, wearing gorgeous outfits and positively dripping with diamonds, gifts from her latest admirers. (Some said it was all really in the line of work, since in this way she attracted the attention of new clients.) The remodeling she had had done in her new home on a fashionable street near the Louvre was probably financed by the latest in a long series of very wealthy lovers, Louis-François I de Bourbon, Prince de Conti, great-grandson of Louis XIV and grandson of Madame la Duchesse, whose father had made a killing from insider trading during the Law affair. She might also have put aside money from the generosity of her long-term benefactor, Conti's brother-in-law the Duc d'Orléans, descendant of Louis XIV's brother and great-grandson of the Marquise de Montespan. (Since the Parisian police were following her every move, we normally have all the details of her finances; the police reports for 1757 and 1758, however, are missing.)

It is fitting that the specter of the 1720 market boom and bust forms a backdrop for the boudoir created nearly four decades later: the dancing girl was displaying her ill-gotten gains at a moment that closely resembled the glory days just before John Law's financial bubble burst. Only months later, France knew another crash, caused once again by mismanagement at the highest level—and by the mounting cost of the Seven Years' War. (People were once again melting the family silver, for example, only this time to help manage a crucial shortage of precious metals.) In a living-on-the-edge-of-the-volcano moment and as a showcase for her apparently considerable personal charms, a very notorious woman had a boudoir designed that immediately became notorious in its own right.

Deschamps's little room was anything but private; she couldn't wait to show off her foray into interior decoration. Thus it was that man-about-town and guide to foreign ambassadors Dufort de Cheverny—always frantic to keep up with the latest trends in Paris, lest a diplomat ask him about a place he hadn't yet seen—quickly procured an invitation to visit Deschamps's new quarters. In his memoirs, the duke provides a positively breathless room-by-room tour.

He reserved his greatest attention for the space that was without precedent, her rose-pink-and-silver boudoir. The room's furniture—a lone *ottomane*—was standard issue. Its wall décor, however, was anything but. Deschamps had taken the principle established by the royalest mistress in the land, the domination of the periphery, to its absolute costliest limit. Every inch of the boudoir's walls and ceiling was covered with mirrors. The duke's reaction: "Stupefaction."

Less than a year later, Deschamps's hymn to interior decorating excess was immortalized in the pages of a periodical by novelist, journalist, and architectural insider Jean-François de Bastide. In the novella *La Petite Maison* (*The Little House*), Bastide tells the tale of the original architecture victims: a marquis who is the proud, proud owner of a house equipped with absolutely every invention dreamed up by modern architecture—every room, every amenity, every gadget, every piece of furniture, every decorating idea—and the beautiful marquise he takes on a house tour in the hope of seducing her. The marquis's dream house naturally contains a boudoir able to test any lady's virtue.

That Bastide's fictional boudoir was intended to evoke Deschamps's is evident from the details—right down to the particular kind of trim (*crépines d'or*) that adorns the sofas in his account and that of Dufort de Cheverny. *La Petite Maison* also points out elements that the count was apparently too thunderstruck to notice—most notably, the intricate design devised to disguise the seams where mirrors were joined: "The joints [of the mirrors] were covered with masterful carving depicting crisscrossed tree branches."

Bastide's story was frequently reprinted, each time bringing the description of the ur-boudoir to new readers. In April 1760, however, curious Parisians got the chance to see its stunning opulence with their own eyes. That month, caught up in what one observer called "the misery of recent times which had been felt by everyone" (he added that the war had kept her foreign clients away from Paris, thereby further "reducing her income"), Deschamps was obliged to auction off her belongings. So many people flocked to see those storied spaces that her street was completely blocked up with carriages, and guards had to stand at her door handing out tickets to those who looked like potential bidders. (She sold her bed exactly as was to a wealthy financier willing to hand over a small fortune for the pleasure of sleeping between its fabled sheets.) Once inside—with the mistress of the house herself playing the role of innocent victim and thus decked out in a "lovely spring dress," there to point out, as she had for Dufort de Cheverny, special features such as that novel mirror design—they were able to see that Bastide had not been exaggerating. Everywhere you looked, "everything was covered with mirrors," many of them framed with the design of interlocking palm fronds already immortalized in fiction by Bastide.

Some of the original boudoir tourists referred to the goods on display as "the wages of debauchery and prostitution," and that lascivious aura thereafter clung to the initially modest little room. In 1780, when Le Camus de Mézières included the first detailed explanation of the interior decoration of boudoirs in an architectural treatise, he had Deschamps's version of the room in mind, rather than earlier incarnations. The most surprising thing about his commentary is the fact that it's not a surprise at all. Much of it is simply an extended, and unacknowledged, quotation from . . . Bastide's description of Deschamps's boudoir in *La Petite Maison*. It's all there—the mirrors, of course, right down to the unmistakable clue: the design of interlocking, crisscrossed branches used to disguise their joints.

Deschamps's boudoir look turned the founding principle of French interior decoration—harmonious simplicity—on end. It thus succeeded in transforming one of the original small spaces reserved for private life into a blatant advertisement for exhibitionistic sexual display. (Numerous commentators pointed out the obvious: with all those mirrored surfaces, couples could see their reflection everywhere they turned.) Naturally, not all boudoirs were transformed into mirror-lined dens of seduction. Nevertheless, in Deschamps's wake the boudoir conjured up two competing visions of how women behaved if they had a room of their own; within decades, the style of the woman of easy virtue had won out over that of the thinking woman, and the boudoir had lost its original mission.

Le Camus de Mézières's discussion, in which he proclaimed the boudoir "the realm of voluptuousness," proves that by 1780, architects were promoting an image of the small room that was a far cry from that of the solitary haven as Blondel conceived it. And by 1832, a French dictionary caught up with the trend and said that women go to their boudoirs in the company of "those with whom they were intimate." By then, the look devised for the original boudoir call girl had won the day. The numerous plates of celebrated boudoirs included in Krafft and Ransonnette's turn-of-the-nineteenth-century volumes devoted to "the most beautiful houses in Paris" feature elaborately decorated rooms in which mirrors play a key role. In 1832, the *Dictionnaire de la conversation* declared that "everyone expects to find mirrors all over boudoirs." And in 1880 in his manual for upholsterers, Jules Deville decreed that the mirrors de rigueur for boudoirs should all be framed with—what else?—a design of sculpted, crisscrossed palm fronds.

The boudoir unveiled in 1757 was thus an early-warning signal of what would happen during the upcoming "reign of the upholsterer." The 1832

Dictionary of Conversation proclaimed the boudoir "the most painstakingly decorated room in the entire house," proving that in the long run, the original chorus girl's boudoir had encouraged the excesses of nineteenth-century upholsterers and decorators.

CHAPTER TWELVE

Dressing for Comfort

IT WAS AS if they were dressed for bed." Louis XIV's sister-in-law, the Princesse Palatine, ever the staunch defender of etiquette, thus summed up the outraged reaction of fashion outsiders to the most visible sign of informality's arrival at Versailles. For the first time anywhere, ever, women of the highest rank had begun to appear in public attired not in their most magnificent and imposing ensembles, but in outfits that, while still beautiful, were designed above all to be comfortable and casual. It was perhaps the greatest fashion revolution of all time—and one fashion revolution seen as politically threatening.

The new garb was a clear affront to the foundations of the age of magnificence, and no less an authority on that question than Louis XIV understood it as such. He waged war on informal dress until the end of his days. In fact, his successor was still fighting the same combat until his death in 1774, exactly a century after the revolution began. In the 1750s, for example, the most influential Western ruler had genuinely weighty concerns to deal with. France was embroiled in the French and Indian War; the Seven Years' War, the conflict Winston Churchill would call the first "world war," was looming. On French shores, however, Louis XV was leading a rearguard effort, trying desperately to force women to wear outmoded dress. Thus, in February 1755, court insider the Duc de Luynes describes him making an official "pronouncement" in favor of formal attire. This was, after all, a man who a decade earlier had made women's clothing—the exact style Louis XIV had tried to impose seventy years earlier—synonymous with his royal authority. "Without outward signs, the king loses his rights," he chided the queen upon learning that she was considering attending a minor ceremony in a provincial city without full robes of state.

You can see why he felt this way. Every innovation of the age of comfort proved that the elite would no longer tolerate the constraints and discomforts of the old way of life. All other inventions, however, remained behind closed doors in the home's new private zone, while fashion would not be locked up. French women appeared in public "as if they were dressed for bed" and thereby proved to anyone with eyes in their head that, as Charles de Peyssonnel summed it up at the age of comfort's end, they found "magnificence a tiresome burden," a burden they were just dying to shake off.

The new look so amazed contemporary observers that all through those decades of controversy, artists depicted women relishing their freedom from the trappings of magnificence. Those images make it abundantly clear that all the king's horses and all the king's men could never have stopped the irresistible rise of comfortable high fashion.

There was, on the one hand, that badge of royal authority, the official outfit (see color plates). Here is Louis XV's wife, Queen Maria Leszczyńska, wearing formal dress no longer identical to the seventeenth-century version, though it followed the same principles. The bodice was the essence of the outfit: it was a masterpiece of the tailor's art, completely and elaborately boned. It was tightly fitted to produce a perfectly smooth surface—a wrinkle was out of the question. That bodice took control over the body of the woman inside it. Thus attired, one woman's body looked very much like the next. The stays were designed to flatten the bust completely, creating a rigid shape that, while it gave a regal air, made women anything but alluring or approachable. Women in formal dress were always portrayed standing, for that is what the garment allowed them to do best. The stays guaranteed perfectly erect posture. When they sat, women didn't need a chair for support; the bodice took care of that. They never sat with real ease; they couldn't bend over, recline, or position themselves fetchingly. Crossing one's legs at the knee was highly uncomfortable; a decorous turn at the ankle was best.

Then there was the alternative (see pages 25, 116, and 117). When you look at depictions of the new fashion—and there were many, since it was the talk of the town—the choice seems a no-brainer. Women in the new garb were likely to be shown relaxing on seat furniture, as if to advertise the fact that comfortable high fashion gave women a far fuller range of motion and thus allowed them to enjoy all the easy seats then being invented. The Marquise de Montespan strikes a come-hither pose on a daybed; the Duchesse de Bouillon uses a prototype for the sofa to the same effect. Women were portrayed as no longer stiffly off-putting, but breezily casual and at ease.

The new look was still another invention of those key years in the 1670s when Louis XIV and Montespan created the Porcelain Trianon and Clagny. Indeed, its creation was announced at the end of the same 1673 press coverage that heralded the beginning of modern furniture and interior decoration and attributed both developments to the Trianon's influence. The timing was important. In 1673, Montespan was pregnant with her first daughter, Louise-Françoise, the future Madame la Duchesse and among the greatest champions of every invention of the age of comfort. Years later, in her tirade against bedroom fashion, the Princesse Palatine was still fuming about how the marquise had "invented" the style "to hide her pregnancy" but how the unusual outfit had simply served to "advertise" her state and thus had won her "added respect" at court. The style's defenders put a very different spin on things.

The official outfit of the age of magnificence proved inconvenient in everyday life; it was excruciating during pregnancy. And the women dear to the Sun King—undoubtedly Montespan first of all—made it clear that they wanted neither to "hide" nor to "advertise" their pregnancies, simply to avoid extreme discomfort. Thus it was that in 1686, the first royal dispensation was granted. His son's wife was pregnant (with the Duc de Berry), and it was not going well. In April, she had spent more than a week confined to her bed when, on April 24, the decree came down: "Since she was putting on weight, henceforth she would wear [comfortable dress]." At first, only mothers of possible heirs to the throne won special treatment, but others began to beg for it. In 1713, the Duchesse de Berry, the wife of the baby born in 1686, was experiencing "discomfort" because her breasts were swollen with milk and was allowed to opt out of that rigid bodice.

By then, fashion plate that she was, the young duchess knew full well that the magnificent look was hopelessly out-of-date. The minute her pregnancy was over, she convened "all the young princesses" to discuss the next fashion season; they "demanded that samples of the new styles be brought to them immediately." You can bet that there wasn't a boned bodice in the lot, for by the end of Louis XIV's reign, there was a fashion industry worthy of the name, and it had long since begun to encourage the taste for breezy comfort.

How could it have been otherwise? A fashion industry needed styles with appeal to as broad an audience as possible. The look of magnificence—extremely uncomfortable, off-putting, and highly expensive because it required such precise fitting—was hardly that. Small wonder, then, that there is no evidence that despite the allure of royal provenance, the formal ensemble known as the "grand outfit" (*grand habit*) or "court dress" (*habit de cour*) was ever imitated outside court circles.

The new bedroom look, on the other hand, was the very essence of marketability. It became the first style ever to be advertised, truly in the modern sense of the term, and thus marked the beginning of fashion as we now think of it—a style that is copied and imitated and influences the way a significant segment of the population dresses. It was so wildly successful that it spread through the ranks of French society and far beyond French borders. Its success, furthermore, proved so durable that under a variety of names, the same basic outfit continued to dominate European fashion until about 1770, when a new look, of English inspiration, finally brought an end to a century during which high fashion was absolutely and exclusively French. Casual dress was the most visible, the most complete, and the largest-scale victory of the age of comfort.

The garment Montespan invented to make pregnancy more comfortable was certainly more dignified than what she is shown wearing on the daybed (page 25) and was probably more like the Duchesse de Bouillon's outfit. The duchess's garment has sleeves, whereas Montespan's does not, but both share a loose shape and simple cut. And therein lies the tale of the first hybrid garments and the original Asian influence on European high fashion.

As soon as Holland and England began trade with the Indies, along with exotic spices merchants brought back exotic garments such as Japanese kimonos. In Europe in the sixteenth and early seventeenth centuries, this startlingly new kind of dress became popular, initially, mainly among men. First in Holland, then in England, and finally in France, every fashionable man most likely owned the new garment. In English, men called them nightgowns, even though they were not for sleeping—"bedgowns" were worn to bed. The loose robe, generally made from imported fabrics, was initially an indoor garment, worn around the house before men got dressed for the day. Gradually, men began to receive visitors in these nightgowns and, by the early eighteenth century in England and Holland, to go out in public, particularly to coffeehouses, in their gowns. By 1711, as Steele observed in *The Spectator*, the fashion had even become a power broker, proof that men thus attired had no need to rush off to their jobs "at eight in a morning," but could hang around in coffeehouses in their nightgowns.

French men, on the other hand, did not follow their example for at least a century. In the 1760s, nightgowns were still indoor wear; only in the 1780s had fashionable men begun "running about town" all day long in their gowns, by then known as *chenilles* because of the velvety silk from which they were often made. French women, however, had a different stake in comfortable dress: they had Montespan's example to show how it could change their lives. Therefore, unlike their counterparts in England and Holland, for whom the original nightgowns were at-home wear, they did what French men did not dare: they took casual fashion into the street. And when they did, the French takeover of high fashion began.

In January 1678, a Parisian paper, the *Mercure galant*, announced an unprecedented phenomenon: "Since everyone in France today wants to be comfortable, people hardly get dressed up anymore. . . . [Court dress] is now used only for ceremonial occasions . . . and no longer when one drops in on one's friends or just to go for a walk." This announcement in a public forum was an opening salvo of the age of comfort. In just five short years, Montespan's example had encouraged the ladies of the court to reject those stiff bodices. Now, when they went out in Paris, they wore instead what the newspaper called "the garment known as a *manteau*."

This was the first time anyone had put a name on fashion that offered an alternative to formal wear. No French women's garments from the seventeenth century have survived, but it's likely that the *manteau* (coat) was closely related to the garment in which Montespan attracted such attention at court. Both appeared on the fashion scene at the same moment; a contemporary dictionary reports that they shared a similar cut. The only real difference appears to have been that the *manteau* was tied or belted at the waist.

Some early *manteaux* came straight from India. In 1672 and 1673, the *Mercure galant* reported another unprecedented event: a Parisian shop was selling clothing from a far-off land; a merchant named Gautier was offering *manteaux* in Indian cotton. Some featured motifs that played on the garment's exotic origins (a mix of flowers and personages); others imitated European designs. Gautier had, for example, a line of Indian skirts printed to resemble *point d'Angleterre*, one of the trendiest patterns of handmade lace. And whereas a skirt trimmed with the real thing cost a fortune, Gautier's Indian knockoffs were, the paper reported, "so inexpensive that almost all ladies have already bought one."

In France, this was the first time that either dress designed for comfort or exotic garments had been seen in public, so it's hardly surprising that the development was considered newsworthy. This was the moment at which men in other countries were first venturing out in their gowns; the sight of noblewomen in Indian *manteaux* would have been even more amazing. The new comfortable look defined the principles evident in every East-West fashion encounter ever since—think legendary couturier Paul Poiret in the 1910s. The loose cut made for a dress that flowed gracefully around the body and gave a sense of easy freedom. East-West hybrids have always appealed because they are exotic, because they are adapted to women's lives, and because they liberate rather than constrict the female form—remember that Poiret invented some of his key designs for his wife Denise's pregnancies.

Under their flowing outer garment, the women of the seventeenth century wore skirts. They also wore stays, but these were no longer built into the dress; they were part of a separate undergarment, one designed to produce a more natural look than the infamous court bodice. (It's likely that some women even wore unboned bodices.) Rather than flattening the body, the new garment—as the image of the Duchesse de Bouillon makes clear—flattered a woman's curves. It was also adjustable, rather than being fitted to produce a wrinkle-free surface, and could thus accommodate changes in a woman's body, as well as allowing greater freedom of movement. Women dressed informally could cross their legs at the knee; they could sit down with ease on any surface; they could lean back in chairs.

This explains why women in the new French kimono look became poster children for innovative furniture designs: they were actually able to enjoy sofas and easy chairs in the way they were meant to be used. This also explains why the women most addicted to comfortable dress—from Montespan to her daughter Madame la Duchesse (whose wardrobe at the time of her death included some thirty-nine informal dresses and not a single grand outfit)— also loved the new seat furniture: they could revel in the way it worked with their clothing. Women were represented as never before—stretching out, lounging about—because these movements were now possible. This explains finally why men who loved comfort-loving women—such as Monseigneur, who adored his half-sister Madame la Duchesse—promoted the creation of well-padded seating.

Comfort thus became a commonly accepted value for fashion. In 1690, for example, a French dictionary decreed that "the best way to dress is to dress comfortably." By then, more and more women had followed in Montespan's footsteps—and not only women of the court. The kimono look was, after all, far cheaper to produce since it required no fitting. In addition, informal wear soon became known as *une indienne*, an Indian gown, since garments were being imported into France already cut and ready to be sewn, which brought down the cost still more. A newspaper article in 1680 concluded that "almost anyone who can sew can put one together" and added that "nothing gives you such a patrician air." There were soon also shops where you could pick one up, all ready to wear.

The original inexpensive ready-to-wear that guaranteed easy freedom and made you look to the manner born—what more could anyone ask? No wonder the *Mercure galant* said that "every woman" in Paris "has already bought one." By the early eighteenth century, French paintings were depicting shopgirls and ladies' maids clad in versions of the same gown worn by the noblewomen standing next to them. And by the age of comfort's end, casual dress had become an absolute social leveler. As Peyssonnel put it, "Those loose gowns . . . cover up social status so that it's become impossible to tell who's who."

And that, of course, was just what two successive kings had dreaded. Not only were women wearing dressing gowns, they were wearing them in the most public places, just as that 1678 article proclaimed. Exactly a century later, the inaugural history of private life confirmed this fact and added that from that moment on, informal dress was all one saw in Paris, while court dress had become a style worn only at court.

In the 1680s, *manteau* began to be used interchangeably with the term *robe de chambre*, bedroom gown or dressing gown. The 1686 decree from Versailles, for instance, said that "from now on, Madame la Dauphine will wear only *robes de chambre*." From then on, informal fashion had a name that, like today's "lingerie dressing," gave a sense of its transgressiveness: it brought the bedroom into the street.

And it was then that casual dress invaded the last bastion of formality, the court. The balance of fashion powers was tipping by the carnival season of 1699. On Friday, February 6, there was a fabulous masked ball at Marly: "the ladies of the court," led by that royal imp the Duchesse de Bourgogne, scampered in "all decked out" . . . in *robes de chambre*. Things went from bad to worse when none other than Monseigneur himself arrived with a group of young royals masquerading as women. They were wearing enormous blond wigs "with much bigger dos than you ever see in real life" . . . and *robes de chambre*. By October of the same year, things had gotten so thoroughly out of hand that for a theatrical performance at Fontainbleau, "all the ladies of the court showed up in *robes de chambre*." And in 1701, when James II of England died and Louis XIV went to pay his condolences to the new king in exile in France, "all the princesses of royal blood" decided to accompany him . . . "wearing *robes de chambre*," something that so shocked Saint-Simon (a man who otherwise never noticed what people had on) that he made a point of noting it. It was clearly time for the Sun King to take charge.

By 1702, he surely thought that he had a new compromise worked out: "At Versailles, which is considered his official residence, everyone who appears in the king's presence must wear the grand outfit; but at Marly women always dress in *manteaux*." The new peace was short-lived. Already in 1704, "the king got really angry" once again about the ladies' conduct at the theater at Fontainbleau: they were either "refusing to dress for performances"—that is, refusing to wear that bodice—or "hiding in corners" so they wouldn't be seen in their dressing gowns. The king, who, as Saint-Simon described it, "insisted on being obeyed," said a few choice words to them, and "all the ladies of the court became most assiduous about the grand outfit."

Nothing, however, not even "outbursts" (to borrow Saint-Simon's word) of royal anger, could keep dressing gowns off his official turf (see below). Consider this depiction of Sunday in the park at Versailles, part of a volume showing people taking in the beauties of those fabled gardens. This is a detail from a scene featuring what was called "the Theater of Water," a spot set up for visitors to admire fountains cascading down steps. Gentlemen point out the sights; mothers hold their children's hands. And there in the midst of it all are two show-offs, women sitting on the theater's terraced steps—gesturing expansively, patting each other on the knee, having a grand old time displaying the fine figures and comfortable pose produced by their decidedly unofficial outfits. (By then, it should be noted, the king may well have decided to switch rather

*A 1714 scene shows people enjoying an outing to Versailles's gardens.
(The gardens were open to the public.) The two ladies happily relaxing on the grass
are flaunting the freedom of movement they enjoy because they are wearing the
comfortable style of dress that was officially banned at Versailles.*

than fight: the inventory of goods purchased for use at Versailles lists dressing gowns, both already sewn up and still in pieces straight from India.)

The *robes de chambre* the ladies were wearing in 1714 had come a long way from the 1670s. For several decades, *robes de chambre* and *manteaux* often had trains like court dress. Ladies pinned them up in a bustle effect as the woman in the upper right in the illustration has done and left only a strip trailing after them. In the 1690s, a new variation—later named the *bayeuse*, or yawning dress, because it was worn open rather than tied at the waist—became fuller and looser still and sometimes featured defined pleats, particularly across the back; these gowns often had no train.

The happy fashion plates at Versailles in 1714 couldn't have known it, but the wide-open style they were sporting was soon to disappear in its turn. About 1718–1720, the dressing gown was reinvented still again. It acquired fetching new three-quarter-length sleeves called, in homage to the Asian influence, pagoda sleeves. These were shorter on the inside where the arm bends; pleats on the outside curved around the elbow. In winter, ladies added a newly invented accessory, *mitaines*, a type of glove that left the bottom half of the fingers exposed; Madame la Duchesse's were fur-trimmed.

Most important, however, was the fact that for the first time, the dressing gown became truly gownlike and thus the first true precursor of the dresses worn today. It was closed up the front to the waist; the woman stepped into it and then fastened it the rest of the way, perhaps, as in de Troy's *The Declaration of Love*, with elaborate cord or frogging fastenings, still another exotic touch previously seen in Europe only on some men's dressing gowns. In an age when, in order to guarantee that perfectly fitted look, ladies in court dress were literally sewn or pinned into their dresses, this was a radical idea. Instead of a gown a lady could not get out of without the help of her maid, the dressing gown now featured the first visible fasteners ever and thus suggested another kind of freedom, dressing on one's own. (A cunning system of ties under the back pleats allowed women to adjust the dress to hug the upper back and thus create a slim silhouette that contrasted nicely with the volume below.)

The informal look also became rounder, fuller, and thus acquired a series of new names, particularly *robe volante*, or flying dress. A few of these dresses, from about 1730, have survived (probably because they were never worn— were women already acquiring more clothes than they could possibly use?). They are the earliest surviving examples of French fashion. One of them, in a glorious French woven silk, is pictured in the color plates. Its shape is perfectly round because it has no train. The style flaunted the fact that it was exclusively for city wear and would never go to court. The pronounced fullness and the

Here is a flying dress worn over round hoopskirts known as paniers, *or baskets.*
The hoopskirts changed the flying dress's shape and made it move
in an even more dramatic, swaying fashion.

way it allowed the fabric to move explain several new names for informal dress
such as *robe flottante* (floating dress) and *robe ballante* from *ballant*, an adjective
meaning "to swing from side to side nonchalantly." Particularly when the
hoopskirt (*panier*, or basket) was added to the mix a few years later, the dressing
gown swayed back and forth and swirled about and with the woman wearing it
(see above).

When we think of hoopskirts in French dress, a model from the late eighteenth century comes to mind—the oval shape that, when worn under a dress
with a flattened front, produced an outlandish shape and forced women to take
mincing little steps and move sideways through doorways, a model so wide at
the top that women could "rest their elbows on them," as the *Mercure galant*
put it. The flying dress was worn over very different hoops—bell-shaped,
round, wider at the bottom—a shape that, like the new bodice, worked with a
woman's body rather than constraining it. These hoops swayed along with the
women wearing them, and the lilting motion lifted their skirts slightly, making
this the first high fashion to display the ankle and the lower calf—and perhaps

a related fad, intricately patterned stockings attached with fancy garters (see color plates). The high fashion created at the moment when Parisians discovered financial risk taking and sudden financial prosperity during the John Law years was therefore the original illustration of the phenomenon recently dubbed a "hemline index": those flying hems truly rose along with the stock market. It also issued in the first period ever during which the leg was the primary erogenous zone.

Round, full skirts that rise up when women move—this seems the stuff of ballet, and indeed that was exactly where the new style originated. In Paris,

A late-seventeenth-century engraving portrays one of the original dancers at the Paris Opera-Ballet in a costume that features a skirt that surely seemed scandalously short in an age when women's dresses normally extended right down to the floor.

hoopskirts were first seen on the stage, that of the Opera-Ballet, one of the pet projects of royal ballet fanatic Louis XIV. There, beginning in the 1680s, women for the first time publicly showed off parts of a woman's body previously kept under wraps (see page 196). Their costumes were given the volume essential to the best twirling effects by small hoops, known as *criards*, or squeakers, because they rustled with the dancers' movements. For an age in which formal dress went right down to the floor, some costumes were very short indeed, true precursors of the midcalf tutu of the nineteenth century.

"Tutu" is thought to come from a child's word for the buttocks; it's not clear that seventeenth-century dancers showed their truly intimate parts (and since, prior to the late eighteenth century, women were very unlikely to wear drawers, they would have been displaying the real thing), but the frisson provoked by that possibility remained attached to all spinning skirts. Ballerinas became sex symbols for men—when the eleven-year-old Louis XV appeared onstage with "dancing girls from the opera," this was considered risqué. To women fighting for freedom of movement in dress, meanwhile, they were fashion icons. The influence of ballet styles on high fashion was openly recognized at the height of the flying dress's popularity, and men were just as open in admitting that they found the new look attractive because it showed off "an adorable foot and a bit of leg."

Thus it was that in the 1720s, casual dress in France became controversial in a new way, as loose garb for loose women. In England, this idea was already exploited in the late seventeenth century, which surely explains why women there never embraced comfortable dress. In France, however, for decades all was calm, even though at several moments such criticism might have seemed inevitable. In the 1680s, for example, casual dress began to be called *déshabillé*, from the verb *se déshabiller*, to undress, yet all understood that "to be undressed," *en déshabillé*, was simply not to wear court dress. In fact, to be *en déshabillé* even received a positive spin, as dressing "without affectation," an "authentic" style. Next came the term *déshabillé négligé*, negligent undress. When artists associated that term with a figure such as the Duchesse de Bouillon and posed her as they did, they were obviously trying to create the link between loose dress and loose women. Still nothing doing. People understood that "negligent" simply added more insouciance to "dishabille": negligence was the original cool and meant you hadn't worked too hard to achieve your look. Then came the stock market craze, and the French attitude changed along with the financial situation and the new clientele for luxury goods.

To modern eyes, the *robe volante* seems more covered up, and thus more modest, than earlier informal styles. Contemporary journalists, however,

claimed that men considered a woman wearing one to be completely undressed, this time in the literal sense of the term. In 1718, when the flying dress
was brand new, Marivaux, writing for the *Nouveau Mercure*, cast the first stone.
He pronounced the gown "a barely decent equivalent of nudity," declared that
it made women seem "dangerous," "risky business," because, thus attired,
they seemed to be saying: "Look at me. . . . I give shape to my outfit, rather
than letting my clothing shape me." That same year, Justus van Effen informed
readers of the Dutch periodical *La Bagatelle* that "the only thing Parisian
women seem to care about when they dress is being comfortable"; they insist
that "their limbs be completely free to move about." Van Effen was no fan of
such notions; he went on to offer this opinion of the *robe volante*: "They choose
such light fabrics that they put as little distance as possible between themselves
and men. It's as if they were dressed in paper, as though they had nothing on."

In warning foreign readers about the dangerous women walking the streets of
Paris, van Effen was also teaching them a brand-new use of the adjective *volant*:
a garment that wasn't lined. In an age when lining was the norm, the sight of an
unlined dress, a *robe volante*, was surely surprising. However, rather than present the women's decision as a desire to be comfortable or to be fashionable—an
unlined garment was far lighter, so the fabric floated with the greatest of ease—
the newsman portrayed it as blatant and intentional provocation.

Within a decade, commentators were characterizing women thus attired as a
threat to public morality: "the garment's very volume immediately makes one
think of nudity"; "these women want to attract attention only to inspire lascivious thoughts." Just as happened with the boudoir, the dressing gown's
original purpose was distorted. Instead of a gown that made pregnant women
comfortable, it began to be discussed as a garment whose voluminousness was
used to hide out-of-wedlock pregnancies—and even to encourage such pregnancies by making it possible to hide them. Thus, when the flying dress hit
the streets of Paris, instead of merely a challenge to court etiquette, women's
desire for less restraining garments became a brazen scarlet letter.

Somehow, in those unstable years of easy money, when people became accustomed to abrupt shifts of fortune and heard previously inconceivable stories every day, what began as a notion whipped up by newsmen to sell copy
became accepted by many as established fact. As a result, the minute you see a
female character in an eighteenth-century French novel wearing a *robe de
chambre* or a *déshabillé*, well, you just know the kind of woman she is. You also
know that she will be found stretched out on an ottoman or a daybed, most
likely in her boudoir, that she will be older and far more experienced than the

innocent young hero—and finally, that she will use the entire arsenal of the age of comfort to have her way with him.

In subsequent decades, novelists fell all over one another in their rush to sensationalize comfortable dress. Thus, in the totally over-the-top *Angola, an Indian Tale*—in which the only thing even remotely Indian is the informal garb favored by its oversexed heroines—"negligence" is the ultimate come-on, and the women know it. They know that every "wrinkle," everything "charmingly out of place," every sign that they are less than perfectly turned out, will be understood by the hero as arranged to turn him on. And in Dominique Vivant Denon's novella *No Tomorrow*, a young man, totally inexperienced in the ways of older women and the complexities of high fashion, thanks heaven for garments that are easily removed.

The women of the age of comfort refused to dignify such male fantasies with a response: they continued to repeat that they were dressing just to please themselves. Thus in 1721, in the midst of all the brouhaha about paper-thin dresses and the dirty thoughts they inspired, the Marquise de Balleroy, stuck in the provinces because of her husband's work and desperate not to lose touch, received a letter informing her that the women of Paris "go absolutely everywhere in *robes de chambre* because it's such a comfortable style." They also calmly went on inventing still more comfortable fashions.

They began by throwing off the absurd big hair look that had been popular in France for decades. As the Duchesse de Bouillon and the ladies on the grass at Versailles show, those who wore the original dress of comfort combined it with a hairstyle that was anything but: they pinned an odd-shaped, fabric-covered flat tower made of wire netting to their heads, piled hair up a bit in front of it, and let lace or fabric cascade down the back. Sometime in the 1710s, big hair began to deflate. By the time ladies began to sway about in floating gowns, they were sporting a style close to the bobs of a similar high-flying decade, the 1920s, among the first hairstyles in history that do not seem outdated today: small, neat caps of curls, close-cropped (three fingers long) and often tightly crimped. They continued to powder their hair, since this was one age that thought gray was beautiful. And they sometimes topped it all off with lace-trimmed hats so tiny that they were barely hats, adorned with a flower or a bow (see color plates).

All through the 1720s and 1730s, newspapers covered new bob styles, from the *papillon* (butterfly) to the *équivoque* (equivocal). In 1729, styles such as the *négligé* were said to be so small "that they can't get any smaller"; in 1730, hair was *a bit* higher and *very* curly in the front. Small hair continued to rule supreme all through the Pompadour years; she helped make her coiffeur, Le Gros de

Rumigny, famous, and he in turn published five volumes of hairstyles that spread the Pompadour look through Europe. (Who knows why the name of the woman who made small hair famous was given to a very big style for men.) Then, in the 1770s, as the age of comfort faded, hair inflated to heights unheard of before or since.

Small hair meant a bare neck and throat, so the women of the 1720s championed a new accessory to help keep cozy on a winter day, the *mantille*—not the Spanish head scarf, but a shoulder mantle, actually more like what we call a shawl. *Reading in a Salon* (see color plates) is a winter scene: the women have come calling in their warmest flying gowns of velvet and silk brocade. The woman on the left is wearing the very *mantille* that the press in 1729 claimed was "worn by all women this winter." It's rounded in the back and ends in two points, each of which is decorated with "a very ornate tassel." It is the in color for *mantilles*, "scarlet edged with gold embroidery." The 1729 article included a plate to illustrate "how to tie the two points in the back," and this lady has followed it to the letter. Madame la Duchesse owned several *mantilles*, one with a fur collar.

The *mantille* may have been an offshoot of another new garment, this time one women actually did wear only in private, the *peignoir*. The peignoir was invented along with the *robe de chambre*; originally, it was merely a cloth, often lace-trimmed, that ladies *en déshabillé* draped around their shoulders while combing their hair (*se peigner*). It evolved first into something like the *mantille*, was always lace-trimmed, and was thus called a "lace peignoir"; by the end of the age of comfort, it had acquired sleeves, was made of a sheer fabric such as fine muslin, edged with lace, came down to about the knees, and tied at the neck with a ribbon. Ladies wore them to protect their outfits from the silvery powder that gleamed on their little curls: the Marquise de Pompadour owned ten of them. (How ironic that the vocabulary of comfortable high fashion—négligé, peignoir—was used to name sexy lingerie.)

It was easy for the women of the age of comfort to ignore what men of letters said about their dress. The opinion of the king of France, however, was another matter altogether. If Louis XIV thought he was bothered by the bodice issue, well, for his successor this was a question that seemed never to go away. And their situations can be precisely compared. Much of our information on Louis XIV's court comes from the diary kept by Versailles insider the Marquis de Dangeau; in the 1730s, his grandson the Duc de Luynes began his own record of life at court. The two diaries are remarkably similar: dust-dry, nononsense lists of the major events of each day. Neither man had an interest in fashion. They took note of it only when positively obliged to do so. Dangeau mentions the struggle between formal and informal dress a handful of times, whereas in the case of his grandson, hardly a week went by when he didn't have a clothing crisis to report.

In the 1730s in particular, Versailles was on full alert on the subject of the grand outfit. It seemed as if every lady of the court had found a pretext to finagle her way out of wearing it—and since Luynes's wife was among the queen's ladies-in-waiting, he didn't miss a single skirmish. There was, to begin with, pregnancy. By the 1730s, it was a given that even the queen could avoid formal dress then. (Since, however, she was the queen of France and "should be seen only in court dress," when in June 1737 she was allowed to receive the Venetian ambassador without the benefit of the bodice, a court official "was charged with writing to explain the reason that prevented the queen from being dressed.") Soon, however, her ladies-in-waiting lobbied for and won the right to skip the bodice during the queen's pregnancies.

They thought of travel next. Initially, a dispensation was granted while women were on the road, since this was not court turf. By 1738, the two days prior to any trip became casual Fridays as well. Then there was the far trickier question of court ceremonies such as baptisms and marriages. In 1737, noblewomen accepted the grand outfit as unavoidable on such occasions. Only two years later, however, the situation had changed dramatically, since for one of the greatest occasions imaginable, the dauphin's marriage, women would agree to the hated dress only if they had a really good seat (very near the altar, for example).

Once she had acquired a taste for comfort, the queen joined forces with the ladies of the court in their struggle—since she was usually such a discreet presence, her forthrightness on this issue speaks volumes. By 1744, she was fed up enough to talk openly about "the discomfort of that outfit." In 1746, she attended mass in the chapel at Versailles, received visitors, and dined with them, all in a *robe de chambre*—"but very nicely done up," Luynes felt obliged to add. The following year, she not only attended mass in the royal chapel in informal dress, but afterward officiated, "standing on the cloth of state," a symbol of royal authority—in the once lowly *robe de chambre*. It was a velvet revolution.

Just three years later, the long struggle was essentially over. When Luynes's wife showed up wearing court dress at an occasion that formerly would have required it, "the king was astonished"—but she was allowed to stay. And as for the royal daughters, they worked out a great way around the whole business. In 1761, Jeanne Genet Campan, the young woman who a few years later would tell the tale of Madame Victoire's love affair with a cushy armchair, explained that they would quickly slip into a hoopskirt, attach a train around their waist, and then "cover up the negligence of it all with a mantle." The ceremony over, they "returned to their rooms, undid a few knots, and took up where they had left off."

Thus, by the age of comfort's end, the grand outfit was as vestigial as the parade bedroom. When the Duc de Croÿ's daughter—she who refused all the formal bedroom nonsense at the time of her wedding—was presented at court in 1762, he had the chance "to see my daughter in court dress for the first time" (and the only time, one would bet). And in 1767, the age's authority on dressmaking, the Roubo of the fashion world, master tailor François Garsault, made its demise official: "This style is out-of-date; it is perpetuated at court." The dressing gown's victory was complete.

In the mid-1740s, when the queen entered the fray, she could hardly have failed to notice something that Luynes had begun to comment on in 1740: her husband was practicing a double standard. He couldn't "abide" anything but court dress as far as his wife was concerned, while his mistresses had already been getting away with murder for years. Thus, one day the king who loved architecture was entranced with his beloved floor plans when one of Pompadour's predecessors, the Comtesse de Mailly, had sashayed in—flagrantly "undressed." The countess had made noises about how "she couldn't possibly remain thus in the king's presence," but he had insisted that she stay.

It's surely no accident that the queen became much bolder after Pompadour came on the scene in 1745. It's hard to imagine that the marquise wore formal dress very often, since at the time of her death she owned only ten court dresses out of nearly ninety gowns. Her dress could not have failed to make the monarch's double standard evident to all. And her taste was typical of the age: in the last model suite Blondel designed for a woman, he built into one corner of the *méridienne* near the ottoman sofa "a large closet" designated specifically "to hold all her *déshabillés*."

True, by the time Pompadour arrived at Versailles, the *robe de chambre* had come a long way. About 1725, the loose back pleats sometimes became double box pleats, less flowing and more structured. Then, when women wrapped the ends of their *mantilles* around and tied them in the back, this gave casual dress something that had disappeared with the original *manteaux*: a waistline. (Bodice-hugging styles might also have been inspired by ballet dress.) In 1730, the year after this began, a volume illustrating "the latest styles" showed flying dresses, flying dresses with *mantilles* tied around the waist, and a completely new kind of informal dress, tightened up and fitted through the torso. The dressing gown had been launched on what was destined to be its final incarnation.

The new look, called both *robe de chambre* and a French dress, *robe à la française*, was also known in English as a "Pompadour gown": it's naturally what the marquise is wearing in Boucher's portrait. As the portrait makes clear, along the way from one marquise (Montespan) to another (Pompadour), the style had lost its free and easy flow—though it still retained the loose back drapery—and had become a dressier look. By Pompadour's day, the style's casualness seems more obviously contrived; you can't miss the fact that she's replaced expensive jewels (of which she naturally owned many) with artificial flowers—on her corsage, around her neck, in her hair. The French dress was, however, still considered informal—and when you compare Pompadour's portrait with the queen's, it's easy to see why (see color plates).

The queen is posed in what is clearly public space, a room whose marble floors and stolid pilasters scream magnificence. She seems so constrained that it's as if she can barely move. The dreaded bodice controls her body, holds her bolt upright and absolutely vertical, at odds with the curving lines of the rococo console table to which she seems to gesture. (She's actually pointing to her crown resting on the table.)

The mistress's portrait, on the other hand, depicts her as a creature of the age of comfort, the embodiment of Comte Dufort de Cheverny's belief that she had helped foster "every invention that made life easier." She's absolutely at one with the evidently interior space in which she's portrayed. Flowers are scattered about the room just as on her person; the fabric of her dress is coordinated with those of her interior. In 1752, near the time of this portrait, Cheverny said of her: "She was all soft curves, her gestures as much as her body," and here her curves match those of that lovely little convenience table as well as the swirling drapes. Even her pose is sinuous, fully at ease and fully at one with the room's contents. She's stretched diagonally across the canvas, leaning seductively on the furniture, and thus shows off both comfortable seating and clothing that gave women the freedom of movement they needed to take advantage of it.

Pompadour's portrait went on very public display in 1757 in the annual painting exhibit at the Louvre. Boucher's canvas was placed at the absolute center of the salon on a special raised platform and was said by some to offer proof that under Louis XV, French painters had become the greatest in Europe. The exhibit was, of course, very visible testimony to the marquise's influence at the French court. It was also seen as testimony to the victory over court dress of the undressed look and all the ease it stood for: Boucher's portrait was described as a triumph of a "natural" style. The most powerful woman in France wanted to be seen wearing not a queen's ransom in diamonds, but simple silk flowers. It was as if the woman who made the straw hat a high-fashion accessory wanted the whole world to see that the 1678 proclamation inspired by her role model, the Marquise de Montespan, had at long last come officially and unequivocally true: "People hardly get dressed up anymore"; "everyone in France today wants only to be comfortable."

CHAPTER THIRTEEN

The Fabric of Their Lives

COTTON—SOFT, EASY care, versatile—what would we do without it? Europeans of the age of comfort were the first Westerners to understand the way we feel.

Until the seventeenth century, Europeans wore all the same natural materials still used today—wool, linen, silk—all of them, that is, but the one foreign to European soil: cotton. When cotton arrived on the scene straight from India, it almost instantly became such a consumer favorite that it threatened to steal the limelight from native textiles. Governments, and none more quickly or more harshly than the French, waged war—and the word is none too strong—against it for decades. Cotton, however, proved unstoppable. At the beginning of the age of comfort, cotton was very occasionally seen (most often as a coverlet on a bed) in a few households—primarily those of merchants dealing in overseas trade. By its end, however, cotton was literally everywhere. It was, to begin with, all over the house—wall coverings, curtains, bedclothes, table linens, upholstery fabrics. It was also on people's backs: every type of dress, except the grand outfit, of course, was made from cotton. Working dress for shopgirls, expensive ensembles for the finest ladies in Paris, the only clothing owned by their poorest counterparts in provincial villages—all were being made in cotton. There had never before been a textile takeover on anything like this scale.

Cotton provides still another example of a phenomenon visible in every area in which comfort became an essential value: the way in which exotic goods seemed to invite casualness. Asian imports—from kimono-inspired dress to Turkish beds and Chinese boudoirs—were seen as the perfect antidotes to Western pomp and circumstance. Having cotton on their backs or Turkish sofas in

their lacquered boudoirs obviously encouraged people to feel freer in their behavior and imparted a glow of luxurious comfort to life in the new interior
rooms.

In other European countries—Portugal, Holland, and England, in that
order—cotton first arrived as still another by-product of the spice trade. In
France, it was marketed on a very limited scale before the ships of any East India
company began bringing cotton to Europe. Marseilles was the traditional port of
entry through which Asian goods arrived in Europe the age-old way, overland
and through the Levant. Prior to the age of comfort, however, nowhere was the
trade in cotton significant. Cotton goods sold in Marseilles tended to remain in
the region; the Portuguese were never really interested in marketing textiles; at
first, the Dutch and the English did not consider this aspect of the Indies trade
significant.

The situation changed dramatically in the second half of the seventeenth
century at the moment when the French finally became a serious player in the
Indies trade. At that point, the volume of imported goods exploded. Cotton
represented but a modest part of English trade at midcentury; by 1684, the East
India Company was exporting to England over a million pieces of Indian cotton annually. In 1691, the directors in London sent this message to their Indian
agents: "You can send us nothing amiss at this time when everything of India is
so much wanted." And already in 1680, the Comtesse de Lafayette—luminous
novelist and astute observer of the changing scene—observed that "in France,
we love everything that comes from India." The budding French fashion industry helped create this situation. As soon as high fashion went casual, cotton
became part of the wardrobe of every woman who followed the dictates of
French fashion. From then on, cotton clothing became increasingly important
in Western wardrobes.

It's easy to understand why the new textile won over European consumers so
quickly: cotton was different from fabrics such as wool and linen in key ways.
To begin with, it was light. For women in particular, whose dresses used many
yards of fabric, the feel of a cotton dress hanging from their shoulders after the
experience of carrying the weight of wool velvet or brocaded silk gowns
would have been a true liberation. Cotton was also washable. The original dry
cleaners—known as *dégraisseurs*, or grease removers—were just then setting
up shop in Paris to help people deal with the buildup of smoke and dirt on their
fine fabrics, proving that people were feeling the need for cleaner garments;
with cotton, they could handle the problem on their own.

Indian textiles had less obvious qualities as well. They were colorfast: their
bright hues lasted through successive washings. (The *Encyclopédie* actually

claimed that their colors got "even brighter" with each washing.) They featured shades previously unknown in Europe, the product of different dyes and dyeing processes. Their tints were brilliant—indeed, the sharp contrasts created by the juxtaposition of several equally intense hues brought a powerful new experience of color to Europe, made its streets and its homes for the first time truly colorful. They also democratized certain shades: prior to the age of comfort, crimson, for example, was a regal hue, a shade expensive to produce and therefore a sign of prestige and rank. Because of imported cottons, red became a commonly used casual accent color.

Cotton fabrics introduced a big new world of pattern unlike anything ever seen in Europe. European woven fabrics tended to have a uniform design, whereas Indian fabrics (produced by a combination of printing and hand-painting) featured a sharp distinction between a solid field and a multicolored motif, something that made its patterns stand out sharply. And as for the kinds of patterns they showed off, well, those may well have produced the biggest textile culture shock of all.

The fabrics of the age of magnificence featured symmetrical designs with rather prim patterns arranged in distinct rows, as if under tight control. Then came Asian textiles—above all from India, though there were also Chinese painted silks and Siamese fabrics as well—and in the space of roughly a decade, the very definition of pattern in textile was revolutionized. The Siamese added stripes to the mix. Then Europeans learned that textiles could be figurative as well—literally so, since the fabrics the Siamese and the Indians exported to France often featured in their scenes what contemporary descriptions refer to as *petits personages*, small human figures—small indeed, often no larger than the animals and vegetation next to them (see color plates). Finally, there were floral patterns—nothing changed the look of European interiors and European fashion more than Asian flowered textiles.

Floral designs had previously played a limited role in European dress and interior decoration—in embroidery such as crewelwork, in the background of tapestries. The flowers depicted in textiles, however, were too symmetrical, too formal, to evoke anything actually found in nature. Asian textiles were the window onto a big new world of flowers. Europeans got their first glimpse of many varieties in imported textiles—peonies, magnolias, camellias—and then proceeded to import the actual plants. Suddenly the Western world went floral to a degree previously unthinkable. Bedclothes began to be flower-decked; next, people covered the walls of entire rooms with flowers; finally, women's dress was taken over by floral and arboreal prints. Wherever this happened, the world of formality disappeared in one fell swoop—to be replaced with a vision of easygoing casualness. The new fabrics appeared tailor-made for the age of comfort, its new private spaces and *robes de chambre* alike; they were as unpretentious as a plain white ceiling. New ways of sitting, lounging, and living seemed to call for new textiles at the same time that those fabrics made it easier for individuals to move in a more relaxed manner. Casual was the new chic, and cotton *was* casual.

The novel designs Europeans suddenly began to see all around them were so arresting that consumers probably thought they were getting an authentically exotic product. The Indian textile industry, however, was a formidable concern: India was the largest producer and exporter of textiles the world had ever seen—and it had played this role for centuries, sending cotton goods to China, Persia, Africa. The Indians were thus past masters at giving foreigners what they wanted; they knew in particular that most often that meant something tailor-made to seem exotic without being completely foreign.

Thus, when the directors of the British East India Company began to issue directives on how to please the newest consumers of cotton, the Indians quickly modified the patterns of textiles destined for the European market— the cotton skirts being sold in Paris in 1673 whose design imitated a trendy European lace pattern are a perfect example of their versatility. The English were thought to prefer a white background, so the red-field textiles the Indians had been sending there quickly disappeared. (They may have been sent across the English Channel instead; at Versailles, they loved red backgrounds—see color plates.) At the same time, no one wanted to lose the feel of the exotic. Thus, the Dutch East India Company's directors, even though they, too, sent out European patterns to be copied, consistently asked that this be done "in the Indian manner" or "after the manner of their country."

The ideas European businessmen came up with in the hope of producing a winning textile often seem pretty amazing. The English directors, for example, asked the Indians to copy a print by French engraver Henri Bonnart illustrating a scene from *Don Quixote*, as well as ideas for cutting-edge mural decorations by Jean Bérain, Monseigneur's favorite designer. Of course, by the time these designs were shipped back to European shores, they had been reinvented by Indian painters, so Western consumers may never have guessed that the fabrics they were wild about were hardly authentically anything—a Frenchman's vision of sixteenth-century Spain as seen through the eyes of a seventeenth-century Indian, for example—as alien to Eastern as to Western eyes, yet somehow fulfilling the desires of Western consumers for just the right touch of partly domesticated exoticism.

Soon, Indian textiles became the vehicle through which Europeans discovered a spectrum of pan-Asian motifs. While there were some legitimately Indian touches—elephants cavorting amid exotic vegetation (so what if they were blue . . . see color plates)—often painted cotton showed Westerners a sort of pan-Asian stew. Some *petits personages* are quite clearly Chinese, for example, while many flowering trees and blossoms are distinctly Japanese. In 1681, the directors in London laid down what was destined to remain the key rule of the cotton game—like couture, it had to have collections: "Ladies will pay twice as much for a new thing not seen in Europe before . . . than they will give . . . for some fashion worn in former years."

By 1681, French noblewomen were stepping out in the streets of Paris in the newly fashionable casual dress. More and more, they chose the equally trendy new textile for their outfits. Like the directors of the English East India Company, those in the French fashion industry—the merchant Gautier, for example—were realizing the advantage of renewing their offerings seasonally. The most influential segment of the French textile industry, the Lyons silk weavers, quickly followed suit. Before long, both Indians and French were on a stepped-up timetable, turning out two and even four collections a year.

In 1735, Jean-Antoine Fraisse published his *Book of Chinese Motifs Inspired by Persian, Indian, Chinese, and Japanese Originals*, a Frenchman's (Fraisse's) version of Asian textiles in the most extensive collection in France, amassed by Madame la Duchesse's son the Prince de Condé. (The prince, too, had made a killing during the Law years.) Fraisse boasted that his copies "of the Chinese style" were so "faithful that they would fool an Indian." His creations prove that French textile designers had understood that the success of the Asian invasion of European markets was based on a clever blend of exotic and familiar motifs and that the French were now following in the footsteps of the Indians. Indeed, during the first half of the eighteenth century, all the major styles of French silks—scholars now call them lace-pattern silks, bizarre silks, and naturalistic silks—are often clearly inspired by motifs found in Indian textiles. Thus, many fabrics made in France—the silk in the flying dress, for example, with its juxtaposition of vivid and boldly contrasting hues, its feathery leaves and strange blossoms—have a feel more exotic than domestic (see color plates). The cross-pollination between East and West was, in fact, so intense that at times it's impossible to be sure where a textile originated—for example, is the wall hanging in *The Garter* an Asian export (Indian? Chinese?) designed for the European market or an Asian wannabe, homegrown French kitsch (see color plates)?

The age of comfort thus unfolded against a backdrop of multihued, multicultural textiles. By the turn of the eighteenth century, the French were surrounded by patterns and shades of a boldness and variety that would have been inconceivable only decades before, by the kinds of fabrics that seem totally incompatible with formality.

Today, we use the term chintz to refer to any upholstery fabric with a floral pattern: the word conjures up a vision of easygoing informality, of chairs one can sink into, of rooms designed to make one feel at home rather than to impress or to intimidate. Those who jump-started the age of comfort had no word for the new textiles when they began buying them. At first, they simply used a generic term for cloth or fabric, *toile*, and said either cotton fabric, *toile de cotton*, or Indian fabric, *toile indienne*. When the trade began to heat up in the 1680s, they learned a new term, *chitte*, a French attempt to reproduce a Hindi word: *chint* (singular), *chintes* (plural), from *chitta*, spotted cloth. (*Chint* surfaced in English as everything from *sit* to *chit* to *cheetes* to *chints*.)

The French never did use "chintz" a lot; they settled on *toile peinte*, painted cloth, or simply *indienne*, Indian (cloth). They knew, however, what they liked: those who could afford it wanted only the finest quality, and that was soon labeled *perse*, Persian cloth. Now, Persian cloth was not really Persian at all; it was made in India and at most shipped to France via Persia. The original "Persian" cottons, however, had a blue background, and the adjective *pers/perse* meant both Persian and blue, so the belief that blue cottons came from Persia was born. All those who chose a blue-and-white decorating scheme to complement their Chinese porcelain—Monseigneur, the Duchesse de Bourgogne— begged their decorators for *perse*.

All the while, those royal *perse* and chintz aficionados surely savored a thrill far more dangerous than that afforded by, say, thumbing one's nose at etiquette by wearing a *robe de chambre*: what they were showing off was just plain illicit. The countless informal gowns stuffing the closets of Madame la Duchesse and Pompadour and the cotton outfits in which the Duchesse de Bourgogne, Monseigneur, and their band "burst into" the carnival ball had one thing in common: they were all against the law—so forbidden, in fact, that anyone less fully under royal protection would have faced criminal prosecution if seen wearing them. The criminals, furthermore, were fully aware that this was risky business. In 1687, when Louis XIV spotted his son and heir sporting a painted cotton vest, he threw a royal fit: "The king ordered that Monseigneur's vest be burned and that the merchant who sold the fabric be fined."

Painted cloth was first seriously marketed in France in the late 1670s and the 1680s, a bad moment for foreign imports. Louis XIV and his finance guru Jean-Baptiste Colbert were putting into place a protectionist policy that would guarantee for decades both the supremacy of the French luxury goods industry and a healthy trade balance for the French economy. As soon as an exotic commodity became fashionable, merchants were ordered to stop importing the foreign product, and French manufacturers were ordered to copy it. When, therefore, the fashion accessory or fabric was clamored for all over Europe, French manufacturers reaped the profits. The craze for Indian cotton, however, could not be so easily managed. French textile workers did quickly begin to turn out ersatz painted textiles. When that happened, however, the producers of traditional French fabrics, Lyons silk weavers in particular, protested that homegrown chintz threatened their livelihood as much as Indian cloth. The Sun King therefore put painted cotton in a class by itself: both the foreign originals and French imitations were banned. The official term was "prohibition," and the ban was to last for nearly a century.

In the seventeenth century, almanacs were illustrated, just as calendars are today. In 1681, one scene depicted two women dressed in *manteaux* made of Indian cotton. The first, a merchant who sells cotton cloth, is begging the other, a fashion trendsetter, not to leave Paris, to which the fashionista replies that it's time to introduce women of other countries to the new look. A caption explained that "the cotton craze" had originated in 1677, which would make it part and parcel of the *Mercure galant*'s January 1678 news flash: "Everyone in France today wants to be comfortable."

By October 1686, the Sun King was convinced that the craze was out of hand and a drain on the French economy: the first law banning cotton went on the books. Merchants were forbidden to sell Indian cotton; the French were forbidden to wear Indian cotton or to use it in their homes. Those who already owned such items could bring them in and have them stamped to prove that they had been purchased before 1686. If they failed to do so and the items were found, they would be confiscated and destroyed. If merchants continued to sell cotton, their business would be shut down and they would be heavily fined. Smugglers were fined half as much—and were condemned to the galleys for three years.

Led by the ever vigilant head of the Parisian police, Nicolas de La Reynie, a crackdown began. In May 1691, La Reynie announced to his inspectors in the provinces that the state had confiscated over fifteen thousand yards of the forbidden merchandise that year alone. (The fabric was burned in December 1692; an even greater quantity had been destroyed the previous year.) In October 1711, the text of the latest ban was pasted up on walls all over the textile-manufacturing center, Troyes. Officers of the law roamed its streets, "grabbing any women and girls they saw wearing painted cloth and forcibly stripping them." In Paris in the early 1700s, the police were entering shops and confiscating cotton goods on the spot. In 1737, they slapped a hefty fine on a female shopkeeper named Jambu; in 1750, they arrested many women merchants, including Dame Louvel, for hiding cotton textiles under their skirts to smuggle them into the city. And by June 1715, the Parisian police were even searching aristocratic residences. At the Marquise de Nesle's home, they confiscated a cotton *robe de chambre*. When she "demanded it back," the then head of the Parisian police, d'Argenson, returned it in person and "cut it into pieces in front of her."

The measures were extreme, but the stakes were huge. In 1692, La Reynie reasoned that because the dictates of French high fashion were followed so slavishly, "all the nations in Europe that formerly bought prodigious quantities of French textiles" were now choosing cotton instead; this, he estimated, had already cost the country the phenomenal sum of five hundred thousand livres, two thirds the cost of the construction of Paris's new bridge, the Pont Royal, in 1685. Representatives from Lyons and Rouen tirelessly begged the government to check the "fury" for cotton that was ruining the French textile industry.

To many, that "fury" appeared unstoppable. In 1723, Savary des Bruslons argued that neither the original ban nor the more than thirty-five decrees that followed it in the next forty years had done a thing "to cure" consumers of cotton madness. By the 1750s, when commentators finally began to debate the prohibition's economic effects in print, all agreed that the French were spending between sixteen and twenty million livres every year on Indian cotton.

Those who favored an end to the ban also considered its human toll. The editors of the *Journal économique* estimated that, whereas every year twelve hundred Frenchmen died in shipwreck or from illness on voyages to the Americas, every year between six thousand and seven thousand Frenchmen died in the war against cotton. (That figure included both soldiers killed by smugglers and smugglers who died after being tortured.) In addition, the state had to bear the expense of "maintaining an infinite number of soldiers to police its frontiers and all through the interior." Economist and free trade advocate Vincent de Gournay formulated a different equation: the government could "force a few thousand [textile workers] to change jobs or be temporarily unemployed"—or it could continue to "wage an endless war on all its borders in its attempt to force twenty million Frenchmen to go against their heart's desire."

Casualties were so high because the French army was no match for the smugglers. Like all native insurgents, they knew the terrain best, were well dug in, and were protected by the locals. Thus in December 1710, the inspector in Brittany, Ferrand, wrote the finance minister in Paris to warn that he couldn't possibly follow orders and confiscate contraband in a warehouse on the island of

Bouin: "Its inhabitants are so formidable that it would take at least two regiments of infantry to do the job."

There was an even more formidable enemy in plain view in Paris. Cut up the Marquise de Nesle's cotton ensemble? One month later, she was spotted by the police strolling in Paris's Tuileries Gardens in a brand-new "outfit made of Indian cotton in an Indian style." The following year, at a meeting of the kingdom's finance council, the Duc de Noailles delivered an "impassioned speech" complaining that the ban would never work as long as "the finest ladies in the land were wearing painted cotton publicly and with impunity." When he finished, the Duc de Saint-Simon stood up and announced that they should simply "arrest Madame la Duchesse, put an iron collar around her neck, and chain her to a post in a public place" as an example to all—at which point, the council members burst out laughing and the discussion was over. It was the *robe de chambre* nightmare, only on a far bigger scale.

The serious use of cotton began—but of course—at the Porcelain Trianon. In 1671, both the king's apartment and that of the Marquise de Montespan had a small room completely upholstered in Indian cotton with a red background—and the coverage was complete indeed: cotton curtains, cotton bedcoverings, huge wall hangings (they were referred to as "tapestries," which is, of course, what the age of magnificence usually hung on palace walls; the switch from dark woven tapestries to bright painted cottons was surely among the most radical of all swerves into informality), the seats of several dozen folding stools, even the walls of the hallway joining the two rooms. In 1675, two bedrooms at Versailles (undoubtedly also for the king and Montespan) had their walls upholstered with cotton, a design in white on a red background. And in January 1686 (were they stocking up before announcing the original prohibition?), a huge shipment of cotton wall hangings was delivered to Marly, and the fabric was referred to for the first time by the French word for chintz, *chitte*.

In 1701, cotton and modern interior decoration began a winning partnership when a bedroom in the Ménagerie was fitted out exclusively with cotton. It contained an early canopied bed, which thus became the first bed to be upholstered in painted fabric; armchairs—still early days for those, too—were covered to match. Everything was upholstered in what would become the most prized decorating fabric of the age of comfort, so-called Persian cotton. (*Perse* was originally offered for sale in Paris in 1680; this is its first recorded use for upholstery.)

This also may well be the first recorded use of cotton to upholster seat furniture. (The Dutch, for example, early proponents of cotton wall hangings, didn't use it on chairs until well into the eighteenth century.) People were

aware that cotton was not a practical choice, that it wouldn't last as long as traditional upholstery fabrics, and that it tore more easily, but this didn't stop
them from using it. To compare the textiles purchased for royal châteaux in
1669 and 1699 is to realize that three decades revolutionized the look of French
interiors. In 1669, it's all velvet, damask, and brocade, made mostly in Lyons;
in 1699, French fabrics represented only a quarter of the orders—everything
else was Indian cotton in colors such as celadon, in all shades of lavender and
purple, and in patterns such as "covered with golden dragons" and "big multi-
colored flowers." And sure enough, in 1729 when that ten-foot-long ottoman
was delivered to Versailles, it was upholstered in *perse*: the young king thus got
his first taste of the floral fabric that he and the Marquise de Pompadour would
do more than any others to send to the top of the decorating pantheon.

From the start, cotton also brought comfort into the everyday life of the king of
France. That 1686 shipment, for example, contained three cotton tablecloths, lots
of napkins, including "twelve with a painted center and border," and the Sun
King's first cotton sheets, "with a design painted on one end." When Louis XIV
decided on "a young look" for the Ménagerie, he clearly understood that the by
then forbidden textile was a favorite with the young royals, so he featured it. The
king who was ordering shops shuttered and *manteaux* cut to pieces thus began a
policy of open textile hypocrisy far more consequential than Louis XV's subsequent wife-mistress sartorial double standard.

With such an example from on high, it's hardly surprising to find that the
king's subjects brazenly flaunted their disrespect for prohibition. In the year
that separated the two editions of Nicolas Blégny's best of Paris books, 1691–
1692—precisely the year when the head of the police wrote proudly about
burning confiscated textiles—the number of merchants who openly advertised
the fact that they were selling cotton textiles increased from one to four. And in
de Troy's hymn to the age of comfort, *The Declaration of Love*, the plump pillow cushioning the lady's flying-gown-clad arm is covered in what is unmis-
takably Indian cotton. This canvas was exhibited to the public at the Louvre,
with de Troy's signature visible on a band on the woman's wrist. An article in
the most-read Parisian paper commented on both that cotton pillow and the
"huge number" of people who had seen it.

Amazingly, however, some individuals wouldn't touch the forbidden fruit.

The example of Pierre Crozat is most telling. He was aware of the advan-
tages of cotton and used it on his table—no fewer than *fifty-seven dozen* cotton
napkins and a proportionately huge number of tablecloths—and on his beds—
dozens upon dozens of cotton sheets. None of them, however, is described, so
all were plain white cotton, which was not affected by the ban. (When unpainted

cotton was confiscated in lots of dry goods, the authorities gave it to the poor.) In the rooms where his leather furniture was found, Crozat chose cotton curtains in keeping with the seating's informality; they were also solid white. Charlotte Desmares was the next most law-abiding citizen of the Crown. She, too, had lots of tablecloths and napkins and sheets to burn—twenty-four dozen plus six dozen for servants. All were plain white. Her curtains were cotton, many of them all white, or at most with a border of the forbidden stuff (borders were usually created by cutting up old textiles); only in a few cases did she cross the line—blue-and-white *indienne*, red-and-white stripes.

Nonaristocrats held back, presumably out of respect for the law; aristocrats, however, were another matter. The Comte d'Evreux did stick to white cotton for his linen: 57 pairs of good sheets, 106 pairs of everyday ones; 55 big tablecloths, 20 small ones, 80, yes, 80 dozen dinner napkins—the French often still used their fingers instead of silverware to pick up food, so they went through lots of napkins—plus 8 dozen coffee napkins. For the décor of private bedrooms, however, he went in for colored cotton: two of them mixed stripes and checks. In the Hôtel d'Evreux, now the Hôtel de Pompadour, as in all her homes, the marquise wanted only the best: in textiles, that was *perse*. By the 1760s, "Persian" cotton no longer meant only floral prints with a blue background; some of Pompadour's *perses*—in the bedroom off her bathroom and the *petit boudoir* next to it, for example—had stripes or checks with a red background. She chose traditional chintz for the chairs in that fabulous garden off the Champs-Élysées. Like Desmares, however, Pompadour was hardly a textile purist: the last furniture she ordered, not yet delivered when she died, included pieces to be covered in white silk as well as others in painted cotton decorated with pseudo-Chinese figures. So while the two original owners of today's Élysée Palace would never have passed inspection by the textile police, neither were they sending all their money to India.

For that, the French could rely on Madame la Duchesse. No one thumbed her nose at her father's justice more flagrantly than the child Montespan was carrying when she introduced Versailles to casual dress. Her father had, after all, encouraged her urge to decorate from the start, though what the king saw in her Parisian mansion cannot have failed to make him understand that his textile hypocrisy was lining the pockets of the very smugglers his soldiers were trying to kill. The quantity of cotton she used on her table and her beds was so vast that it took four pages in her estate inventory to list it all. Even more impressive is the number of rooms done up entirely in painted cotton—her little writing room (a mix of checks and *petits personages*), her boudoir (floral), her bath (gray flowered cotton)—as well as the quantity of seat furniture upholstered in cotton (four sofas with flowering branches on a white background, an ottoman and matching armchairs in a blue floral on white, to cite but two examples). And her passion for foreign textiles was common knowledge: Saint-Simon knew he could bring down the house just by mentioning her name.

Sartorial taste exactly matched decorating style. Crozat's wardrobe contained not a single item in cotton, not even a dressing gown, while the count owned quite a bit of white cotton: 110 *chemises* (longer than the modern shirt, this was the basic garment men wore under vests and jackets) and 50 more in muslin, the feather-light, semitransparent cotton that began taking the fashion world by storm in the 1730s, plus a painted cotton dressing gown. Ten of Pompadour's 78 French dresses were in *perse*, 4 more in muslin; she owned 6 other casual outfits in painted cotton, a daring amount considering her very public position, but nothing in comparison with Madame la Duchesse: 37 of her 39 *robes de chambre* were made from forbidden cloth, with patterns ranging from a floral in shades of violet to a grapevine motif that was surely a special request for the French market to black-and-white stripes or a multicolored mix of trees, fruit, and flowers on a white ground.

Like her mother before her, Madame la Duchesse was creating the style of the future. In the mid-1780s, a young French woman, Henriette-Lucy Dillon, was given a huge—it filled many "vast closets"—and hugely expensive trousseau before her marriage to the future Marquis de La Tour du Pin; she remarked with evident satisfaction that "there wasn't a single silk dress." Her trousseau was a perfect indication of how the cotton craze had transformed French fashion. Elsewhere in Europe, upper-class women used chintz, like the *robe de chambre*, strictly as indoor wear; only European fabrics were considered acceptable for street wear. In France, however, the finest ladies in the land did not hesitate to wear painted cotton in public. In the Dutch journalist van Effen's shocked reaction to the flying dress, for example, he attributed its indecency in large part to "the Indian material" in which French women "dressed so lightly"; he called it a "next-to-nothing fabric."

Cotton was a natural for the styles of the age of comfort—*robe de chambre*, negligent undress, *robe volante*. Its "next-to-nothing" diaphanousness meant that cotton ensembles such as the swaying, swinging *robe ballante* flowed and moved; this was the first time that a fabric became an integral part of the choreography of high fashion. And the lighter cotton got—muslin, gauze—the tighter its bond with French high fashion became. In the 1720s and 1730s, the *Mercure de France* was full of tips such as how to superimpose a dress of pink muslin on an underskirt in white to create "a charming effect."

That love affair was among the principal reasons why, during the decades of prohibition, the French were at the center of the European cotton trade. In France, cotton spread through the ranks of society as no other fabric ever had. Already in 1709, the government inspector for the textile industry in Rouen reported that because they had seen "women of quality" wearing them, women of the middle and even the lower classes "who used to wear textiles from Rouen" now wanted only cotton. They were able to get what they wanted because cotton, among its other qualities, could go low as easily as high. The influential economist and contributor to the *Encyclopédie* François de Forbonnais explained that while the highest-quality goods were reserved "for affluent individuals," "less expensive cottons were widely used," and "the lowest quality made up the everyday dress of the common folk"—and even they could also afford "a nicer outfit for dressy occasions." Indeed, by the 1780s, well over half the clothing owned by female servants working in Paris was made of cotton.

The fashion industry was but the first reason for France's ever increasing dependence on Indian textiles. The demise of the parade bedroom and the rise of interior decoration created another important market for painted cloth. Cotton was first used on beds in Holland and England; in France, it was almost unheard of prior to its arrival at the Trianon. A study of Parisian households found only two mentions of painted cloth bed coverlets prior to 1671. In the age of comfort, however, cotton became synonymous with the new private bedroom. Tester beds such as the *duchesse* bed (page 170) showcased painted cloth; often the bed and the outside of the canopy were covered in, say, a floral print, the backboard and the lining in a different color and a contrasting pattern (a check, for instance).

The seat furniture in the room was upholstered to match, as were the walls. What Louis XIV had called a "youthful look" had thus become a dominant style in the original modern bedrooms. From there, cotton upholstery fabric spread to related interior rooms, such as boudoirs, and to less intimate spaces. By 1770, master upholsterer Bimont pronounced "the different qualities of painted cotton" an excellent choice for seat furniture that was "comfortable, appealing, and in the best taste." By then, as in all domains related to style and décor, "the best taste" in the use of textiles had come to be considered a typically French look.

In the early decades of the eighteenth century, people would surely have recognized that the fabric in the lady's flying dress in *The Declaration of Love* (see color plates) was French-made (it's a so-called lace-pattern silk). Some may also have noticed that it was not purely French; its design contained motifs inspired by the exotic flora in Indian textiles. Those same observers would just as surely have known that this fabric (see color plates) was a cotton hand-painted in India; they might also have realized that its little sprigs of flowers and lacy motifs were borrowed from contemporary French silks such as the one in *The Declaration of Love*.

Today, nearly three centuries later, these distinctions no longer count. Here is the identical early-eighteenth-century Indian pattern, this time in a modern reproduction by a French textile manufacturer (see color plates). The cozy look the fabric is being used to create—the same cotton floral print on the walls, the furniture, and the curtains around the bed—is Louis XIV's "youthful look" all over again. It's also one that decorators would now call French without considering for a second that the textile that makes it possible might hardly be authentically French. And if would-be decorators today saw this image (see color plates), it's unlikely that they would ever guess that the multicolored fabric is in fact a painted and dyed Indian cotton made for the European market circa 1700, while the blue-and-white one is that early-eighteenth-century Indian textile as it was copied and marketed in France circa 2000.

Thus, three centuries later, the invasion of the European market by Asian cottons that made eighteenth-century French government officials fear for the future of their country's textile industry has played itself out in a manner no one could have foreseen: the "youthful look" created for young royals at the turn of the eighteenth century is now being copied in parts of the globe that people at the Sun King's court rarely considered. And the original look of comfort is now just where Louis XIV and Colbert wanted it in the first place— fully under French control.

CHAPTER FOURTEEN

The Comfortable Body

PERHAPS THE BIGGEST difference in the way French men and women of the eighteenth century are depicted from their contemporaries in other European countries has to do with body language. The French of the age of comfort didn't invent all the attitudes in which they are portrayed, but they did create some of them—draping an arm over the back of a sofa, for instance. They reinvented postures such as relaxing into a chair that had not been seen since antiquity, and they first made informal poses—including reclining nonchalantly in a chair and stretching out on a chaise longue—typical.

Demeanor was able to change, on the one hand, because of the various inventions of the age of comfort—interior rooms in which life could be more informal, seat furniture that provided increased support for the body, clothing that allowed for a wider range of motion. On the other hand, demeanor changed because certain individuals—the same ones who first championed the sofa and cotton and bathrooms and who slept in the original modern beds—moved about in ways that caused their contemporaries to take note.

The age of magnificence was characterized by bodily rigidity: aristocrats spent an enormous amount of time upright and on their feet; virtually all their movements were regulated by ever more numerous and intricate rules. These codes of comportment dictated the correct way of performing actions ranging from entering a room to sitting down, from helping oneself to food to dancing. Absolute knowledge of these rules and the ability to carry them out to perfection were considered, furthermore, essential to being seen as an aristocrat. In such an atmosphere, the idea of moving spontaneously—lolling about on a piece of furniture, sitting on the grass—would have had an obvious appeal, particularly for those who had been educated in a less rigid manner—a royal mistress, for example, or the foreign bride of a French prince. Thus, when the notoriously high-spirited Duchesse de Bourgogne arrived at the French court and shocked that defender of tradition the Princesse Palatine with antics such as "bursting out in song in the middle of dinner and then dancing on her chair," the king's sister-in-law declared that "no one could have had a worse upbringing" and worried that the court as she knew it was coming to an end.

Etiquette naturally survived everything the young royals were able to dish out; to foreign visitors, Versailles remained the epitome of formality and ceremony. In a rearguard attempt to stop the spread of body language that both felt and looked comfortable, within decades the rules were rewritten to forbid the postures and the chair manners first seen at court in the late seventeenth century: Don't cross your legs at the knee. Don't drape your arms around the top of a chair. Don't lean back nonchalantly.

Something essential had changed, however. Just as by the early eighteenth century rooms were divided into public and private, so there were soon two kinds of body language. For public ceremonies, the rulers of Versailles continued to observe the strict rules of deportment, and even the Duchesse de Bourgogne managed to be "serious, stately, and respectful." Meanwhile, in their interior suites, the air of grave dignity that had formerly been the only way of life often fell away; more and more, people learned to relax. "In private," the Duchesse de Bourgogne could be found "sometimes perched on the arm of the king's chair," at others, "flitting and fluttering all around it," acting, in other words, as if the Sun King's armchair were just another comfortable chair, rather than a substitute for his throne.

The comfortable body, like comfortable fabrics and comfortable dress, did not remain confined to those private rooms and back corridors for long. First, casual behavior was observed at formal occasions. In 1705, for instance, the Princesse des Ursins was sashaying into balls carrying her King Charles spaniel (the breed had become fashionable because of England's King Charles) "under her arm just as if she were in her own home; no one could believe such informality, which even the Duchesse de Bourgogne wouldn't have tried to pull off—much less the sight of the king petting the little dog." Then, in the heady years before and during the stock market boom, the new body language spread to the modern city Paris was becoming—even to public spaces such as the Tuileries Gardens, where anyone and everyone could see what was going on.

The ways of sitting and lounging that then developed were recorded for posterity virtually on the spot: French artists were so taken with the easy flow and curving lines of the new attitudes that they began engraving and painting scenes showing real people—rather than mythological or allegorical figures—in contemporary settings, wearing fashions of the moment, using newly invented furniture, carrying and deporting themselves in ways unthinkable in previous decades. Artists depicted the manner in which new pieces of furniture facilitated daily life, as well as ways of wearing the new informal dress. This painting, now referred to as genre painting, might well be known as the painting of modern life or the painting of private life, since it recorded all the inventions of modern architecture and modern design. These wildly new depictions of the human body were displayed in the most public venues then available and thus proved to all and sundry that, in France, the body, too, was being modernized.

The initial signs of the brave new world of deportment date from the early 1670s. They indicate that, virtually at the same moment, informal body language began to be displayed both in private and in public.

The first clue to the revolution brewing inside the palace comes from a series of images of the Marquise de Montespan reclining (see page 25). In them, the woman responsible for many of the ideas key to the age of comfort provides the original demonstration of the chair behavior that would continue to shock and intrigue her fellow countrymen and foreign observers alike for decades. A vocabulary quickly developed to designate the startling ways in which people began using the new seat furniture. (At first, it usually signified intense disapproval.) Thus, one no longer merely "sat" in a chair—instead, the minute large comfort armchairs appeared on the scene, people began to revel in the possibilities they offered. They "rocked back" in them; they "leaned back to a half-inclined position"; they "crossed their legs" (meaning crossed them at the knee); they even dared to "stretch their legs out on the seat of another chair" or "drape them over the arm of the chair" in which they were sitting—all of which were pronounced, by the first person to record them for posterity, "indecent postures."

Things only went from bad to worse as seat furniture became more expansive. A pose such as Montespan's was characterized as "to stretch out full length" or even "lying down," as in lying down in bed. Both these expressions, by the way, were first used to describe the daybed and sofa behavior of those royal relaxers par excellence, Monseigneur and the Duchesse de Bourgogne. The Princesse Palatine left a memorable portrait of the dauphin's sofa manners that makes it clear that he played a key role in its invention because he was truly to the sofa born: "He was capable of spending an entire day lying down [couché] on a sofa or in a big armchair . . . without saying a word."

The numerous engravings and paintings that soon began to feature seat furniture prove that the crown prince's tendencies were not the aberration his hidebound aunt imagined them to be: people were almost never depicted simply sitting on a sofa. Look at *Noblewoman on a Sofa* (see page 114): with one arm draped across its back and one leg propped up on it, she is the height of nonchalance. And this previously unheard-of pose became one of the basic ways of using the new easy seats: witness this mid-eighteenth-century engraving (see below). Unlike her precursor of the 1680s, defiantly proud of her startling

*Here is a depiction of the casual behavior that comfortable seating had
immediately encouraged and that, by the mid–eighteenth century,
individuals such as the young woman shown here were able to take for
granted. She seems oblivious to the fact that the mule has
slipped off the foot so nonchalantly extended in front of her.*

new demeanor, her French-dress-attired heir can take such behavior for granted. She's so fully absorbed in her letter that she seems not to notice that she's not only stretched her leg out, but let her mule slip from her foot.

There was good reason for her naturalness. By then, as numerous sofa images attest, the French were taking advantage of the new "reading rooms" created by architects such as Blondel and of new seat furniture and had begun a practice we now call curling up with a good book. The original modern readers are always portrayed just as is the woman shown here: leaning with their back against a well-cushioned surface and a leg or legs stretched out in front of them, holding a book or letter open on their lap. These are the earliest depictions of a new type of reading, reading not as a scholarly or an educational activity, but as a purely recreational pursuit, a way to spend one's leisure time, an activity as casual as the sofa itself. This concept's novelty was confirmed in 1779 by the original history of private life: "A century ago, no one would have thought of reading as a form of entertainment."

As the eighteenth century unfolded, artists depicted a full range of new sofa behavior that put the comfortable body on display. The three canvases by de Troy that illustrate this book (see color plates) show off bearing inconceivable elsewhere in Europe, particularly for women: leaning far forward—smoothly, effortlessly, seductively (*The Garter*); reclining indolently, supported by a variety of padded surfaces rather than rigid stays (*The Declaration of Love*); lounging around in and on low armchairs—an arm across the back, leaning over a chair, leaning forward on an arm, stretching out almost to a recumbent pose, deeply sunk into the arms of comfort (*Reading in a Salon*).

The new seat furniture encouraged another position then still rare for men— and unheard of for women: crossing one's legs. This late-seventeenth-century scene (page 224) is set inside the Parisian shop of Jean Magoulet, embroiderer to the queen. Two merchants are displaying an embroidered jacket and several embroidery designs for the inspection of a wealthy couple. Thanks to its large-pane windows, the shop is spacious, airy, and light. And to put his customers further at ease, Magoulet has furnished it with lots of big comfort armchairs. His strategy has worked: the lady feels so much at home that she has relaxed into her chair and crossed her legs. This is perhaps the earliest depiction of a woman adopting this posture in a public place, and the pose was surely familiar to Magoulet's well-heeled clientele, for he used this image in the most public way possible. Such engravings were known as *enseignes*, shop signs, because they copied the image on the sign outside the shop. They were printed on very large sheets of paper and used to wrap the customer's purchases. Like today's Tiffany blue box or shopping bags with a store's logo, they thus advertised the

JEAN MAGOULET Brodeur
Demeurant Rue S.tBenoist alhôtel
Germain des prez   fait et
en Or Argent et Soye tant pour
meubles et Esquipages
ordinaire de feüe La Reine
de Bruxelle port de labaye S.t
vend toutes sortes de Broderies
Hommes et Femmes que pour
des plus a la mode.

This scene shows a woman adopting a posture virtually unheard of in the late seventeenth century: she has crossed her legs casually at the knee, and she has done so in a public place. (She is seated in an embroiderer's shop, looking over samples of his work.) The newly fashionable large armchairs must have encouraged her to relax into them; her comfortable pose was made possible by the casual cut of her dress, which didn't restrict her movements.

shop to anyone who saw the package being carried about and reminded the buyer of its address.

All this, however, was nothing next to what was going on right in the open in the parks and on the lawns of Paris, in the woods and all over the great outdoors of France. Indeed, of all the new behavior associated with the age of comfort, none is more startling than the desire to act as if every expanse of grass were one big sofa all ready for public lounging. Some of the original evidence of this behavior, too, comes from those portraits of Montespan in the early 1670s. Several show her in her daybed pose—stretched out, however, not on a piece of furniture, but on the well-manicured lawn of a lovely garden or park. And French artists were not simply creating a contemporary equivalent of Renaissance allegorical canvases. They were inspired by actual behavior.

In 1671, the Marquise de Sévigné was doing just as Montespan did, only in real time and in the real world. In March, she was visiting a close friend in Livry in the countryside near Paris; while out for a stroll, she was overcome by the sudden urge to write a letter. The letter survived, so we know that rather than do the expected for a lady of her station, known for her beautiful clothes and equally beautiful ways—go inside, sit at a desk, and put pen to paper—the marquise just plumped right down on the grass and started to write to her beloved daughter: "seated on the same *siège de mousse* [mossy seat] where I sometimes watched you completely stretched out."

That mossy seat is the first recorded instance of the desire for more expansive seating that was about to fuel the creation of all modern forms of seat furniture. It is also the first recorded instance of a kind of behavior that suddenly became rampant at the turn of the eighteenth century: public lounging. All through the age of comfort, French men and women in droves—or so letters, memoirs, and the visual record tell us—began to follow Sévigné's example and find comfort all over the great outdoors. I have no idea exactly what a *siège de mousse* looked like or how it was made. I do know that in no time at all, outdoor seat furniture proliferated: there were turf or lawn benches (*bancs de gazon*) and even moss beds (*lits de mousse*) and turf or lawn beds (*lits de gazon*). Individuals sometimes sat on this "furniture" in the manner of those ladies in casual dress perched on the terraced steps of Versailles's Theater of Water (see page 193). More often, however, they used it exactly as they did its indoor equivalent, or as people "sit" on the grass today: they stretched out leaning on an arm, reclined back supported on both arms, or lay prone with their hands under their head.

The signs of this behavior are everywhere evident. In novels, if a heroine was "a bit tired," without further ado, she simply took a nap on a "mossy bed," even if she was clad in her finest "negligent undress," even if she found herself in the middle of Paris's Tuileries. Heroes of novels were more likely to seek out a mossy bed or a turf bench for a seduction scene. And in real life, people were acting the same way. Thus, the Duc de Croÿ recounts the day in 1752 when he ran into an acquaintance in the Tuileries: they started talking, and de Croÿ immediately "sat down on the grass with him."

The person who did more than anyone else to preserve for posterity this new body language in all its variations was Pierre Crozat's favorite artist, who lived and painted under Crozat's luxurious roof for years, Antoine Watteau. Early in his career (c. 1709), Watteau worked in the genre that first commemorated sofa-related body language, the fashion plate. Immediately after this (c. 1710), his drawings began to feature women sitting on the grass and wearing each successive style of informal dress from the *robe de chambre* to the *manteau* to the *robe volante*. And soon after that (c. 1712), Watteau's paintings began to highlight women similarly dressed and in similar poses. The first of many such scenes was probably *The Perspective* (now in Boston's Museum of Fine Arts), where the grass depicted was actually the lawn of Crozat's country home, the Château de Montmorency. Only one of the ladies is standing; all the others are lounging on the lawn as though this were the most natural idea in the world, with no thought to the effects of grass stains on all those yards of gorgeous silk. (Was it possible that the law-abiding Crozat didn't allow his guests to wear cotton—or his in-house painter to depict it?)

The notion that reclining on the lawn was just average behavior is even more flagrant in Watteau's *The Champs-Élysées* (c. 1717). The scene, set in a wooded area bordering the gardens of the Hôtel d'Evreux, then under construction, features in the foreground four ladies in fabulous dressing gowns in the open-front style worn by the ladies at Versailles in 1714. In the background, we can glimpse lots of others, all enjoying the grassy expanse in the same way. From his windows and while strolling in his garden, the count may well have looked out above all upon a veritable legion of fashionable ladies showing every passerby that the age of comfort had not only created a body language without precedent, but had succeeded in making it seem the most basic instinct in the world.

All through the following decades, French painters continued to promote just that vision: people got dressed to the nines in gorgeous outfits—only to treat any expanse of grass as though it were the best-padded sofa in the world. Even de Troy, who normally preferred to feature real couches and chairs, in the same exhibit with *The Declaration of Love* and *The Garter* showed a canvas in whose foreground lay a figure "asleep on a turf bed." In 1737, Carle van Loo received a royal commission for a painting to be hung in the dining room of Louis XV's small suite in the château at Fontainbleau and chose a subject appropriate for a royal hunting fanatic: a hunting party taking a lunch break. The women are wearing particularly fetching riding habits with short coats cinched tightly at the waist and adorable little bow ties. Their billowing skirts in glowing silks are spread all around them, for the entire hunting party is sitting on the ground, ready to dig into picnic baskets brimming with hams, game pies, and roast rabbits.

In the 1730s and 1740s, first Nicolas Lancret and then Boucher expanded the vision of the kind of casual behavior possible on a Sunday in the park. Lancret created a series of canvases, one of which is now in Washington's National Gallery of Art, in which famous ballerinas give impromptu performances. Their audience is lying all over the ground, while the ballerinas, clad in the short skirts and hoops that were actively influencing contemporary fashion, twirl for their entertainment. As for Boucher, well, he added bare feet to the mix and thereby intensified the focus on the leg as the new erogenous zone. The many scenes he called pastorals because they allegedly represent shepherds and shepherdesses (many of whose outfits are actually quite similar to French dresses) depict couples on the grass and barefoot in the park.

It was also Boucher who gave sofa behavior in the park its finest moment. We know that the Marquise de Pompadour was a proponent of all seat furniture, both indoor and out. At her Château Bellevue, she personally drew up the plans with her landscape architects, Lassurance and Garnier d'Isle, for the only turf sofa whose construction can be documented: "They prepared for her a kind of rustic throne, made up of gravel and turf." In 1758, Boucher painted her portrait on that "rustic throne": her pose is virtually identical to the one she adopted when half reclining on a daybed. This time, however, she is propped up on a flower-strewn, mossy, natural surface, one very similar to the terrain on which her self-avowed model Montespan was portrayed. This time, she props her arm not on a plump cushion, but on a pile of exceedingly well-thumbed books. Boucher has made the marquise once again a poster child for her age. The world was one giant sofa, always ready with a well-cushioned surface on which to curl up with a good book.

Also in the mid–eighteenth century, Comte Dufort de Cheverny commented that contemporary French painters (he mentioned Boucher in particular) were redefining the concept of "ideal beauty." That redefinition may in fact be the ultimate result of the new body language. Under the influence of sofa behavior, artists had shifted their attention from timeless, idealized bodies to a radically different and radically contemporary depiction of the body. With, for example, La Toilette (A Lady at Her Toilet, c. 1716), Watteau seems to have invented the modern nude. It's as if the depiction of the female body had suddenly been shifted from the allegorical mode that makes today's viewer wonder if women ever really looked like that to a casually intimate vision of a body that still seems very familiar indeed.

The scene is remarkable above all for its ordinary, everyday quality. We're in one of the new, interior rooms, and the woman is positioned on a chaise longue. She's nude, but not in a Manet-like, overtly provocative pose. In the manner of Degas's depictions of women in slightly awkward positions as they dry themselves after a bath, the woman is leaning sideways, her arms stretched over her head in order to slip into a chemise. A maid is visible in the background, but she's not helping. The woman is smiling quietly, and her body forms one big, loose arc: she seems to be reveling in the new freedom of dressing herself.

Her body represents indeed a new kind of ideal beauty, the appeal of a body informally rather than rigidly positioned, of a woman free to be seen in an awkward stance (getting a garment over one's head is never the most graceful process) because she was in a setting both private and cozy, of a body clearly at ease and relaxed. With his depiction of a comfortable nude body, Watteau paved the way for all the scenes of sofa behavior to come, such as de Troy's *Declaration of Love* with which this study began: he indicated why the French were using furniture as no one else in Europe did.

Master chair maker Roubo argued that "sitting bolt upright," as the English did, was "much too tiring a posture." As Roubo saw it, the eighteenth-century French were neither strained nor ill at ease because their furniture allowed them to avoid proper English bearing. Watteau further suggested that the impetus for comfort came from the bodies on the furniture. In the new rooms, surrounded by the beginnings of the world of modern convenience, people had begun to feel newly comfortable in their bodies. All the creations of the age of comfort—from new kinds of furniture to new styles of dress—were shaped to suit this comfortable body.

L'Art de Vivre

IN 1743, SHORTLY before Arthur Devis painted his portrait of Mr. and Mrs. Bull, Sir Horace Mann wrote Horace Walpole to bemoan the situation evident in the Bulls' very stiff and proper English drawing room (see color plates): "Surely no people understand the art of living so little as we do." The two correspondents would undoubtedly have agreed with a sentiment that their fellow countrymen had begun to express in the 1730s, as soon as the signature accomplishments of the age of comfort—from interior architecture to interior decoration to well-padded seats—had gained prominence: the only way to make up for English insufficiency was to "imitate the French," since they have "given the *ton* [the tone, or style] to all Europe." In 1790, Arthur Young provided a succinct formulation of the attitude shared by all those with firsthand experience of the way of life practiced in Paris: "In the art of living, the French have generally been esteemed by the rest of Europe, to have made the greatest proficiency."

"The art of living," the phrase used by many in the eighteenth century to sum up all they saw as lacking in their own countries and yet so gloriously present in France, is no longer much in use. At that time, however, everyone knew what was meant by the French expression *l'art de vivre*, first widely used in the early eighteenth century. It referred most obviously to such characteristic inventions of the age of comfort as interior decoration and new types of furniture, as well as to two areas in which the French had set the pace since the 1670s: food and clothing. Those "proficient" in the art of living followed the French way in food and dress, in furnishing and decorating a home.

The expression conveyed, however, a sense of less tangible contributions as well. For instance, in his comment on the French, Young went on to say that "their manners have been accordingly more imitated, and their customs more adopted than those of any other nation." By the age of comfort's end, it was therefore a commonly accepted belief that furniture and décor profoundly modified the way people behaved and that with their new furniture designs and the original interior decoration, French architects and craftsmen had changed "manners" and even "customs"—standard behavior or habitual ways of doing things—not only in France, but in all the nations where a French look had been adopted. The notion that private rooms and sofas and white ceilings and less formal dress had had a significant impact on the habits of people all over Europe was thus the second dimension of the art of living. French commentators, however, agreed that the concept was more complicated still.

In France, many things were changing at the moment when the home and its contents were being reimagined. Those were, most notably, the decades when the Enlightenment was taking shape as a radically new philosophical and political movement. They witnessed the publication of the first works to champion Enlightenment causes. The networks and strategies essential to the spread of Enlightenment ideals were then developed, the groundwork was laid, and work was begun on the quintessential monument to the goals and the philosophy of the movement: the seventeen huge folio volumes of text plus eleven volumes of plates that constitute Diderot and d'Alembert's *Encyclopédie* (1751–1772). (A supplement later added four volumes of text and one more of plates.)

The *Encyclopédie* was intertwined with the invention of comfort in complex ways. The two projects, to begin with, shared many contributors. Most notable, perhaps, is the example of Jacques-François Blondel, the architect who in his collections of floor plans and his treatises recorded for posterity the accomplishments of modern French architecture. Blondel was responsible for entries related to architecture and interior decoration for the *Encyclopédie*, thus guaranteeing that modern French architecture and design would be promoted to the *Encyclopédie*'s international audience as the enlightened vision for the modern home.

Other collaborations, while less official, were no less significant. One of the staunchest advocates of comfort's every invention, for instance, the Marquise de Pompadour, was an equally staunch defender of the *Encyclopédie*; she worked tirelessly to convince Louis XV to allow its publication to resume after its opponents had succeeded in having it shut down. In perhaps her two most famous portraits—by Boucher in 1756 (see color plates) and a monumental pastel by Quentin de La Tour (1755)—the marquise chose (and the verb is no accident, for the sitter carefully choreographed every aspect of these poses) to be represented with a massive folio volume of the *Encyclopédie*; in the Boucher portrait, this is the large tome under the writing table conspicuously bound with the marquise's coat of arms; in the de La Tour portrait, its title can be deciphered on the spine. Both portraits were exhibited to the public at the Louvre and served therefore as very visible reminders of her allegiance to the enterprise at one of the moments when it was under heaviest fire from its critics. The marquise may not have dared to wear cotton in her portraits, but she did not hesitate to use them to give a public endorsement to a philosophically progressive publication.

In addition, the *Encyclopédie* was by its very nature on the same wavelength as the creators of comfort. Its subtitle, *Dictionnaire raisonné des sciences, des arts et des métiers* (*A Rational* [or *Synthetic*] *Dictionary of Sciences, Arts and Crafts*), says it all: the enterprise conceived by Diderot and d'Alembert put the craftsmen and artisans without whom neither furniture nor bathrooms nor many other things could have entered the modern age on an equal footing with scientists and artists. The *Encyclopédie* devoted equal coverage to the progress made by contemporary French craftsmen and to the accomplishments of contemporary scientists and artists. Indeed, given the step-by-step approach with which it uses a combination of text and plates to explain crafts as diverse as ribbon making and furniture making—the illustration of an upholsterer's shop (page 123) is one such plate—it could even be argued that the *Encyclopédie* devoted its most prominent coverage to the progress made in diverse fields by contemporary French craftsmen.

Progress, of course, was an Enlightenment buzzword: the clearest sign of hope for future generations was offered by the improvements in various domains that the encyclopedists saw all around them and duly charted for their readers. This meant that every accomplishment seen as essential to the art of living—from new forms of seating to running water—was also seen as contributing to the spread of enlightenment. This becomes clear in the early history of a word that entered modern languages—first French and then English—during the years when the *Encyclopédie* was being published: civilization.

As it gradually won recognition in French, the concept went through three stages. It originally referred to the process of making individuals civil—that is, able to live well in society, sociable. It then came to signify the process as a result of which a society was able to progress to a higher state of material, social, and cultural development. Finally, by the time the *Encyclopédie*'s final volume had appeared, the word was also used to designate what we call *a* civilization—that is, a society characterized by its degree of material, social, and cultural advancement.

It's surely no accident that the modern concepts of civilization and a civilization developed in tandem with the *Encyclopédie*. The notion of progress was crucial for both of them; the notion that simultaneous artistic and material progress led to social development was equally crucial for both. In the second half of the eighteenth century, thinkers all over Europe took for granted the idea that progress in the conditions for everyday life (increased convenience, increased comfort) was an essential proof of a society's degree of civilization.

And thus it was that all the inventions characteristic of the age of comfort—from its showpieces such as "distribution" or interior, modern architecture to less obvious candidates such as large-paned windows—were presented without question as evidence of eighteenth-century France's superior degree of civilization. Not everyone used the emerging word civilization; some spoke instead, as Mann did, of the "art of living"; others said *mœurs*, mores or customs and usages. All agreed, however, that along with contemporary discoveries in science and medicine and the prominence of contemporary French art and literature, factors such as better lighting in their homes and more kinds of comfortable and convenient furniture had played a role in making France both the worthy heir of ancient Greece and the country that was civilizing Europe.

The expressions *art de vivre* and art of living, as those who used them in the eighteenth century were well aware, referred to the Latin *ars vitae* or *ars vivendi*, which in turn translated a concept from Greek Stoic philosophy. The ancient art of living, as those in the eighteenth century also well knew, was a philosophical stance, an internal mental state according to which individuals could use rational thinking (as opposed to religious faith) to transform their way of life. The new *art de vivre* updated this concept. Those who used it made no apology for including the decorative arts and crafts in the concept's orbit; they argued that it was only in a comfortable environment that individuals were truly capable of rational thinking. The simultaneous spread of Enlightenment values and the values of comfort was seen as confirmation of this view.

In the *Encyclopédie*, Voltaire argued that "every country has a national character" and that "the essence of the French today" was to be "the most civilized nation" in Europe, "a model for all neighboring countries." This was the case because "the effortless casualness of French ways is beloved by all Europeans." (Voltaire, of course, was something of an expert in such matters: when Françoise de Graffigny was a houseguest of Voltaire and Emilie du Châtelet in December 1738, in her letters describing the experience she gave equal praise to their efforts at making Newton better known in the French-speaking world and to the architecture and interior decoration of their château Cirey—its adorable bathing suite and its charming "little nest" of a niche bedroom.)

It's ironic that Voltaire expressed these views in an article entitled "The

French," because the belief in French civilization was not at all a form of nationalistic propaganda. The belief was in fact shared by individuals all over Europe, members of the first generation to feel that they were citizens of Europe or citizens of the world and not merely of a particular nation-state, the first generation able to describe themselves with a word just coming into general use, as "cosmopolitans." Indeed, the belief in France's civilizing role as the new Greece seems to have played a key role in the creation of that European consciousness, a role it continued to play for well over a century: witness Nietzsche writing to August Strindberg in December 1888, "There is no other culture than the French . . . it is, by necessity, the right one."

Those who followed in Voltaire's footsteps made even bigger claims; they were also far more specific about the role in the civilizing process played by the creature comforts that as the eighteenth century went on were increasingly no longer reserved for the most affluent segment of society, but were transforming daily life for an ever broader part of the French population. Thus, Louis-Antoine, Marquis de Caraccioli, the Neapolitan ambassador to Versailles, claimed in his aptly titled *Voyage de la raison en Europe* (*The Travels of Reason Throughout Europe*) that "progress in the arts and sciences" all over the continent had created a new kind of European, "citizens of the world." This meant most obviously a higher degree of societal development: "All the nations of Europe are now much more civilized." Caraccioli then explained how this had come about. He pointed out in particular that in the civilizing process, "the smallest things have their significance": "those who dressed in French fashions began imperceptibly to copy their language and their manners." To be more civilized, or so this very cosmopolitan Italian was among the first to claim in print, was thus to live in a French manner.

Four years later, in the equally appropriately named *Essay on Progress in the Arts and Human Reason During the Reign of Louis XV*, Gudin de La Brenellerie explained that during Louis XV's monarchy, "human reason had reached a state of perfection" at the same time as, "with an astonishing rapidity," "comfort had replaced magnificence." The layout of homes ("distribution," of course), interior decoration, lighting, heating—all had been brought "to such a point of perfection that it seems impossible that the degree of comfort that we enjoy today can ever be surpassed." He laid particular stress on what he called "the mechanical arts" and said, for example, that it took "as much genius to invent a machine to pump water as to imagine the concept for a new tragedy." This simultaneous "progress" in matters intellectual and in the art of comfort meant in turn that the French had created a veritable "science of manners" in which "their mastery is recognized all over Europe." "The Swiss, the Italians, even the English admit that the elegance of French manners is gaining ground every day." Also in 1776, Caraccioli argued in similar fashion that as a result of having acquired "comfortable and convenient" French beds and tables, "Europe had become French."

The following year, Caraccioli concluded his triptych with *Paris, the Model for Foreign Nations*, in which he argued more plainly than ever before that by transforming the way in which people lived their daily lives, the age of comfort at the same time had helped transform the way Europeans thought. Prior to 1700, "Europeans valued only magnificence and never comfort," whereas now, all because of the inventions and the new way of life emanating from Paris, "the compass of the world," the old ways of behaving—"Italian grandiloquence, German protocol, Spanish arrogance"—had all fallen by the wayside. Now, thanks to "the most comfortable country in the world," there was a universal European style: "Europeans have learned to relax." "People thought they were merely adopting a new style of dress, but their customs and usages were completely transformed along with their clothing."

In the decade that followed, Europeans heard variations on this argument from all sides. The author of the original history of private life, Le Grand d'Aussy, for example, explained to his readers that "the manner of thinking characteristic of the French" had been shaped by factors such as architecture, furniture, and dress. "The French way of life" was now universally recognized to be superior to all others; as a result, "enlightened" Europeans were adopting all the "interior arts" developed in France and were embracing "the comfortable life" that these arts produced in the hope of becoming more like the French. In 1784, Antoine de Rivarol suggested that French had become Europe's new lingua franca because of the powerful attraction of the French art of living: "France is currently wielding the kind of dominion that no country has ever enjoyed." The combined influence of "the products of the mind and the products of craftsmen" had put Europe under French domination.

There you have it, the union of philosophy and furniture, of Enlightenment and comfort, the belief that as part of the same civilizing process, Europe had become both more rational and more casual. France had produced the first modern civilization, the first civilization ever to be referred to by that newly coined word, because the French had taught their fellow Europeans simultaneously how to enlighten their minds and how to make their bodies more comfortable.

The years during which this vision, according to which the French *art de vivre* possessed civilizing powers, was put into place were good ones for the Enlightenment. Supporters of the American Revolution such as Beaumarchais's close collaborator Gudin de La Brenellerie, for example, saw the moment around 1776 as a triumph for its values. (This timing explains why, in all the discussions of comfort's civilizing effects on Europe, England is presented as the only country in any way reluctant to champion French ways.) And in 1784, the moment when the new vision was most loudly trumpeted, no one could have guessed that just around the corner loomed the events that would ultimately prove most problematic for the image of the Enlightenment as a civilizing force, as well as for that of the beneficial effects of a comfortable, relaxed art of living. The years during and immediately after the French Revolution witnessed the massive destruction and deterioration of the fabric, the stuff—from buildings to furniture to water piping—crafted and put into place by the age of comfort. In the Revolution's aftermath, comfort knew another of the moments of backsliding that characterize its checkered history.

In some areas, activity picked up again fairly quickly. Artisans responsible for interior decoration and furniture design, for example, were soon back at work. Specialists agree that the new models they produced were never again as comfortable—they were overstuffed and failed to provide proper support—and that décor quickly became oppressively fussy; but the fields did at least survive. In one area, at least, soon after the Revolution it may even have seemed that pre-Revolutionary conditions would be improved on: in the 1790s, a new fireplace design, the work of an Anglo-American, Benjamin Thompson, Count Rumford, advertised as the long-awaited cure for smoking hearths, came into far more widespread use than previous models. (Historians argue that Rumford fireplaces did not put an end to the problem of smoke and that their design was infinitely inferior to Gauger's model.)

In most realms in which comfort had reigned, however, any return to what could have passed for the old ways was short-lived. In Paris in the early nineteenth century, for example, there were a few grand bathrooms. (They are not well documented, so we can't be sure that they were in fact equipped with running water.) By the 1830s, however, any trace of indoor plumbing was gone. From then on, those living in the greatest homes in Paris were surrounded by a much lower level of comfort and convenience than their predecessors a century before. The English soon became the leaders in the realm of comfort. As the century progressed, they reinvented the wheel and patented new, merely functional versions of devices that had already been in use in eighteenth-century Paris in far more sophisticated incarnations. The new fixtures were hygienic and a vast improvement on what they replaced, but personal hygiene was no longer a pleasure. The age of comfort, however, was not just an aberration. Three centuries later, its standards and its definitions of comfort have once again come to the surface.

Is it possible that sofas and writing desks actually helped pass on a message of philosophical enlightenment? Could relaxed posture and well-cushioned chairs have played a role in the spread of civilization? Was casual high fashion really in the service of the Enlightenment? I can say only that Europeans of the final pre-Revolutionary decades seemed to find such reasoning perfectly plausible. In his memoirs, Comte Dufort de Cheverny described the quintessential Enlightenment reformer, Pablo de Olavide y Jáuregui, arriving in Paris about 1760 with the goal of "dragging Spain out of the darkness in which it was stagnating." He naturally bought vast quantities of books to bring home, but he also "stripped Paris bare of all its most beautiful furniture" and had it shipped to Madrid. The same reasoning could help explain all those niche bedrooms Jefferson added at Monticello upon his return from France in 1789, as well as the four *bergères* and two *lits de repos* (plus forty-four chairs of various kinds, most with the rounded *cabriolet* back) that he brought all the way from Paris to these shores. In his mind, they may well have represented more than simple decorating choices. He could have seen in them both the intellectual values and the *art de vivre* that had so attracted him to eighteenth-century Paris, potent if humble reminders of the city that had witnessed the invention of a new way of life.

ACKNOWLEDGMENTS

A great many people—historians, curators, archivists, independent scholars—shared with me data, images, opinions, and references. Without their generosity, the foundation on which all scholarly communities are built, I could never have completed this work.

Two architects were tremendous resources from the start. Alan Chimacoff answered questions great and small, gave me as much practical detail as I could handle, even worked wonders with Photoshop. Amy Gardner asked great questions and was willing to read early drafts.

Someone ignorant of the ways of the museum world quickly comes to dead ends. All doors, however, open before Michael Fried, and he graciously got some key ones to open for me. The late Philip Conisbee was a model of scholarly generosity. He always responded to requests for help, and he always sent me to just the right person. Colin Bailey saved the day at one crucial juncture, Keith Christiansen at another. Philippe Borde answered questions about portraiture. Christian Michel was a model of patience in the face of many requests for information. Nicolas Milovanovic showed me hidden corners of the Château de Versailles. Anne de Thoisy-Dallem introduced me to the Musée de la Toile in Jouy-en-Jonas. Pascale Gorguet Ballesteros opened the reserves of the Musée Galliéra to me. Bertrand Rondot gave me a wonderfully observant and beautifully prepared tour of the furniture collection of the Musée des Arts Décoratifs. Aurélie Samuel introduced me to the textile collections of the Musée Guimet. Véronique Belloir made possible one of the great experiences in my scholarly life with a visit to the reserves of the Musée des Arts Décoratifs. She showed me just the garments I needed to see and fine points I might have missed. I owe many of these contacts to someone who seems to know everyone in French museums and who has been unfailingly generous to me for years: Barbara Spadaccini-Day.

Several scholars answered questions about a subject I found particularly elusive, Indian textiles: Aditya Behl, Deborah Kraak, and Xavier Petitcol. I thank all of them for offering their opinions and helping identify textiles. Sandy Rosenbaum put me in touch with experts in the field.

I am enormously grateful to the Maison Pierre Frey-Braquenié and the Maison Georges Le Manach for allowing me to reproduce historic textiles in their collections. Sophie Rouart, archivist for Pierre Frey, graciously showed me their collection and gave information on the dating of items in it. She even helped out with a last-minute emergency. Anne Biosse Duplan of the Maison Georges Le Manach welcomed me there so that I could photograph items in their collection. And Alain Damlamian was the ideal photographer.

No library proved more valuable to my research than Paris's Arsenal—small wonder, since the library houses the collections of the individual who commissioned the original history of private life, the Marquis de Paulmy. Sabine Coron provided most generous assistance with their extensive collection of engravings. Everyone on the sixth floor of the University of Pennsylvania's Van Pelt Library helped out in countless ways, as they always do. Special thanks are due to Lynne Farrington and John Pollack for having scans made from works in the collections. Emmanuelle Toulet, *conservateur-en-chef* of the archives at the Château de Chantilly, greatly facilitated my research on Madame la Duchesse. Elizabeth Chew at Monticello graciously provided a photocopy of the Grévin packing list of Jefferson's possessions. And Phillippa Plock of Waddesdon Manor provided information on trade cards in their collection. Thanks are also due to Chloe Wigston-Smith for having spotted just the cards that would interest me.

Several colleagues answered questions, provided references, and talked me through gray areas. Daniel Roche was, as always, a phenomenal source of information. David Leatherbarrow was a spirited interlocutor on subjects ranging from the chair to the upholsterer. English Showalter helped me track down references in Françoise de Graffigny's correspondence. And Christian Jouhaud helped with everything from deciphering difficult eighteenth-century handwriting to interpreting difficult eighteenth-century documents.

Jean Nérée Ronfort is truly in a class by himself. No one knows more about French furniture, and no one could have been more generous in sharing knowledge of all kinds, from information on particular techniques to information on particular *ébénistes*. He also used his vast personal database to locate estate inventories for me.

Lance Donaldson-Evans and Jerry Singerman read drafts, gave feedback with a smile, and made great suggestions for changes. Anne Lutun and Arcana Albright provided expert research assistance. Kathy Belden's reading guided me through a final shifting and rethinking of the manuscript's parts. Alice Martell was once again the perfect reader: no one could be more careful; no one could pull off the difficult task of being simultaneously tough and encouraging more successfully than she does. I feel lucky to be able to work with her.

Mrs. Charles Wrightsman graciously allowed me to study works in her collection. The Marquise de Contades opened her home to me and took me on a tour of the private rooms of the Château de Montgeoffroy, among the very few places where the architecture, furniture, and interior decoration of the age of comfort have been preserved intact. As I stood for just a moment, alone in one of those interior hallways of which eighteenth-century architects made such ingenious use, I understood why I had felt compelled to devote years of my life to this project.

Finally—and in this case last means anything but least—no scholars could have been more generous with their time and expertise or more intelligent in their guidance than four curators from the Victoria and Albert Museum. Lesley Miller planned my visit there, gave me hands-on experience with eighteenth-century textiles, and continued to help with tricky examples for years. Antonia Brodie gave wonderfully thoughtful answers to my questions and spent an afternoon with me in the museum's reserves, teaching me how French and English furniture worked. Rosemary Crill communicated both her enthusiasm and her encyclopedic knowledge of Indian textiles with unfailing patience; she was always willing to help date elusive examples. Susan North answered questions, helped unravel dilemmas of the history of fashion, and was willing to read part of my manuscript. Theirs was scholarly generosity well beyond the call of duty.

Philadelphia, September 12, 2008

NOTES

Introduction: The Age of Comfort

4   THE MARQUISE DE MAINTENON Noailles, 2:186.

5   A PRIVATE KITCHEN WAS ADDED Antoine, 528. Salmon documents the changes Louis XV and Pompadour made to Versailles, 70–71, for example.

5   HE HAD AN AVIARY Luynes, 10:439.

5   A NEWSPAPER ARTICLE *Mercure de France*, July 1755, 11.

7   JEFFERSON Crowley, 142.

7   THE FRENCH NEWSPAPER *Le Mercure galant*, "extraordinaire," January 1678, 508.

7   FORTY YEARS LATER van Effen, *La Bagatelle*, July 11, 1718, 155; van Effen speaks of *"la commodité."*

7   A COURT INSIDER Dufort de Cheverny 1: 135–136.

7   PEOPLE ASK ARCHITECTS Briseux 1728, preface, n.p. Herrmann contests the attribution to Briseux of this anonymously published work; other scholars accept it.

8   "ART COMPLETELY UNKNOWN" Courtonne, 92. Speaking with particular reference to distribution and to "the art of the plan," Blondel used statements similar to Briseux's as a rallying cry for French architects and repeated them virtually verbatim in the prefaces to *Architecture française* and *Cours d'architecture* and in the article "architecture" for the *Encyclopédie*. On the invention of the modern notion of comfort by eighteenth-century French architects, see Thornton 1978, 10; Thornton 1984, 17; Rykwert 1980.

8   "THAT WHICH IS LESS GRAND" D'Aviler 1691, 2:375; 1:180.

9   "THE LEAST LIVABLE" Soulavie, 57–58; see also Blondel 1752, 4:123.

9   DESIGNED FOR CONVENIENCE Such furniture is now often called *meubles de commodité*. See Verlet, 175–205.

10   COMFORT ARMCHAIRS *Inventaire* for 1672, 2:271, 483; 2:298, 678, and so forth.

11   THE FIRST GREAT THEORETICIAN Roubo, 2:607–608, 638. On the invention of comfortable seating in eighteenth-century France, see Giedion, 7.

11   "POSTURE FOR THE LOWER BACK" Roubo, 2:18–19,615. Andry de Boisregard 1:70–72; on him, see Rykwert 1982, 23–24.

12 "AFFAIR OF THE STOOLS" Saint-Simon, 2:904–905.

12 "THE RIGHT TO SIT DOWN" Sévigné, January 12, 1689, 3:471.

12 "LOOKS AT ALL LIKE A COURT" August 2, 1705, Palatine 1981, 361.

12 "COMFORTABLE WELL-BEING" Caraccioli, 287.

12 "THE ENGLISH ICON STYLE" Roy Strong coined the phrase to describe English Renaissance portraiture.

14 "MULTI-COLORED" *Inventaire*, 2:104:22.

14 "READY FOR BED" Palatine 1857 (1:218); 1981 (622).

15 IN 1751 Graffigny, 11:383; Showalter, 253–254.

16 THAT PHRASE ACQUIRED Crébillon 1736, 44.

17 THE BEGINNING OF THE END Dennis, 1–2.

17 A WORD NOT YET AVAILABLE article "personnalité," *Supplément à l'Encyclopédie*, 4:303. On *déshabillé*, Féraud.

18 THE PAINTING KNOWN AS The title is not de Troy's but comes from an article in the *Mercure de France*, September 1725, where it was called "*une déclaration d'amour*," 2:225.

19 RICHARD BULL'S POSE D'Oench, 53–54. On de Troy, Léribault, 58–62. Chippendale's 1754 phrase was probably borrowed from Blondel's 1737 *Traité d'architecture dans le goût moderne*.

20 *TOMBER AMOUREUX* Marivaux, July 16, 1723; Guyot Desfontaines, 95. The expression appeared sporadically in English before 1723 but first became commonly accepted in the 1720s after it had entered the French language.

20 *COUP DE FOUDRE* Crébillon 1751, 184; Crébillon 1763, 3:376–377; Académie Française dictionary 1798.

Chapter One: A Short History of Modern Comfort

23 "LOVED TO BUILD" Saint-Simon, 3:361.

23 THE KING INSISTED Saint-Simon, 3:361; Sévigné 1:157. The Trianon, which was destroyed in 1686, was located about a half hour from the main château. In 1670, that construction project was but a gleam in the monarch's eye.

24 AN "ENCHANTED," "MAGICAL" PALACE Sévigné, June 14, 1675, 1:734; July 3, 1675, 1:749; August 7, 1675, 2:38.

24 ARCHITECTS SOON PRONOUNCED D'Aviler 1691, 2:331; Blondel 1774, 2:31–32; Blondel 1771, 3:87–88; Le Camus de Mézières, 108. Clagny was demolished in 1769; it stood on the site of today's Versailles train station.

24 THE GUEST LIST Saint-Simon, 1:302.

24 SO TAKEN WITH Historians contend that Clagny was at the origin of Louis XIV's decision to transform his father's modest hunting lodge into the Château de Versailles. Hautecœur, 2:537.

26 A SECOND MARRIAGE The marriage was truly secret; no one has ever found any document proving that it took place. On the other hand, no one, beginning with those at court in the 1680s, has ever seriously doubted that it occurred. The marriage would have been morganatic. Since Maintenon was hardly of royal birth—even the rank of marquise was bestowed on her by the king—she was obliged to renounce any inheritance.

26 THEIR MOTHER MIGHT REGAIN Saint-Simon, 2:968–977.

27 THE FIRST PIECE OF FURNITURE *Inventaire*, 2:540:1143; see also 2:539:1061.

27 TO GET AWAY FROM IT ALL Sévigné, 3:873.

27 IN 1686 ALONE Deville, 2:362:1193.

27 THE KING'S SISTER-IN-LAW Palatine 1857, 1:262.

27 "BRING ME NEW SKETCHES" The letter was signed "Louis, Fontainbleau, 10 September 1699." Watson 1956, 1:xxvi.

27 LOTS OF COMFORTABLE SEATING *Inventaire*, 2:459:2003.

27 "EVEN THOUGH HE STOOD" Saint-Simon said that because of this he was "a prince who defied characterization," 4:97.

28 A SEVEN-FOOT-LONG *Inventaire*, 2:356:1174. Among other exceptional models made for the dauphin, see especially 2:404:1486, the first true sofa at Versailles.

28 A COFFER DESIGNED Ronfort, 49.

28 THE FINEST DESIGNERS See Dangeau's report on his radical remake of his apartment in the first château at Meudon, 7:10–11. On Bérain's importance, Kimball, 59 ff.

28 DESCRIBED HER Sévigné, March 1680, 2:881, 886; April 1680, 2:889, 901–902; July 1689, 3:456.

28 COMMISSIONED A PORTRAIT Bordes suggests that the dauphin and Mignard collaborated on this unusual vision of family life at Versailles; someone made the decision to efface the bust of Louis XIV originally seen in the background, thereby removing the only hint of dynastic celebration (79–80). Mignard's payment for the painting was listed in the *Comptes des bâtiments* on January 13, 1688 (3:5). The painting probably hung in the formal bedchamber of the queen, occupied after the queen's death by the dauphine; it was in the inventory of its contents in 1695, by which time the room had passed on to the Duchesse de Bourgogne. The placement of an informal portrait in a ceremonial room was still another proof of the dauphine's commitment to remain "a real person."

29 CONTEMPORARY COMMENTATORS Saint-Simon, 4:403; 2:273–274; 1:341; 5:516.

29 IN THE 1690S Bullet 1691, 87; Bullet 1695, 12–15.

30 IN TIME, ALL ENDED WELL For a detailed history of the place, Ziskin, 5–14.

30 "CROZAT THE RICH" I found only one contemporary expression of scorn for the sudden, dramatic invasion of new money: in 1706, Germain Brice, describing Crozat's home on the Place Vendôme, commented laconically: "Bad taste reigns in certain circles," 1:187.

31 ONE HUNDRED THOUSAND LIVRES Sourches, January 20, 1707, 9:251.

31 "LITTLE BAR OF GOLD" Saint-Simon, 14:364.

31 TO LIVE WITH HER FATHER Saint-Simon, 2:891–892.

31 "HIS LAST REMAINING PLEASURE" Princesse des Ursins, December 11, 1706, 270.

31 EVERY LOAF IN SIGHT Palatine 1999, 412–413.

32 "ITS SOUL LEFT THE COURT" Saint-Simon, 4:408.

33 LANCRET Holmes, 58–60.

33 SAVVY ARCHITECTS On Bullet's activities, Langerskiöld, 21, and Pénicault, 70–71. On Mansart, Ziskin, 13. On Boffrand, Kimball, 130n.56; Neumann, 142; Brice 1713, 3:153.

33 THE ROYAL BRIDGE Piganiol de La Force, 8:311; Brice 1706, 4:146.

33 The Faubourg Saint-Germain developed in two distinct phases. The first phase, near the Saint-Germain-des-Prés church, was a seventeenth-century phenomenon. The second phase, which continued well into the eighteenth century, moved the city farther east, onto land never before developed.

34 THE BUILDING BOOM Hautecœur describes the increasingly frenzied land speculation in the Faubourg Saint-Germain, III:36–38, 47–48.

34   THE ARCHITECT ALEXANDRE LE BLOND D'Aviler 1710, 185*5–6, plate 63L.

35   THE MOST CELEBRATED ARTISTS OF THE DAY Some think that Watteau may have used Des-
     mares as a model in a number of his best-known paintings. Kalnein and Levey, 20.

35   HER PERSONAL FORTUNE Balleroy, March 30, 1721, 2:304–305.

36   FROM HER BOX AT THE OPERA Palatine 1999, 597–598. Marie's employer was Madame Bé-
     gon, widow of Louis XIV's *intendant de la marine*, or secretary of the navy.

36   SELL THE FAMILY PLATE *Correspondants de la marquise de Balleroy*, March 9, 1720, 2:132.

36   *NOUVEAUX RICHES* Montesquieu, *Lettres persanes*, letter 126, 2:149.

36   "MILLIONS" Mercier, 7:949.

37   PARIS HAD BEEN REBUILT Law, 3:401. On Law's system, see Velde.

37   A CONTEMPORARY COMMENTATOR Piganiol de La Force, 1:31. His *Description de Paris* is,
     along with Brice's guide, the most frequently reedited tourist guide to contemporary
     French architecture throughout the eighteenth century.

37   NEXT-DOOR NEIGHBOR *Correspondants de la marquise de Balleroy*, 2:103.

37   MARIETTE ILLUSTRATED J. Mariette, figs. 159–161 (plates 488–491 in Hautecœur's reedi-
     tion).

37   BRICE PRAISED Brice 1725, 1:298–299.

37   BLONDEL . . . RECOMMENDED Blondel 1771, 3:120–121.

37   SOMEONE SEEN BY HER CONTEMPORARIES Dufort de Cheverny, 1:320.

38   WHEN BLONDEL VISITED Blondel 1752, 3:156–157. See also Kalnein, 242.

38   SIX TELESCOPES D'EVREUX, 34V, for example.

38   A MAJOR BREAKTHROUGH Blondel 1752, 1:267; Patte 1754, 6; Dennis, 101.

38   PROFITED MOST HANDSOMELY Saint-Simon, 6:576.

38   "LA REINE DES PLAISIRS" Saint-Simon, 2:934.

39   "TACITURN" In October 1718, the Princesse Palatine said it was like "pulling teeth to get
     the little king to say even a few words," Palatine 1857, 2:9. See Antoine, 108–109, for
     other contemporary reactions to Louis XV during his early years in Paris.

39   "MOST FULLY ALIVE" Antoine, 513.

39   ON HIS FIRST DAY Antoine, 111.

39   BY THE TIME OF HIS DEATH La Luzerne, 4–5.

40   SPLIT PERSONALITY Campan wrote in 1768 that "making clear the separation between
     Louis de Bourbon and the king of France was the aspect of his royal existence that the
     monarch found most essential," 22.

40   "SETTING ASIDE" Dufort de Cheverny, 1:319.

40   HAPPY FAMILY LIFE In 1745, Françoise de Graffigny pronounced it "bourgeois" for a king
     to love his wife, 6:253.

40   HER WILL Le Roi, 222.

41   "OFFICIALLY DECLARED MISTRESS" Dufort de Cheverny, 1:69; Graffigny, March 1745,
     6:253. The term *maîtresse declarée* seems first to have been used to describe the regent's
     mistresses. See *Correspondants de la marquise de Balleroy*, November 19, 1722, 2:497. In
     1746, the Duc de Croÿ described Pompadour as a "*maîtresse très declarée*," 1:56.

41   SHE READ EVERYTHING Croÿ, 1:336; Mitford, 217.

41   NO MAJOR DECISION Croÿ, 1:62–63; 1:147; 1:189.

41   "CONSTRUCTION MAD" Pompadour said that she had "*la folie de bâtir*." Pompadour, *Let-
     tres*, 1:63. These letters are said to be apocryphal; they were first attributed to Crébillon

and later to Barbé-Marbois. The statement reflects therefore either Pompadour's self-image or her contemporaries' image of her.

42 SHE TURNED HER NEW SUITE Salmon, 74–76; d'Argenson, 6:113; Blondel 1752, 4:118.

42 ONE FREQUENT GUEST Croÿ, 1:72–74, 91–92, 95–96, 196.

Chapter Two: An Architecture of Comfort

45 HIS GUIDE IN 1717 Brice 1717, 3:1–2. See also Brice 1706, 1:384–385 and Brice 1725, 1:168, for accounts of very recent and ongoing construction.

45 IN 1742 Piganiol de La Force 1742, 1:39. His original guide (1715) covers only royal châteaux.

46 VOLUME AFTER VOLUME Just to give one point of comparison, from 1600 to 1690, only a half dozen works devoted to domestic or residential architecture were published in France, whereas between 1691 and 1787, forty-four such publications appeared (Neuman, 130n.12). And these figures do not include publications on design and interior decoration.

46 VIRTUALLY AT THE MOMENT OF See, for example, Brice 1706, 1:384–385, for his account of Antoine Lepautre's recent remodeling of the Hôtel de Beauvais.

46 BEGAN TO GRUMBLE See Patte 1754, 115, for his view that French architects were not paying enough attention to "exterior decoration." See also Blondel 1771, 1:xix.

47 GREAT BUILDINGS SHOULD BE I'm quoting Blondel 1752, 1:21, but I could just as easily quote Courtonne, 92; Patte *Monuments*, 6; Briseux 1728, "introduction"; or even Brice, 1713 ed., 2:31. On the role played by these architects in making interior space livable, see Etlin. On the changing role of the architect in the eighteenth century and Blondel's contribution to that change, see Rykwert 1980, 15, 417; Gallet, 18–20.

47 COULD HAVE NO REAL MEANING see, for example, the plans in Le Muet's 1623 architectural manual.

48 WHAT THE ARCHITECT BOFFRAND Boffrand 1745, 11.

49 IN ENGLAND Robin Evans provides a particularly eloquent account of the relation between Puritanism and the development of private space in English architecture, 74–78. Early-eighteenth-century literature, Richardson's novels in particular, illustrates vividly the fearfulness that motivates a desire for private life (the fear of corruption, scandal, and so forth).

49 IN 1690 Furetière's 1690 dictionary defines "private life" in the entry for *privé*.

49 ONE YEAR LATER d'Aviler 1691, 2:375.

49 IN THE SECOND HALF The equation between private life and private space is found in Mercier's *Tableau de Paris* (1781). Other particularly instructive uses of "private life" are found in Rousseau's *Julie* (1761), Mirabeau's *Ami des hommes* (1756), and the introduction to Le Grand d'Aussy's *Précis d'une histoire de la vie privée des Français* (1779).

49 THEY OFTEN USED Blondel 1771, 4:208; 1752, 1:33.

50 MOST POPULAR Kalnein, 219.

50 BY 1752 Blondel 1752, 1:27. Blondel provided a detailed description of the triple division of interior space in his article "Architecture" for the *Encyclopédie*. In 1737, Blondel referred to the semiprivate realm as the "company" suite, or *appartements de compagnie*, 1:157. On this usage, see also Luynes, 14:113. The semiprivate rooms were more likely to be referred to as the "society" suite, or *appartements de société*, even by Blondel.

51 THE MOMENT IN 1747 Croÿ, 1:72–73.

52   FOR DIDEROT The French title is *plan du rez-de-chaussée d'un grand hôtel*. Still today in France our first floor is called the *rez-de-chaussée*, or ground floor, our second floor is therefore the first floor, and so forth. When translating from French, I will follow U.S. usage when referring to the floors of a house. The term *hôtel* originally referred to the home of a member of the nobility; homes of nonaristocrats were known as *maisons*, houses. When nonaristocrats began constructing dwellings every bit as grand as those of the nobility, the rigid distinction between *hôtel* and *maison* began to break down. For examples of the disappearance of the distinction between *hôtel* and *maison*, see Coquery, 235–236.

54   152 CANVASES Wildenstein, 7.

54   THOSE WHO DID BUSINESS AT HOME d'Aviler 1710, 185*8; Blondel 1737, 2:159; 2:178; Blondel's article "*cabinet*," *Encyclopédie*, 2:488.

54   VARIOUS CIRCULATORY DEVICES *Dégagement* is first defined architecturally by Furetière (1691) and the Académie Française (1694). These original entries are brief, but by the 1771 edition of the Trévoux dictionary, the term received full-blown treatment.

55   PASSAGEWAY The term passageway was gradually upstaged by *couloir*, hallway, during the second half of the eighteenth century. (*Couloir* first appeared in the 1762 edition of the Académie Française dictionary.)

55   SMALL STAIRCASES On Louis XV and back stairs, see Dufort de Cheverny, 1:319, and Antoine, 885. See also Luynes's account of the reconstruction of the living quarters at the Château de Fontainbleau by Louis XV in 1737, 1:264.

55   ONE ACCOUNT OF Félibien, 4.

55   ARCHITECTS THUS Blondel 1737, 1:159.

56   A 1736 NOVEL Marivaux's *Vie de Marianne*, part 5, 248–249.

56   CHARLOTTE DESMARES Desmares, 10V.

56   POMPADOUR Cordey, 27.

57   CALL BELLS BEGAN Girouard 1978, 264.

57   SERVANTS' LIVING QUARTERS Many plans in Mariette indicate servants' rooms; the earliest example seems to be the Hôtel de Noailles (1715). On servants' quarters, Benhamou, 3–8.

57   *MERCURE DE FRANCE*, February 1755, 168.

57   CEILINGS WERE Blondel 1771, 4:384; Le Camus de Mézières, 126. See also Etlin, 147n.16.

57   THE SALON On the Italianate *grand salon*, see, for example, the definitions in Furetière's 1691 and the Académie Française's 1694 dictionaries. In 1798, the Académie added the new, downsized definition of the salon. Blondel says that a "medium-sized" salon should be roughly twenty-six by twenty-six, which, while still big, is no longer overwhelming, 1771, 5:101.

58   "WHEN YOU'RE ENTERTAINING ONLY" Briseux 1761, 22.

58   "RATS' NESTS" Croÿ, 1:253.

58   LOWERED BY A FULL THREE FEET de Croÿ, 1:528–529.

58   IN THE EARLY 1760s Dufort de Cheverny, 1:327.

58   Dufort de Cheverny saw the subdivided salon at Louis La Live de Bellegarde's Château de La Chevrette; the panels were controlled by springs, 1:86.

58   CHILDREN ATTRACTED On the "invisibility" of children and the invention of childhood as a category, see Ariès, esp. part I, chapter 2, and part III, chapters 1 and 2.

59   IN OCTOBER 1715 Palatine 1857, 1:192–193.

59   IN 1737 Blondel 1737, 1:165–166.

59   THE ENTIRE LEFT WING The 1694 edition of the Académie Française dictionary mentions
     "l'appartement des enfants."

59   WITHIN A DECADE OR SO Eleb-Vidal and Debarre-Blanchard, 64, 185; Pardailhé-
     Galabrun, 36–37.

59   LE CAMUS DE MÉZIÈRES Le Camus de Mézières, 217–221.

60   MORE AND MORE PEOPLE Cavallo and Chartier, especially chapters 10–11.

60   "TO INDUCE EVERYONE" Blondel 1737, 1:160.

61   "WRITING ROOM" Blondel 1737, 1:156.

61   "THE KING WRITES" Luynes, 7:5.

62   MANY OF THE AGE'S Dufort de Cheverny, 1:271–272. This scene of seduction took place
     about 1760. For an earlier, related scene, 1:166–167.

62   A TERM UNKNOWN "Rococo" began to be used at the very end of the eighteenth century.
     It was first defined in the 1842 supplement to the Académie Française dictionary, already
     in a pejorative sense: the adjective *frivolous* was featured. In 1772, Blondel used his pe-
     riod's closest equivalent of rococo, *rocaille* (that which follows the lines of shells and
     rock formations): "A few years ago our century seemed to be the age of *rocaille*," 3:lviii.

62   *GOÛT MODERNE* Brice 1706, 1:384–385.

62   *GOÛT NOUVEAU* Courtonne, 111. (The adjective *new* was also featured in countless guides
     to interior decoration published at the turn of the century.)

62   IN 1737 Blondel 1737, 2:149.

62   BLONDEL'S SEMINAL The term *maison de plaisance* in Blondel's title was then a synonym
     for *maison de campagne*, country house or vacation house. See the Académie Française's
     1694 dictionary entry, *plaisance.*

64   PATTE Patte 1767, 6–7.

64   ENGLAND On the reluctance of English architects to introduce the new values of comfort
     and on the introduction of interior architecture there, beginning in the 1770s with the
     publication of the work of Robert Adam, see Thornton 1984, 18–19, 138–139, 145. On the
     English critique of early-eighteenth-century English architecture as "comfortless splen-
     dor," see Wright 1962, 139–140, 80. In England, the boom in architectural publications
     began later than in France and was openly associated with Palladianism. Colen Camp-
     bell's 1715 *Vitruvius Britannicus, or British Architecture* was the first book to show modern
     British buildings; it was also a plea to return to the antique simplicity of the Palladian
     style. In 1738, when Blondel published his manifesto for the new architecture, England
     saw instead the publication of the first complete, accurate translation of Palladio's 1570
     work, *The Four Books of Architecture.* On the spread of French values to Germany and
     Italy, see Thornton 1984, 139–140.

64   "RICH CROZAT" Blondel 1752, 3:106, on both remodelings of the Crozat home. Ziskin in-
     cludes proposed plans from the 1740s for both number 17 and number 19, 131–132, 136–136.

64   THE MODERN MARKETING The best sources for ads of all kinds from the 1740s on are the
     Affiches de Paris and *Annonces, affiches et avis divers.* The ads I quote are, in order, from
     Affiches de Paris, June 2, 1746; January 18, 1751; *Annonces, affiches,* June 12, 1760; Decem-
     ber 14, 1772; *Affiches de Paris,* June 16, 1746.

65   IN THE SUMMER OF 1790 All these ads are from the daily *Le Journal de Paris*: Saturday,
     July 31, 1790; Sunday, November 28, 1790; Thursday, December 30, 1790; Sunday, Au-
     gust 11, 1792.

Chapter Three: The Bathroom

67 FROM THE MIDDLE AGES The history of bathing, Havard, 4: 842; Vigarello, 7–41; Wright 1960, 5–29.

68 SOME RENAISSANCE PALACES Thornton 1978, 321; Thornton 1980, 91.

68 HIS DIARY ENTRY Héroard, 2: 1935.

68 PART OF CLAGNY On Clagny's "sumptuous" bath, Saugrain 1716, 358.

68 SIT-DOWN MEAL *Le Mercure galant*, April 1680, 177–191.

69 IN ENGLAND Girouard 1978, 256.

69 AN ENGLISH VISITOR Young, 291.

69 STANDARD BUILDING GUIDE d'Aviler 1710, 185*10, *13; 1738, 218.

69 THE MODERN BATHROOM Blondel 1752, 1:273–277.

69 THIS SINGULAR SITUATION Saint-Simon, 1:187.

70 "THE MOST METICULOUS" Saint-Simon, 2:694–695.

70 SHE ADDED A SUBSTANTIAL Blondel 1752, 1:239.

70 THEIR DÉCOR Madame la Duchesse, IV, 4R.

70 "UNBRIDLED AMBITION" Saint-Simon, 7:357.

70 A VAST BATHING SUITE Blondel 1752, 1:278; Massonie, 200–201.

70 THE FIRST ARCHITECT Blondel 1737, 1:72–74; 2:129–135.

72 IN 1743 Briseux 1743, 7–8.

72 THE *ENCYCLOPÉDIE* Blondel's article *"bains,"* 2:19.

72 THE AD FOR A HOME *Annonces, affiches, et avis divers,* February 4, 1765, 86.

72 "WHEN A PERSON OF MEANS" Ronesse, 91. *Salle de bains* seems to have first been used by Briseux in 1728 and first included in a dictionary in 1771 (Trévoux), though it was still defined there as "the main room in a bathing suite."

73 THE NEW BATHTUBS *Encyclopédie,* article *"baignoire,"* 2:15; Blondel 1737, 2:130; d'Aviler 1755, 45.

73 THE 1710 EDITION D'Aviler 1710, 185*11–12.

73 THERE WAS ONE Blondel 1752, 3:92.

73 *ENCYCLOPÉDIE* article *"citerne"* by Jaucourt, 3:488–489.

73 PUMPS WERE INSTALLED D'Aviler 1755, 122–123.

75 BY 1779 Hurtaut and Magny, 2:678–679. Other estimates, Auxiron 1765, 23; Ronesse, 62, 90n.

75 THE CITY OF PARIS Pardailhé-Galabrun, 132–133; Roche, 142–144; Vigarello, 153.

75 LISTER MARVELED OVER Lister, 154.

75 A FOR-SALE AD *Journal de Paris,* October 30, 1790.

75 IN 1723 Balleroy, April 12, 1723, 2:332.

75 IN 1778 On the Périers, Hautecœur, 3:203–204; Pardailhé-Galabrun, 133; Sauvage, 40. On water supply projects, Vigarello, 156–157.

75 BY OCTOBER 13, 1781 Périer, 6, 4, 23–26.

75 MUNICIPAL PIPING Hurtaut and Magny, 2:678: 11,814 *toises*; a *toise* equals six feet.

75 ANOTHER CONTEMPORARY SPECIALIST d'Auxiron 1769, 7.

76 "INEXPENSIVE" Périer, 22.

76 WE DON'T KNOW Estimates on the total number of tubs in Paris—Pardailhé-Galabrun, 138; Roche, 157—are based on architectural treatises and do not take into account the fact that many plans found there are inaccurate. Many, for example, show early versions of the homes described and do not include later additions, when baths were often added.

76 "EVERY NEW HOME" Ronesse, 90–91n.

76 ALREADY IN 1728 Antoine, 527; Feray, 204.

76 THE MARQUISE HAD Salmon, 76–78.

76 WHEN SHE TOOK OVER Cordey, 22.

76 AT MÉNARS Cordey, 160.

76 AND AT BELLEVUE Biver, Salmon, 100.

77 ABOVE THE DOORS Laing, 255–258.

77 LEVEL *Mercure de France,* July 1768, 178–182; September 1768, 185–186. A bath with the first model cost twenty to twenty-two *sols,* with the second ten to twelve. Level's tub used five *voies* of water, at a cost of two *sols* per *voie,* a conventional tub eight. A *voie* was "the amount of water a man can carry in two buckets" (Académie Française dictionary, 1762).

77 THE TUB Garsault, 36.

79 FINALLY, HE IS See *"bain"* in the 1762 edition of the Académie Française dictionary and the 1771 edition of the Trévoux dictionary.

79 FROM THE 1830S Girouard 2000, 232–235.

Chapter Four: The Flush Toilet

81 A CRIMSON VELVET CURTAIN Deville, 1:450; *Inventaire,* 2:350:1130.

81 IN 1708 Hautecœur, 4:202–203.

81 THE DUCHESSE DE BOURGOGNE Saint-Simon, 4:400.

82 DUC DE VENDÔME Saint-Simon, 2:694.

82 THE PRINCESSE D'HARCOURT Saint-Simon 2:271–272.

82 STANDARD BEHAVIOR AT VERSAILLES Hautecœur, 2: 201.

82 LESS THAN MAGNIFICENT Viollet-le-Duc, 6:163–164.

82 VENDÔME TRIED TO FORCE Saint-Simon, 2:694–695.

82 THE PRINCESSE DE CONTI Blondel 1752, 1:239.

83 "VENTILATION PIPING" d'Aviler 1691, 181; plates 61, 62.

83 *VENTOUSE* Furetière's dictionary.

83 BULLET, TOO, PUBLISHED Bullet 1691, 82.

83 FOUR YEARS LATER Bullet 1695, 12–15, 17.

84 BY 1710 d'Aviler 1710, 185*9–10.

84 "COMFORTABLY OFF" d'Aviler 1710, 185*6.

84 IN 1728 Briseux 1728, 1:71–72. Briseux's plans for "modern" homes still include many closestools.

84 BLONDEL'S 1737 Blondel 1737, 1:29,73,87.

84 THE 1755 UPDATING d'Aviler 1755, 81.

86 MONSEIGNEUR Kalnein, 203–204.

86 MADAME LA DUCHESSE Havard, 2:954.

86 FINANCIERS LOVED Barbier 3:226–227; Blondel 1752, 3:111.

86 CHARLOTTE DESMARES Blondel 1752, 1:267, 238; *Encyclopédie, "aisance,"* 1:240.

86 MARIE-ANNE DESCHAMPS Barbier, 7:246.

86 COMTE DUFORT DE CHEVERNY Dufort de Cheverny, 1:276.

87 SMALL CLOTHS APPEAR Le Camus de Mézières, 134.

87 THE GREAT FURNITURE DESIGNER Havard, 2:950; Hunter-Stiebel, 56.

87 WHEN THE NEWS OF THIS d'Argenson, 3:264.

87 POMPADOUR SOON GOT EXACTLY Salmon, 80–82, 92.

89 IN THE SECTION Roubo, 2:263–264.

89 THE TANK CONTAINED Giraud, 23, 25, 26.

89 GIRAUD'S WORK ENDS Giraud, 58–62.

91 IN AUGUST 1739 Barbier, 3:195.

92 BLONDEL AND ROUBO Blondel 1771, 2:136; Roubo, 1:203.

92 IN THE 1720S Kalnein, 248–249; see J. Mariette for their plans.

92 IN ENGLAND BY THE 1730S Girouard 2000, 233; Wright 1960, 104.

92 HARRINGTON REPEATEDLY INSISTS Harrington, 85, 160.

92 NO PATENT MENTIONS Wright 1960, 106.

92 MASS-PRODUCED Wright 1960, 107–110.

92 THE HAVARD BROTHERS Louis Havard, 6–7.

92 "LOO" Some say "loo" derives from "Waterloo."

Chapter Five: Heating

93 EVERYDAY LIFE IN DECEMBER 1708 Saint-Simon, 3:312.

93 "NEVER IN THE MEMORY" Palatine 1857, 2:12.

94 ANCIENT SITES Wright 1960, 6–14, 19.

94 MEDIEVAL HOMES Havard, 1:773.

94 THE FRENCH MIRROR-MAKING INDUSTRY DeJean, 199–200.

94 ENCYCLOPÉDIE article "cheminée" by Blondel, 3: 281.

96 GAUGER EXPLAINED Gauger, 163.

97 SYSTEM OF DUCTWORK Gauger, 216–217, 42–43, 52.

97 QUALITY OF LIFE Gauger, 42, 54, 99, 216.

98 HISTORIANS CONTEND Castarède Labarthe, 104, 114, 121.

99 IN HIS 1728 Briseux 1728, 62–64.

99 HE WENT FURTHER Briseux 1743, 1:7.

99 BOFFRAND Loyer, 185.

99 IN 1760 Dufort de Cheverny, 365.

99 FUMISTE Académie Française dictionary, 1762 edition.

99 "THE COMFORT" Franklin, 2.

100 FRANKLIN'S MODEL Franklin, 2, 11, 24.

100 IN HIS 1786 Fossé, 2.

100 "FILLED WITH THE SMOKE" Biver 101; d'Argenson, 6:205.

100 AND AS GAUGER Gauger, 63.

100 BRONCHITIS Palatine 1857, 2:10.

101 WHEN SHE DIED Dufort de Cheverny, 1:324.

Chapter Six: Easy Seats

102 "THIS ARMCHAIR WILL BE THE RUIN" Campan (Genet), 32–34.

103 THE ANCIENT GREEKS Giedion, 309–310, 260.

103 THE FRENCH WORDS Havard, 3:756.

104 LE BRUN THUS BECAME Some Italian Renaissance architects may have designed furniture, as Inigo Jones may have done. See Thornton 1978, 93, 52. French architects were the first of their profession who considered the importance of furniture design to be self-evident.

104 THE WORD *MEUBLE Inventaire du mobilier*, 2:270:476, 2:415:1576. Compare the definitions in Richelet (1680), Furetière (1691), and the Académie Française (1694) dictionaries with those found a half century later in the Trévoux dictionary. See Furetière's definition of *emmeublement* and the Académie Française's for *ameublement*, the word invented in the late seventeenth century to convey the new meaning.

105 THE PARISIAN NEWSPAPER *Mercure galant*, December 1682, 17, 19, 33.

105 THE FOREMOST SWEDISH ARCHITECT Nicodemus Tessin, 280.

105 IN 1769 Roubo, 2:602.

105 FURNITURE ALSO ENTERED Furetière's dictionary (1691) declares that furniture is essential to "a dwelling's comfort."

107 "BIG COMFORT ARMCHAIRS" *Inventaire du mobilier*, 2:271:483; 2:272:491; 2:298:678; 2:240:301; Havard, 1:900.

108 A PARISIAN NEWSPAPER *Mercure galant*, 1673, 4:341.

108 THE "GIGANTIC BACK" Janneau 1993, 54.

108 THE ARMREST WAS MOVED Havard, 2:col. 651.

108 AS ROUBO EXPLAINED IT Roubo, 2:608–609, 638, 614, 643.

110 THE MAKING OF A *CABRIOLET* Roubo, 2:634, 637.

110 EVEN THOUGH FRENCH CRAFTSMEN Thornton and Tomlin, 21, 24; Thornton 1978, 174. In the seventeenth century, remarkably similar armchairs were in use in England and in France. Many of those in England are known to have been purchased in France or made by French cabinetmakers working in England.

110 KNOWN AS FRENCH CHAIRS Thornton 1978, 198; Beard, 83.

110 THE BEST FRENCH CHAIRS Victoria, 2.

110 THE *ENCYCLOPÉDIE* article *"fauteuil,"* 6:439.

111 THE DUCHESSE DE BOURGOGNE Havard, 2:642.

111 THE *BERGÈRE* Roubo, 2:643.

111 CHARLOTTE DESMARES Desmares, September 11, 1725, 1V, 3V.

111 AS FOR THE MARQUISE DE POMPADOUR Cordey, 136, 140, 154–158.

111 SHE HAD BEEN SUFFERING Cordey, 50.

111 ROUBO EXPOUNDED Roubo, 2:642–643.

113 THE MOST POPULAR PAPER *Mercure de France*, July 1755, 10.

113 THEY DOUBLED IT UP Roubo, 2:650.

113 FOUR PROTOTYPES Janneau 1993, 44.

113 A MOST STRIKING *LIT DE REPOS Inventaire du mobilier*, 2:267:445.

113 IN LATE 1683 *Inventaire du mobilier*, 2:339:1061; 2:346s:1095; 2:347:1107; 2:356:1174.

115 THE PRINCE DE CONTI Havard, 4:1038; Saint-Simon, 3:616; 1:388, 403; 3:372, 870.

115 "DOUBLE WINDSOR CHAIRS" Walpole, October 3, 1743, 18:332.

115 THE DUCHESSE DE BOUILLON Saint-Simon, 1:891; 4:783,788.

118 THE ENGLISH QUICKLY Furniture historians see the English sofa as a French import. Thornton 1978, 17, 213; Bowett, 252; Beard, 82–83; Edwards, 3:70–105.

118 IN 1745 Walpole, October 3, 1745, 18:315. Chippendale identifies certain sofas as "mortal sins" (4, plate 32).

118 HORACE MANN Walpole, 18:332.

118 IN 1770 Mrs. Delany, 205.

119 THE PRINCESSE DE ROHAN Saint-Simon, 1:170; 6:435.

120 SOMETIME AROUND 1680 *Chantourné* first appears in the inventory of royal furniture in 1687; from then to 1691, it is used four times to describe either carved headboards on beds or backs on sofas, 2:381:1356; 2:394:1416; 2:402:1459; 2:404:1486. The technique was discussed for the first time in print in d'Aviler 1691, 1:169, 2:449. Jean Néré Ronfort has on file a reference to a daybed with a *chantourné* headboard made for Mademoiselle de Blois in 1679.

120 SUPPORT FOR THE ARMS *Inventaire du mobilier,* 2:381:1356; 2:438:1808.

120 LOUIS XIV CHOSE *Inventaire du mobilier,* 2:459:2003.

121 EVERY TECHNIQUE ON WHICH THE UPHOLSTERER'S Thornton 1978, 217.

121 OVER WHICH THE FRENCH Beard, 82–83.

121 MADAME VICTOIRE'S Thornton 1984, 102.

121 UPHOLSTERY *EN CHÁSSIS* Blondel 1752, 1:123.

122 THE FRENCH SILK INDUSTRY Miller, 181. In 1738, Graffigny noted that Voltaire and Emilie du Châtelet changed the fabric twice a year at Cirey, 1:197.

122 IN THE 1692 EDITION Blégny 1692, 1:284. There were several distinct kinds of *tapissiers*, and only *tapissiers-marchands* were supposed to sell furniture; these distinctions were not always carefully upheld. Havard, 4:1246.

123 THE TWO MOST POPULAR MODELS Havard, 3:1205; Jarry, 224.

123 IN THE CHÂTEAU DE MÉNARS Cordey, 158.

124 ROUBO DID HIS BEST Roubo, 2:652–653.

124 IN MAY 1690 Sévigné, May 24, 1690, 3:883.

124 "SOFA" WAS FIRST MENTIONED Furetière, entry "canapé."

124 THE FOLLOWING YEAR Callières, 112–113.

125 THE MARÉCHAL D'HUMIÈRES Havard, 4:1038.

125 CRONSTRÖM *Relations artistiques,* 67, 79, 81, 106.

125 LOUIS XV Havard, 4:1038.

125 CHARLOTTE DESMARES Desmares, September 11, 1725, 3V, 4V.

127 POMPADOUR Cordey, 9–22.

127 SOFAS IN DINING ROOMS Madame la Duchesse, 22V.

127 IN BLONDEL'S VISION Blondel 1737, 2:134.

127 FRANÇOISE DE GRAFFIGNY'S Graffigny, 1:197.

128 MANSART Ronfort, 72–73.

128 KNEW FULL WELL Blondel 1752, 1:122; Roubo, 2:600–601.

128 ONE FRENCHMAN REMARKED *Mercure de France,* 11.

128 THE COMTE D'EVREUX Dezallier d'Argenville, 94; Luynes, 12:325.

128 "TWELVE ARMCHAIRS" Crozat, 13R.

128 THE LOUVRE MUSEUM The Louvre armchairs from Crozat's ensemble are Inv. OA11200–201. The Getty Museum owns a stool from the ensemble, accession number 84.DA.970.

129 BY 1776 Caraccioli, 120–124.

Chapter Seven: Convenience Furniture

131 TODAY'S ALL-PURPOSE Giedion, 305.

131 THE ORIGINAL CHESTS OF DRAWERS *Inventaire general du mobilier,* 2:171:473; 2:172:487; 2:175:514. They were called at first *tables en bureau.*

131   SOON KNOWN AS *COMMODES* Deville, 1:90; Havard, 1:888–889.

132   THE TRUNK WAS RAPIDLY DISAPPEARING Pardailhé-Galabrun, 106–107.

132   LE BLOND EXPLAINED D'Aviler 1710, 185*11.

132   ARCHITECTS CHAMPIONED INSTEAD Blondel 1752, 1:122. The *Encyclopédie*'s entry *"cabinet"* also contains an attack on storage furniture. In 1690, d'Aviler used built-in *ormoires* in the pantry off the kitchen, plate 63C.

132   THE WORD ALREADY DESIGNATED Havard, 1:149–164.

132   MARQUISE DE POMPADOUR Salmon, 79, 83.

134   LOCKING MECHANISMS Havard, 4:991.

134   SECRET COMPARTMENTS Briseux 1743, 2:165–167.

134   SMALL TABLES CAME INTO USE Janneau 1952, 7–11.

134   SMALL TABLES WERE OFFICIALLY NAMED The 1798 edition of the Académie Française dictionary (entry *"volant"*); Havard, 1:454. Eighteenth-century French furniture was divided into two categories: stationary furniture, pieces either too large to be moved about easily or considered an integral part of a room's décor (these were called *meubles meublants*, or furniture that furnished), and pieces that were moved about.

134   THE PROTO-ELEVATOR Salmon, 71, 76. The earliest proto-elevator dates from about 1680. Dangeau, 3:395.

135   BY 1769 *Mercure de France*, July 1769, 208–210.

135   THE TINY GAMING TABLES *Le Mercure Galant*, December 1682, 36, 39.

135   IN 1684 Piton, 174.

135   THE MARQUISE DE MAINTENON Deville, 1:457 and ff.

135   CHARLOTTE DESMARES Desmares, September 25, 1746, 4V, 5R, 11V.

135   THE MARQUISE DE POMPADOUR Cordey, 50–55.

135   LAZARE DUVAUX Courajod, 2:42:432.

136   JOHN BYNG Byng, 3:156–157.

136   DESIGNERS MAKE THE BREAKTHROUGH Thornton 1978, 25; Havard, 4:1126.

136   NORMALLY TWENTY INCHES WIDE Roubo, 2:740.

136   CHARLOTTE DESMARES September 11, 1725, 4R, 5R.

136   THE MARQUISE DE POMPADOUR Salmon, 342–344; Watson 1966, 1:204–207; Havard, 4:1126; Courajod, 2:65:647; Biver, 44.

138   EARMARKED FOR GROOMING The earliest mention of a *cabinet de toilette* I have found is in Lafayette's 1678 novel *La Princesse de Clèves*, 186. *Cabinets de toilette* and *toilettes* appear frequently in Blondel 1737.

138   THE *TABLE DE TOILETTE* Havard, 4:1126; Janneau 1952, 18; Roubo, 2:740. Graffigny, 1:199, refers to one simply as a *toilette*. Both *cabinet de toilette* and *table de toilette* appear often in Pierre Crozat's probate inventory, 192V, for example.

138   CHARLOTTE DESMARES September 11, 1725, 4V.

138   THE ONE PRODUCED FOR LOUIS XV Meyer, 1:122–130.

138   *SECRÉTAIRE*, OR SMALL DESK It's hard to date the use of *secrétaire* to mean small desk; however, when Graffigny described one at Cirey in 1738, the usage was clearly already established, 1:198.

138   ROUBO EXPLAINED Roubo, 2:734–736.

138   THE RAREST EXOTIC WOODS Havard, 1:8.

139   IT'S A CAREFULLY ORCHESTRATED Scott 2005, 250–256.

139   IT'S IDENTICAL TO Hunter-Stiebel, 56, 98; Watson 1966, 1:254; Laing, 269. On the same
        day in 1750 on which she bought six night tables, Pompadour also bought ten writing
        tables.

Chapter Eight: 1735: Architect-Designed Seating Begins

140   THE PRACTICE OF STAMPING OR SIGNING Augarde, 52, 55–56.

141   QUANTITIES OF EVERYDAY ITEMS My descriptions of Meissonnier's designs are based on
        the plates in his *Oeuvres*.

142   THE MOST IMPORTANT PAPER OF THE DAY *Mercure de France*, July 1736, 1690, and ff. On
        Meissonnier's room, Kimball, 159. On Meissonnier, Donnell.

Chapter Nine: The Original Interior Decorators and the Comfortable Room

144   TWO SWEDES WHO FOLLOWED *Relations artistiques*, 209, 44.

145   PRIOR TO THE SEVENTEENTH CENTURY'S FINAL DECADES Feray, 1–10.

145   FRANÇOISE DE GRAFFIGNY DESCRIBED HER VISIT Graffigny, February 9, 1751, 11:390.

145   "TODAY, THE MOST MODEST" Gudin de La Brenellerie, 90.

145   THEIR LETTERS DOCUMENT *Relations artistiques*, 209, 29. In 1717, Nicodemus Tessin
        wrote, in French, what he rightly saw as the first treatise on interior decoration.

146   TESSIN'S SON CARL Carl Tessin, July 11/22, 1740, 97–98.

146   THE *ENCYCLOPÉDIE* *Encyclopédie*, article *"décoration,"* by Blondel, 4:702–704.

146   THE FRENCH THUS CAME TO DOMINATE Thornton 1984, 14–17,48–49; Kimball, 3.

146   ARCHITECTS SUCH AS Le Roux's *Nouveaux lambris de galeries, chambers, et cabinets* (un-
        dated but c. 1710) and Le Pautre's *Cheminées à la royale* (1698) were among the most suc-
        cessful of the early decorating pattern books.

147   VIRTUAL TOURS Brice's guide was reissued so often that readers could follow decorating
        projects as they unfolded. In the 1717 edition, for example, work on a gallery for Louis
        XIV's legitimated son, the Comte de Toulouse, was "under way" (1:168), whereas in
        1719 its "magnificent" décor was newly finished, 1:407. Piganiol de La Force, 9:43.

147   PIERRE-JEAN MARIETTE P.-J. Mariette, 2:101.

147   THE CONTEMPORARY PRESS *Mercure de France*, June 1724, 2:1391.

147   BOUCHER Laing, 195–197, 224–229.

147   FREDERICK THE GREAT Fahy, 162, 284.

148   LARGELY ENGRAVED BY I agree with Kaufmann, 59, who takes Blondel at his word
        (Blondel 1747, 62n.) and credits him with "the vast majority of the plates," 59.

149   HE WAS CRAZY ABOUT SOFAS Blondel 1737, 2:108.

150   SHOULD NEVER BE REMOVED Blondel 1752, 1:122.

150   THEY COULD NOT SIMPLY REST ON THEIR LAURELS Blondel 1752, 2:119, 108, 87–88.

150   MARIETTE ADDED A SECTION D'Aviler 1738, 3.

150   PUBLICATION AFTER PUBLICATION Briseux includes "interior decoration" in the title of his
        1743 volume, whereas in 1728 he did not mention the term. Boffrand 1745, 41.

150   ALL AGREED THAT Patte 1767, 64; Gudin de La Brenellerie, 1:90.

150   PATTE . . . PRAISED Patte 1754, 64. Patte uses the terms *légèreté* and *gravité*.

151   "WAYS OF DECORATING" *Mercure galant* 1673, 4:332–341.

151   PLAFOND The expression *plafond dans le goût moderne* is Blondel's.
151   MARIETTE HEAPED SCORN d'Aviler 1738, 399–400.
152   ITS FEBRUARY 1755 ISSUE *Mercure de France*, February 1755, 159–160.
152   BLONDEL ILLUSTRATED Blondel 1771, plate 26.
152   PARISIANS FROM ALL INCOME BRACKETS Ballot, 18.
152   IN STRONG COLORS Feray, 164; Pardailhé-Galabrun, 171–172.
152   THE MÉNAGERIE *Inventaire du mobilier*, entries for 1701.
152   D'AVILER d'Aviler 1691, 1:228.
152   LE ROUX DECLARED Le Roux, title page.
152   WHITE, WHITE, AND WHITE Feray, 160; Scott 1995, 2; Boffrand, 62, 64, 97–98, plates 53–54.
152   GILDING Beard 1983, 10.
152   BULLET GAVE Bullet 1691, 10.
153   THEIR WOOD FRAMES WERE PAINTED Ronfort, 43; A. N. *Journal du garde-meuble de la couronne* (013306, #1182).
153   WALPOLE GRUMBLED Walpole, December 25, 1765, 31:87; 23:312; 32:261.
153   BRISEUX CLAIMED Briseux 1741, 2:174, 176–181.
153   PATTE Patte 1754, 64.
153   D'AVILER d'Aviler 1691, 180.
153   TESSIN ANNOUNCED *Relations artistiques*, 165.
154   TESSIN EXPLAINED *Relations artistiques*, 165.
155   BOFFRAND DICTATED Boffrand, 45.
155   GLASS WAS VERY RARELY Crowley, 38–44.
155   BY THE MID–SEVENTEENTH CENTURY Belhoste and Leproux, 15.
155   ITS MEMBERS CRITICIZED *Procès verbaux* of the Académie Royale d'Architecture, 1:124; 3:93.
155   TESSIN Tessin 1926, 276.
155   PIERRE BULLET Bullet 1691, 262.
155   AND IN 1703 *Relations artistiques*, 322.
156   TO OPEN AND CLOSE *Mercure galant*, 1673, 4:339; Belhoste and Leproux, 28–31.
156   A "LARGE" PANE OF GLASS Blondel 1771, 6:454–455.
156   IN 1738 d'Aviler 1738, 386.
156   THE PALAIS BOURBON Blondel 1752, 1:267. Dufort de Cheverny describes a huge skylight used to light a windowless semiprivate reception room, 1:366.
156   A LARGE MIRROR ABOVE A DOOR Blondel 1737, 1:27.
156   A NEWS FLASH *Mercure galant* 1673, 4:302–303.
158   HALL OF MIRRORS *Mercure galant*, September 1686, 324.
158   SIMPLE COTTON CURTAINS *Inventaire du mobilier*, 1701.
158   CURTAINS WERE PART OF EVERY ROOM Le Mire 1991, 82.
158   CHARLOTTE DESMARES Desmares, July 11, 1725, 4R; September 25, 1746, 8V, 9R.
158   MONSEIGNEUR'S PORCELAIN CABINET Ronfort, 43.
158   ADS IN THE CONTEMPORARY PRESS *Mercure de France*, December 1750, 1:211.
158   POMPADOUR Duvaux, 2:244.
158   UNTIL THE SEVENTEENTH CENTURY Havard, 4:118–122.
159   FONTAINEBLEAU Kimball, 26.
159   EVELYN Thornton 1978, 46.
159   PALATINE Palatine 1985, November 22, 1710, 435.

159 WHEN VERSAILLES'S ARCHITECTS *Comptes des bâtiments*, 1:1013; 2:430; 2:610; and so forth.

159 MADE IT OFFICIAL *Procès verbaux* of the Académie Royale d'Architecture, 3:8.

159 BULLET Bullet 1691, 268–272.

159 THE FIRST EDITIONS d'Aviler 1710, 1: 351; d'Aviler 1738, 1:405.

159 MONTESPAN *Comptes du bâtiment*, 1:1150.

159 MONSEIGNEUR Ronfort, 41.

160 TESSIN Tessin 1926, 276.

161 BLÉGNY'S Blégny, 2:123.

161 TESSIN *Relations artistiques*, 20.

161 "SIMPLICITY" Blondel 1737, 2:101.

161 HARMONY Blondel 1737, 2:103, 122–123.

161 IDEAL FROM THE STANDPOINT *Encyclopédie*, article "*cabinet*," 2:488.

161 TESSIN *Relations artistiques*, 30.

162 BLONDEL Blondel 1737, 2:61.

162 ROUBO Roubo, 2:654.

162 BLONDEL DESIGNED Blondel 1737, 2:103,108.

163 HE MEANT THE ARCHITECT Blondel 1737, 2:106; *Encyclopédie*, article "*menuiserie*," 10:349–357.

163 JAUBERT ANOINTED Jaubert, 2:9–10. *Décorateur* was first included in a dictionary in 1832: "Someone whose profession is the interior decoration of apartments." Earlier entries, such as that in Johnson's dictionary, do not refer to the new profession.

163 POMPADOUR TABLES Duvaux, 2:42:432.

163 THE ENGLISH Delany, April 11, 1752, 110, also 321.

163 BECAME A SYNONYM FOR "Rococo" first appeared in a dictionary in the 1842 edition of the Académie Française; the entry calls "the pompadour style a nuance of the rococo."

163 BLONDEL Blondel 1771, 3:120–121.

164 IN 1780 Le Camus de Mézières, 113.

164 "THE REIGN OF THE UPHOLSTERER" Giedion, 364–365. On the struggle between architects and upholsterers, Thornton 1984, 11.

Chapter Ten: The Bedroom

165 IN ANTIQUITY Daremberg and Saglio (*lectus, torus, cubile*). The age of comfort produced the first history of the bed, by Le Grand d'Aussy, 154–166.

166 HE SENT SKETCHES BACK TO STOCKHOLM Thornton 1984, 57; Dee and Walton, 76–81.

166 *CHÂSSIS* Havard, 1:658; 3:372–441.

166– WORDS . . . THEN CAME INTO GENERAL USE The definitions of *chambre* in Furetière's 1691

167 and the Académie Française's 1694 dictionaries show that it was evolving from a generic term, a room, to bedroom. The 1762 edition of the Académie Française dictionary includes *chambre à coucher*, proving that the evolution was complete. For some early uses of *chambre à coucher*, see Saint-Simon, 3:399; 7:275.

167 ANTOINE COURTIN Courtin, 47.

167 DUC DE LUYNES Luynes, 2:175.

167 DUC DE CROŸ Croÿ, 1:76; 2:30.

168 LE CAMUS DE MÉZIÈRES PROUDLY CHRISTENED IT Le Camus de Mézières, 111.

169 THE BED WAS TUCKED AWAY For the earliest illustration of a niche bed, see Thornton 1984, 71.

169 NEW ARCHITECTURE'S VALUES Blondel 1752, 1:177.

169   LE CAMUS DE MÉZIÈRES CALLED IT Le Camus de Mézières, 111.

169   TO MAKE THE BED Blondel 1771, 4:386.

169   PIVOTED Roubo, 2:670.

171   BON BROTHERS *Mercure galant*, 1673, 3:298–299.

171   THE PRINCESS SLEPT OFF Perrault, 133.

171   THE MÉNAGERIE *Inventaire du mobilier*, 2:459:2006.

171   CAME IN THREE SIZES Roubo, 2:667–681.

172   THOMAS JEFFERSON Stein, 51.

172   POMPADOUR'S FAVORITE Cordey 23–24.

173   THE *GARDEROBE* Havard, 2:934.

173   LE BLOND d'Aviler 1710, 185*9.

173   LE CAMUS DE MÉZIÈRES Le Camus de Mézières, 88, 131.

173   A PERFECT BEDROOM SUITE *Encyclopédie*, article *"cabinet,"* 2:488; Le Camus de Mézières, 88,131.

173   SAINT-SIMON Saint-Simon, 4:758.

174   ADOPTED BY BOFFRAND Boffrand, pl. 12.

174   BY COMPARING THE TREATMENT Briseux 1728, 2:29, 2:33, 54, 71. Briseux 1743, 1:23–24, 49, 126; 2:5; 135, pl. 95. See also Ziskin, 50.

174   GUEST QUARTERS Briseux 1743, 1:23.

174   LE CAMUS DE MÉZIÈRES Le Camus de Mézières, 219–220.

175   CHARLOTTE DESMARES Desmares, July 11, 1725, 1R, 2V; September 11, 1725, 2RV; September 25, 1746, 4V, 5R.

175   A FOOTSTOOL WAS USED Havard, 3:681.

175   PIERRE CROZAT Crozat, 9RV, 10RV.

176   THE COMTE D'EVREUX Evreux, 21V, 22R, 23R, 24R, 16V, 17V, 25R, 33R, 20V.

176   POMPADOUR Cordey, 27–28, 53, 52, 22.

Chapter Eleven: The Boudoir

178   BRISEUX Briseux 1741, 1:22.

179   INITIALLY, THE BOUDOIR Roubo uses *méridienne* and boudoir as synonyms, 40:202.

179   BLONDEL Blondel, article *"cabinet," Encyclopédie*, 2:488. ("Boudoir" is not used in the *Encyclopédie*.)

179   *RECUEILLEMENT* ORIGINALLY MEANT Furetière's 1690 dictionary.

179   IT WAS ONLY IN THE MID–EIGHTEENTH CENTURY *"boudoir,"* Académie Française dictionary, 1762, 1832; Trévoux dictionary, 1753 edition.

179   WHEN FRENCH NOVELS FEATURED For pouting literary characters, see, for example, Marie-Jeanne Riccoboni's *Lettres de Mistriss Fanni Butlerd* 1757.

179   HÔTEL D'HUMIÈRES Blondel 1752, 1:273–277.

179   BRISEUX Briseux, 1:24.

179   EMILIE DU CHÂTELET Graffigny, 1:198.

179   THE QUEEN Kimball, 246–247.

179   MADAME LA DUCHESSE Madame la Duchesse, 68V.

179   THE MARQUISE DE POMPADOUR Cordey, 23; Piganiol de La Force, 9:42–43.

179   WAS PLACED IN VARIOUS LOCATIONS See Lilley for more information on the placement of boudoirs.

179   BLONDEL OFTEN MADE Blondel always called the room a *méridienne*, never a boudoir. See his 1737 work and Thornton 1984, 95.

180   POMPADOUR PUT A BOUDOIR Blondel 1752, 4:plate 2; Salmon, 80.

180   RUMOR HAD IT Croÿ, 6:207; 1:358–359.

180   MADAME LA DUCHESSE Madame la Duchesse, 68V.

180   EMILIE DU CHÂTELET'S Graffigny, 1:198.

180   AT BELLEVUE Salmon, 100–101.

182   MARIE-ANNE DESCHAMPS Benabou, 369–376; Capon, 137–146.

182   FRANCE KNEW ANOTHER CRASH Barbier, 7:198–202.

182   DUFORT DE CHEVERNY Dufort de Cheverny, 1:271–272.

183   JEAN-FRANÇOIS DE BASTIDE Bastide, 375.

183   DUFORT DE CHEVERNY Dufort de Cheverny, 1:272. Bastide the journalist reported on the Deschamps affair, Capon, 171.

183   ITS FABLED SHEETS Capon, 174–175.

184   SOME OF THE ORIGINAL BOUDOIR TOURISTS Barbier, 7:245–247.

184   LE CAMUS DE MÉZIÈRES Le Camus de Mézières, 116–123.

184   AND BY 1832 Entry *"boudoir,"* Académie Française dictionary, 1832 edition.

184   THE NUMEROUS PLATES Krafft and Ransonnette, for example, plate 80, no. 2; plate 89; plate 93, no. 2.

184   IN 1832 *Dictionnaire de la conversation*, Druckett, 7:468.

184   JULES DEVILLE Deville, 1:244–245.

Chapter Twelve: Dressing for Comfort

186   LOUIS XIV'S SISTER-IN-LAW Palatine 1857, August 9, 1718, 1:443; Palatine 1838, 60–61.

186   AN OFFICIAL "PRONOUNCEMENT" Luynes, 12:350.

186   "WITHOUT OUTWARD SIGNS" (*"Où il n'y a rien, le Roi perd ses droits"*) Luynes, September 3, 1744, 6:65.

187   CHARLES DE PEYSSONNEL Peyssonnel, 1:149.

188   1673 PRESS COVERAGE *Mercure galant*, 1673, 4:339–346.

188   HIS SON'S WIFE Dangeau 1686, 1:322–325.

188   THE DUCHESSE DE BERRY Dangeau, 14:390; 14:48; 15:457; Saint-Simon, 4:172.

188   THERE WAS A FASHION INDUSTRY Crowston, 30–35; DeJean, 35–41.

188   THE FORMAL ENSEMBLE KNOWN AS Saint-Simon uses *grand habit*, 2:152, 275; as does Palatine 1857, 1:13, 81, 130. By the mid–eighteenth century, Luynes still does, 1:93, 109, 262, also occasionally *habit de cour*, 3:284; 9:296; 16:259. Also *robe de cour*, Balleroy, 2:512, and *habit habillé, Mercure de France*, March 1729. The *Mercure galant* indicates that *grand habit* was still a new term in January 1708, 279–280.

189   IN ENGLISH Lemire 1991, 18.

189   MEN BEGAN TO Cunningham, Fennetaux, and Swain.

189   BY 1711 *The Spectator*, April 26, 1711, 3:209.

189   IN THE 1760S Académie Française dictionary, 1762 ed.

189   IN THE 1780S Peyssonnel, 1:146–147. Entry *"chenille,"* Académie Française dictionary, 1832 ed.

190   IN JANUARY 1678 *Mercure galant*, January 1678, *extraordinaire*, 508–509.

190   A CONTEMPORARY DICTIONARY Académie Française dictionary, 1694.

190 SOME EARLY *MANTEAUX Mercure galant*, 1672, 278; 1673, 4:340–346. It's possible that Montespan copied Indian *manteaux*, but the two original casual looks appear to have arrived at exactly the same moment.

191 WORE SKIRTS The French said *jupe*, a skirt, while the English called the garment a "petticoat" and used "skirt" for men's coats.

191 UNBONED BODICES Willett and Cunnington, 88.

191 MADAME LA DUCHESSE Madame la Duchesse, 241V–247V.

191 A FRENCH DICTIONARY Furetière, entry "commode."

191 *UNE INDIENNE Mercure galant*, May 1680, 350; Savary des Bruslons, 2:1708; Nemeitz, 1:331–332.

192 PEYSSONNEL Peyssonnel, 1:34–35.

192 THE INAUGURAL HISTORY OF PRIVATE LIFE Le Grand d'Aussy, 252.

192 THE CARNIVAL SEASON OF 1699 Palatine 1985, 251–252.

192 FONTAINBLEAU Dangeau, 7:172.

192 SAINT-SIMON Saint-Simon, 2:144.

192 "AT VERSAILLES" Palatine 1857, 321.

192 "THE KING GOT REALLY ANGRY" Saint-Simon, 2:527–528.

194 THE INVENTORY OF GOODS *Inventaire du mobilier*, 2:104:22; 2:107:58.

194 THE *ROBES DE CHAMBRE* Crowston, 34–42; Ribeiro 1995, 57.

194 THE *BAYEUSE* Luynes, 10:192.

194 DE TROY'S A principal source of information on eighteenth-century fashion, the *Mercure de France*, pronounced de Troy the absolute authority on dress in the 1720s and 1730s, April 1735, 716.

194 A SERIES OF NEW NAMES The *Mercure de France* speaks of *robe volante*, March 1729, 612. Contemporaries also called it a *manteau volant* (Hénissart) or a *robe flottante* (*Cas de conscience*). Palatine speaks of *robes ballantes* (first on April 12, 1721), *robes battantes*, a term I can't explain (first on August 9, 1718), and *robes flottantes*, Palatine 1838, 24. Saint-Simon and Luynes still use *robe de chambre*.

195 "REST THEIR ELBOWS" (*à coudes*) *Mercure galant*, October 1730, 2312.

197 *CRIARDS Mercure galant*, October 1730, 2312. The earliest engraving of a dancer with a very short skirt is dated 1681.

197 WEAR DRAWERS Willett and Cunnington, 52, 65.

197 LOUIS XV APPEARED ONSTAGE Barbier, 1:105.

197 THE INFLUENCE OF BALLET STYLES *Mercure galant*, March 1729, 618.

197 MEN WERE JUST AS OPEN La Morlière, 424–425.

197 IN ENGLAND Ribeiro 2003, 248, 274.

197 *EN DÉSHABILLÉ* Académie Française dictionary, 1798.

197 *DÉSHABILLÉ NÉGLIGÉ* Académie Française dictionary, 1694. Furetière (1690) doesn't yet record this usage.

198 "RISKY BUSINESS" *Nouveau Mercure*, March 1718 (101–102). Marivaux invented the short-lived adjective *risquable*. Justus van Effen, *Bagatelle*, June 18, 1718, 170; July 11, 1718, 155.

198 THE ADJECTIVE *VOLANT* Académie Française, 1694, and Trévoux dictionaries.

198 TO ENCOURAGE SUCH PREGNANCIES Hénissart, 21; *Cas de conscience*, 5, 9.

199 *ANGOLA* La Morlière, 1:1, 77, 88, 113, 153; 2:158.

199   VIVANT DENON *Point de lendemain*, 93.

199   THE MARQUISE DE BALLEROY Balleroy, 2:335.

199   NEWSPAPERS COVERED NEW BOB STYLES *Recueil de différentes modes*, plates; *Mercure de France*, May 1726, 952–955; March 1729, 615; October 1730, 2316.

200   THE VERY *MANTILLE Mercure de France*, May 1726, 951; March 1729, 614.

200   MADAME LA DUCHESSE Madame la Duchesse, 251V.

200   WHILE COMBING THEIR HAIR entry "peignoir" in Furetière, 1690, Académie Française, 1694, and Trévoux, 1771, dictionaries. See also van Loo's 1769 portrait of Pomadour's brother, the Marquis de Marigny, and his wife in the Louvre.

200   POMPADOUR Cordey, 79,81.

201   IN JUNE 1737 Luynes, June 1737, 1:262.

201   SOON, HOWEVER Luynes, September 1737, 1:361.

201   TRAVEL NEXT Luynes, November 1738, 2:279.

201   IN 1737 Luynes, September 1737, 1:352.

201   THE DAUPHIN'S MARRIAGE Luynes, August 1739, 3:16–19.

201   BY 1744 Luynes, September 1744, 6:64.

201   IN 1746 Luynes, May 1746, 7:320.

201   THE FOLLOWING YEAR Luynes, August 1747, 8:284.

201   JUST THREE YEARS LATER Luynes, October 1750, 10:347.

201   IN 1761 Campan, 23–24.

202   DE CROŸ's Croÿ, 2:92.

202   GARSAULT Garsault, 45.

202   COULDN'T "ABIDE" Luynes, May 1740, 3:185.

202   "UNDRESSED" Luynes, April 1740, 3:170.

202   POMPADOUR Cordey, 74–82. I count only *robes de chambre*; she owned other informal styles.

202   BLONDEL Blondel 1771, 4:387–388.

202   IN 1730 *Mercure de France*, "*modes nouvelles*," October 1730.

203   *ROBE À LA FRANÇAISE* Ribeiro 1995, 57; Ribeiro 1985, 98. "Pompadour gown" Lemire 1991, 215.

203   DUFORT DE CHEVERNY's Dufort de Cheverny, 1:319, 69.

203   BOUCHER'S PORTRAIT *Mercure de France*, October 1757, 2:155–159; Laing, 267; Scott 2005, 250–256.

Chapter Thirteen: The Fabric of Their Lives

206   COTTON FIRST ARRIVED Irwin and Brett, 23.

206   THE VOLUME OF IMPORTED GOODS EXPLODED Bruignac-La Hougue, Gittinger, Irwin and Brett, and Lemire 1991.

206   BY 1684 Lemire 2003, 68.

206   ALREADY IN 1680 Lafayette 1942, 2:99–100.

206   *DÉGRAISSEURS* Furetière's dictionary, 1727; Hurtaut and Magny, 2:639. On fabric services in Amsterdam, Hartkamp-Jonxis 1994, 74n.1.

206   *ENCYCLOPÉDIE Encyclopédie*, article "*toile peinte*," 16:370.

207   DYEING PROCESSES An overview of eighteenth-century knowledge of Indian dyeing techniques, especially to produce reds, *Journal économique*, June–September 1756.

207   SIAMESE FABRICS Kimball, 139.

207   ASIAN FLOWERED TEXTILES Lemire 2003, 69.

208   DUTCH EAST INDIA Hartkamp-Jonxis 1989, 81–82.

208   TO COPY A PRINT Irwin and Brett, 9, 4; Lemire 1991, 13.

209   A SPECTRUM OF PAN-ASIAN MOTIFS Irwin and Brett, 32.

209   RENEWING THEIR OFFERINGS SEASONALLY DeJean, 47–49; Miller, 181; Fraisse, introduction.

209   PERSE Savary des Bruslons, perse 3:799; Encyclopédie; Havard, 4:248–256; Irwin and Brett, 11. Only in 1832 did a French dictionary admit the truth about perse.

210   A PAINTED COTTON VEST Dangeau, 2:67.

211   ALMANACS d'Allemagne, 1:53.

211   BY OCTOBER 1686 Depitre suggests that since many of the workers in the French cotton industry were Protestants, the 1686 ban was a footnote to the 1685 revocation of the Edict of Nantes, which drove Protestants from France, v–vi.

211   IN MAY 1691 Correspondance des fermiers généraux, 1:305. The amount destroyed was 11,800 aunes.

211   IN OCTOBER 1711 d'Allemagne, 1:64.

211   IN PARIS IN THE EARLY 1700S Code des toiles, 47, 51.

212   AND BY JUNE 1715 Correspondance des fermiers généraux, 3:577.

212   DE LA REYNIE REASONED Correspondance des fermiers généraux, 1:305.

212   HAD ALREADY COST THE COUNTRY Correspondance des fermiers généraux, 1:227.

212   REPRESENTATIVES FROM LYONS Correspondance des fermiers généraux, 1:142–143.

212   IN 1723 Savary des Bruslons, 2:1153.

212   BY THE 1750S Forbonnais, 11; Moreau, 215.

212   THE EDITORS OF Journal économique, July 1755, 66–67, 77.

212   THAT FIGURE INCLUDED Depitre, 84.

212   VINCENT DE GOURNAY Gournay, 75–77.

212   IN DECEMBER 1710 Correspondance des fermiers généraux, 3:334.

213   SPOTTED BY THE POLICE Correspondance des fermiers généraux, 3:577.

213   DUC DE SAINT-SIMON Saint-Simon, 5:870–871.

213   THE SERIOUS USE OF COTTON Inventaire du mobilier, 2:266:441; 2:306:747; 2:366:1228; 2:117:216. Merchants spoke of chitte or chint a bit earlier, but 1686 marks the first use by nonprofessionals.

213   MÉNAGERIE Inventaire du mobilier, 2:452:1916.

213   PERSE WAS ORIGINALLY Mercure galant, May 1680, 350–351.

213   TO UPHOLSTER SEAT FURNITURE Morellet, 106; Deville, 1:471:194.

214   THAT 1686 SHIPMENT Inventaire du mobilier, 2:118:232.

214   THE YEAR THAT SEPARATED Blégny 1691, 26; Blégny 1692, 2:13.

214   AN ARTICLE IN Mercure de France, September 1725, 2:225–227.

214   PIERRE CROZAT Crozat, 13RV, 11R.

215   CHARLOTTE DESMARES Desmares, July 11, 1725, 8V, 9R.

215   COMTE D'EVREUX Evreux, 11R, 13RV, 15RV, 45R.

215   POMPADOUR Cordey, 15, 22–23, 48, 136–137.

215   MADAME LA DUCHESSE Madame la Duchesse, 40–44RV, 62V, 68V, 133R, 104V.

216   THE COUNT OWNED QUITE A BIT Evreux, 46R, 47V.

216   POMPADOUR Cordey, 74–77.

216   MADAME LA DUCHESSE Madame la Duchesse, 241V, 242 RV, 243 R, 244 RV, 245V.

216   HENRIETTE-LUCY DILLON La Tour du Pin, 82.

216   DID NOT HESITATE TO WEAR Hartkamp-Jonxis 1989, 82.

216   VAN EFFEN'S van Effen, June 18, 1718, 170.

216   *MERCURE DE FRANCE Mercure de France*, October 1730, 2314.

217   ALREADY IN 1709 *Correspondance des fermiers généraux*, 3:142–143.

217   FORBONNAIS EXPLAINED Forbonnais, 5–6.

217   BY THE 1780S Roche 1994, 144.

217   IN FRANCE, IT WAS ALMOST UNHEARD OF Nicolas Courtin notes that cotton first appeared in 1650 and 1669 and became more frequent after 1700.

217   MASTER UPHOLSTERER Bimont, 14. On the use of cotton as an upholsterey fabric elsewhere in Europe, see Lemire 1991, 17.

Chapter Fourteen: The Comfortable Body

219   REINVENTED POSTURES Giedion, 310.

219   CODES OF COMPORTMENT Annas, 35, 45.

220   THE PRINCESSE PALATINE Palatine 1985, October 22, 1698, 244.

220   DON'T CROSS YOUR LEGS Londeau, 29, 38.

220   DUCHESSE DE BOURGOGNE Saint-Simon, 4:403.

220   PRINCESSE DES URSINS Saint-Simon, 2:580.

221   "INDECENT POSTURES" *S'y bercèr, se renverser à demi-couché*, Callières, 40.

221   THE DAUPHIN'S SOFA MANNERS *Étendus tout de leur long, couché*, Palatine 1985, 361, 424; Palatine 1838, 174.

223   "READING ROOMS" Blondel 1737, 1:160.

223   THE ORIGINAL HISTORY OF PRIVATE LIFE Le Grand d'Aussy, 196.

223   *ENSEIGNES* Savary des Bruslons, 2:323–324.

225   THE MARQUISE DE SÉVIGNÉ Sévigné, March 24, 1671, 1:199.

225   IN NOVELS Durand, 1:250, 254; La Morlière, 426; Crébillon 1735, 183; Duclos, 202; Denon 1777, 79.

225   THE DUC DE CROŸ Croÿ, 1:288.

225   ANTOINE WATTEAU Grasselli and Rosenberg, 77–226, 277–279, 300–303.

226   EVEN DE TROY Wildenstein, 39.

227   AT HER CHÂTEAU BELLEVUE Piganiol de La Force, 9:39.

227   "IDEAL BEAUTY" Dufort de Cheverny, *le vrai beau*, 1:117.

228   MASTER CHAIR MAKER ROUBO Roubo, 2:634.

Coda: L'Art de Vivre

229   SIR HORACE MANN Walpole, 18:331–332.

229   "IMITATE THE FRENCH" *London Magazine*, November 11, 1738, 552.

229   ARTHUR YOUNG Young, 292, 289.

231   PUT THE CRAFTSMEN AND ARTISANS *Encyclopédie*, Diderot, "art," 1:714; "métier," 10:463.

231   THE EARLY HISTORY On the early history of *civilisation*, see Febvre. It was first used in 1755 by the economist Mirabeau. In 1772, Johnson still refused to admit "civilization," though it did appear in Ash's 1775 dictionary, by which time it was common in French.

232   THE ANCIENT ART OF LIVING Sellars, 6–7, 40–41.

232   VOLTAIRE ARGUED Voltaire, *Encyclopédie,* 7:285.

232   FRANÇOISE DE GRAFFIGNY Graffigny, 1:208–209.

233   AS "COSMOPOLITANS" Entry "cosmopolite," Académie Française dictionary, 1762, J. F. Féraud, dictionary, 1787.

233   NIETZSCHE Nietzsche, 8:539.

233   TRANSFORMING DAILY LIFE On the spread through French society in the second half of the eighteenth century of the architecture of comfort, see Roche 2000, 77, 102–103.

233   CLAIMED IN HIS APTLY TITLED Caraccioli 1772, iv–v, 419–420.

233   FOUR YEARS LATER Gudin de La Brenellerie, 1:61, 91; 2:166, 145–146, 170.

234   ALSO IN 1776 Caraccioli 1776, 119–120.

234   THE FOLLOWING YEAR Caraccioli 1777, 119–120, 206, 353–357.

234   LE GRAND D'AUSSY Le Grand d'Aussy, ix, 140–141.

234   ANTOINE DE RIVAROL Rivarol, 40–41.

236   IN HIS MEMOIRS Dufort de Cheverny, 1:310.

236   THAT HE BROUGHT ALL THE WAY Stein, 24.

BIBLIOGRAPHY

Allemagne, Henry d'. *La Toile imprimée et les indiennes*. 2 vols. Paris: Librairie Gründ, 1942.

Andry de Boisregard, Nicolas. *L'Orthopédie, ou l'Art de prévenir et de corriger dans les enfants les difformités du corps*. 2 vols. Paris: Veuve Alix, 1741.

Annas, Alicia. "The Elegant Art of Movement." In E. Maeder, ed. *An Elegant Art*. New York and Los Angeles: Los Angeles County Museum of Art/Harry N. Abrams, 1983: 35–58.

Antoine, Michel. *Louis XV*. Paris: Fayard, 1989.

Argenson, René-Louis de Voyer de Paulmy, Marquis d'. *Mémoires et journal inédit du marquis d'Argenson*. 5 vols. Paris: P. Jannet, 1857–1858.

Ariès, Philippe. *Centuries of Childhood: A Social History of Family Life*. New York: Vintage Books, 1962.

Arminjon, Catherine, ed. *Madame de Pompadour et la floraison des arts*. Montreal: Musée David M. Stewart, 1988.

Augarde, Jean-Dominique. "Histoire et signification de l'estampille des meubles." *L'Estampille* 182 (June 1985): 52–57.

Auxiron, Claude François d'. *Projet patriotique sur les eaux de Paris, ou Mémoire sur les moyens de fournir à la ville de Paris des eaux saines*. N.p.: 1765.

———. *Comparaison du projet fait par M. de Parcieux pour donner des eaux à la ville de Paris à celui de M. d'Auxiron*. Amsterdam/Paris: Musier, 1769.

Aviler, Augustin Charles d'. *Cours d'architecture*. Paris: Nicolas Langlois, 1691.

———. *Cours d'architecture*. Ed. Alexandre Le Blond. Paris: Jean Mariette, 1710.

———. *Cours d'architecture*. Paris: Jean Mariette, 1738.

———. *Dictionnaire d'architecture civile et hydraulique*. Paris: Jombert, 1755.

Balleroy, Marquise de. *Correspondants de la marquise de Balleroy*. Ed. E. de Barthélemey. 2 vols. Paris: Hachette, 1883.

Ballot, Marie-Juliette. *Le Décor intérieur au XVIIIe siècle à Paris et dans la région parisienne*. Paris: G. Van Oest, 1930.

Barbier, Edmond Jean François. *Chronique de la régence et du règne de Louis XV*. 9 vols. Paris: Charpentier, 1851–1857.

Bartoli, Piero. *Admiranda Romanarum antiquitatum*. Rome: de Pace, 1693.

Bastide, Jean-François de. "La Petite maison." *Le Nouveau spectateur* 2: 363–412. Paris: Rollin & Bauche, 1758.

Beard, Geoffrey. *Upholsterers and Interior Furnishing in England: 1530–1840*. New Haven: Yale University Press, 1997.

————. *Stucco and Decorative Plasterwork in Europe*. New York: Harper & Row, 1983.

Belhost, J.-F., and G.-M. Leproux. "La Fenêtre parisienne au XVIIe et XVIIIe siècles." *Cahiers de la Rotonde* 18 (1997): 14–43.

Benabou, Erica-Marie. *La Prostitution et la police des mœurs au XVIIIe siècle*. Paris: Perrin, 1987.

Benhamou, Reed. "Parallel Worlds: The Places of Masters and Servants in the *Maisons de Plaisance* of Jacques-François Blondel." *Journal of Design History* 7, no. 1 (1994): 1–11.

Bimont, J. F. *Principes de l'art du tapissier*. Paris: Lottin, 1770.

Biver, Count Paul. *Histoire du château de Bellevue*. Paris: Librairie Gabriel Enault, 1933.

Blégny, Nicolas de. *Le Livre commode*. Paris: Veuve D. Nion, 1692.

Blondel, Jacques-François, and J.-F. Bastide. *L'Homme du monde éclairé par les arts*. 2 vols. Paris: Monory, 1774.

————. *Cours d'architecture*. 6 vols. Paris: Desaint, 1771–1777.

————. *Architecture française*. 4 vols. Paris: C.-A. Jombert, 1752–1756.

————. "Discours sur la manière d'étudier l'architecture et les arts qui sont relatifs à celui de bâtir." *Mercure de France* (August 1747): 57–74.

————. *Traité d'architecture dans le goût moderne: De la distribution des maisons de plaisance*. 2 vols. Paris: C.-A. Jombert, 1737–1738.

Boffrand, Germain. *Livre d'architecture*. Paris: Guillaume Cavalier Père, 1745.

Bordes, Philippe. "L'Essor d'un genre continental: Portraits de famille dans les cours européennes, 1665–1780." *Studiolo* 4 (2006): 77–96.

Bowett, Adam. *English Furniture: 1660–1714*. London: Antique Collectors' Club, 2002.

Brice, Germain. *Description de la ville de Paris et de tout ce qu'elle contient de plus remarquable*. 2 vols. Paris: Michel Brunet, 1706.

————. 2 vols. Paris: François Fournier, 1713.

————. 3 vols. Paris: François Fournier, 1717.

————. 4 vols. Paris: J. Gandouin, 1725.

[Briseux, Charles Etienne]. *Architecture moderne ou l'art de bien bâtir pour toutes sortes de personnes*. 2 vols. Paris: Jombert, 1728.

————. *L'Art de bâtir des maisons de campagne*. 2 vols. Paris: Prault, 1743.

Bruignac-La Hougue, Véronique de. "Les Indiennes: Origine et diffusion." In *Touches d'exotisme*. Paris: Musée de la Mode et du Textile, 1998: 41–55.

Bullet, Pierre. *L'Architecture pratique*. Paris: E. Michallet, 1691.

————. "Observations sur la nature et sur les effets de la mauvaise odeur des lieux ou aisances." N.p.: 1695.

Byng, John. *The Torrington Diaries, Containing the Tours Through England and Wales Between the Years 1781 and 1794*. 4 vols. London: Eyre & Spottiswoode, 1936.

[Callières, François de]. *Les Mots à la mode*. The Hague: Abraham Troyel, 1692.

Campan, Jeanne Genet, known as Madame. *Mémoires*. Ed. Jean Chalon. Paris: Mercure de France, 1988.

Capon, G., and R. Yve-Plessis. *Fille d'opéra, vendeuse d'amour: Histoire de Mlle. Deschamps.* Paris: Plessis, 1906.

[Caraccioli, L. A. de]. *Paris, le modèle des nations étrangères.* Paris: Veuve Duchesne, 1777.

———. *L'Europe française.* Paris: Veuve Duchesne, 1776.

———. *Voyage de la raison en Europe.* Paris: Saillant, 1772.

Cas de conscience: On demande s'il est permis de suivre les modes, si l'usage des paniers peut être souffert? Paris: 1728.

Cavallo, Guglielmo, and Roger Chartier. *A History of Reading in the West.* Tr. Lydia Cochrane. Cambridge, U.K.: Polity Press, 1999.

Chippendale, Thomas. *The Gentleman and Cabinet-Maker's Director.* London: Printed for the author, 1762.

Code des toiles, ou Recueil d'édits, declarations, tariffs, sentences, arrêts et règlements concernant la police des toiles. Paris: d'Houry, 1761.

Comptes des bâtiments du roi sous le règne de Louis XIV. Ed. J. Guiffrey. 5 vols. Paris: Imprimerie Nationale, 1881–1901.

Coquery, Natacha. *L'Hôtel aristocratique: Le Marché du luxe à Paris au XVIIIe siècle.* Paris: Publications de la Sorbonne, 1998.

Cordey, Jean. *L'Inventaire des biens de Madame de Pompadour rédigé après son déces.* Paris: Pour la Société des Bibliophiles Français, 1939.

Correspondance des contrôleurs généraux des finances avec les intendants des provinces. Ed. Arthur Michel de Boislisle. 3 vols. Paris: Imprimerie Nationale, 1874–1897.

Courajod, Louis, ed. *Le Livre-Journal de Lazare Duvaux.* 2 vols. Paris: Société des Bibliophiles Français, 1873.

Courtonne, Jean. *Traité de perspective pratique.* Paris: 1725.

Coutin, Antoine. *Nouveau traité de la civilité qui se pratique en France parmi les honnêtes gens.* Paris: H. Josset, 1671.

Cranz, Galen. *The Chair.* New York: Norton, 1998.

Crébillon, Claude Prosper Jolyot de. *L'Écumoire, histoire japonaise.* 2 vols. London: Aux Dépens de la Compagnie, 1735.

———. *Les Égarements du cœur et de l'esprit.* 1736. Paris: Folio, 1977.

———. *Ah! quel conte.* 1751. 4 vols. London: Duffort, 1779.

———. *Le Hasard du coin du feu.* 3 vols. The Hague: 1763.

Crowley, John E. *The Invention of Comfort: Sensibilities and Design in Early Modern Britain and Early America.* Baltimore and London: Johns Hopkins University Press, 2000.

Crowston, Clare. *Fabricating Women: The Seamstresses of Old Regime France, 1675–1791.* Durham, N.C., and London: Duke University Press, 2001.

Croÿ, Emmanuel, Duc de. *Journal inédit, 1718–84.* Ed. Vicomte de Grouchy and P. Cottin. 4 vols. Paris: 1906–1907.

Crozat, Pierre. "Inventaire." May 30, 1740. Archives Nationales. ET/XXX/278.

Cunningham, Patricia. "Eighteenth-Century Nightgowns." *Costume* 10 (1984): 2–11.

Dangeau, Philippe de Courcillon, Marquis de. *Journal.* Ed. M. Feuillet de Conches. 19 vols. Paris: Firmin Didot, 1854.

Daremberg, C., and E. Saglio. *Dictionnaire des antiquités grecques et romaines.* 5 vols. Paris: Hachette, 1877–1919.

Dee, Elaine Evans, and Guy Walton. *Versailles: The View from Sweden*. New York: Cooper-Hewitt Museum, 1988.

DeJean, Joan. *The Essence of Style: How the French Invented High Fashion, Fine Food, Chic Cafés, Style, Sophistication, and Glamour*. New York: Free Press, 2005.

Delany, Mrs. (Mary Granville). *A Memoir: 1700–1788*. Ed. G. Paston. London: G. Richards, 1900.

Dennis, Michael. *Court and Garden: From the French Hôtel to the City of Modern Architecture*. Cambridge: MIT Press, 1986.

Denon, Dominique Vivant. *Point de lendemain*. 1777. Ed. Michel Delon. Paris: Gallimard, 1995.

Depitre, Edgard. *La Toile peinte en France au XVIIe et au XVIIIe siècles*. Paris: Librairie des Sciences Sociales et Politiques, 1912.

Desmares, Charlotte. "Donation." September 25, 1746. Archives Nationales. ET/LXIV/329.

————. "Vente de meubles." July 11, 1725. Archives Nationales. ET/LXIV/294.

————. September 11, 1725. Archives Nationales. ET/LXIV/294.

Deville, Jules. *Dictionnaire du tapissier*. 2 vols. Paris: Claegen, 1878–1880.

Dezallier d'Argenville, Antoine-Nicolas. *Voyage pittoresque de Paris, ou Indication de tout ce qu'il y a de plus beau dans cette grande ville*. Paris: De Bure, 1749.

D'Oench, Ellen. *The Conversation Piece: Arthur Devis and His Contemporaries*. New Haven: Yale Center for British Art, 1980.

Duchesse, Louise-Françoise de Bourbon, known as Madame la. "Inventaire des biens et effets." June 22, 1743. Château de Chantilly. 2-A044.

Duckett, M. W., ed. *Dictionnaire de la conversation et de la lecture*. 52 vols. Paris: Belin-Mandar, 1832.

Duclos, Charles. *Confessions du comte de ****. 2 vols. Amsterdam: 1741.

Dufort de Cheverny, Jean-Nicolas, Comte de. *Mémoires*. Ed. R. de Crèvecoeur. 2 vols. Paris: Plon, 1909.

Durand, Catherine Bédacier. *La Comtesse de Mortane*. 2 vols. Paris: Veuve Barbin, 1699.

Edwards, Ralph. *The Dictionary of English Furniture*. 3 vols. London: Country Life Ltd., 1954.

Eleb-Vidal, Monique, and Anne Debarre-Blanchard. *Architectures de la vie privée*. Brussels: Aux Archives d'Architecture Moderne, 1989.

Etlin, Richard. " 'Les Dedans,' Jacques-François Blondel and the System of the Home, c. 1740." *Gazette des Beaux-Arts* XCI (April 1978): 137–147.

Evans, Robin. *Translations from Drawing to Building*. Cambridge, Mass.: MIT Press, 1997.

Evreux, Louis de La Tour d'Auvergne, Comte d'. *Inventaire après déces*. January 29, 1753. Archives Nationales. ET/LXVIII/446.

Fahy, Everett. *The Wrightsman Pictures*. New York: Metropolitan Museum of Art: 2005.

Febvre, Lucien. "Civilisation: Evolution d'un mot et d'un groupe d'idées." *Civilisation: Le Mot et l'idée*. Paris: Félix Alcan, 1930: 1–55.

Félibien, André. *Les Divertissements de Versailles donnés par le roi à toute sa cour au retour de la conquête de la Franche-Comté en l'année 1674*. Paris: Coignard, 1674.

————. *Les Plans et descriptions des plus belles maisons de campagne de Pline le Consul*. Paris: F. and P. Delaulne, 1699.

Fennetaux, Ariane. "Men in Gowns: Nightgowns and the Construction of Masculinity." *Immediations* 1 (spring 2004): 77–89.

Féraud, Jean-François. *Dictionnaire critique de la langue française*. Marseilles: J. Mossy, 1787–1788.

Feray, Jean. *Architecture intérieure et décoration intérieure en France des origines à 1875*. Paris: Berger-Levrault, 1988.

Fiennes, Celia. *The Journies*. Ed. C. Morris. London: Cresset Press, 1947.

[Forbonnais, François de]. *Examen des avantages et des désavantages de la prohibition des toiles peintes*. Marseilles: Carapatria, 1755.

Fossé, Charles-Louis de. *Cheminée économique, à laquelle on a adapté la mécanique de M. Franklin*. Paris: Jombert & Dessene, 1786.

Fournier, Edouard. *Le Vieux neuf*. 2 vols. Paris: E. Dentu, 1859.

Fraisse, Jean-Antoine. *Livre de desseins chinois tirés d'après les originaux de Perse, des Indes, de la Chine, et du Japon*. Paris: Lottin, 1735.

Franklin, Benjamin. *An Account of the New Invented Pennsylvanian Fire-Places*. Philadelphia: B. Franklin, 1744.

Gallet, Michel. *Stately Mansions: 18th-Century Parisian Architecture*. New York: Praeger, 1972.

Garsault, François. *L'Art du tailleur*. Paris: Delatour, 1769.

Gauger, Nicolas. *La Mécanique du feu, ou L'Art d'en augmenter les effets et d'en diminuer les dépenses*. Paris: Jean-Jacques Estienne et Jean Jombert, 1713.

Giedion, Siegfried. *Mechanization Takes Command: A Contribution to Anonymous History*. 1948. New York: Norton, 1969.

Giraud, Pierre. *Commodités portatives*. Paris: Cailleau, 1786.

Girouard, Mark. *Life in the English Country House: A Social and Architectural History*. New Haven and London: Yale University Press, 1978.

———. *Life in the French Country House*. New York: Cassell & Co., 2000.

Gittinger, Mattibelle. *Master Dyers to the World: Technique and Trade in Early Indian Dyed Cotton Textiles*. Washington, D.C.: Textile Museum, 1982.

[Gournay, Vincent de]. *Observations sur l'examen des avantages et des désavantages de la prohibition des toiles peintes*. Marseilles: Carapatria, 1755.

Graffigny, Françoise de. *Correspondance*. Ed. J. A. Dainard et al. 12 vols. Oxford: Voltaire Foundation, 1985–2009.

Grasselli, Margaret Morgan, and Pierre Rosenberg. *Watteau, 1684–1721*. Washington, D.C.: National Gallery of Art, 1984.

Gudin de La Brenellerie, Paul-Philippe. *Aux Mânes de Louis XV: Essai sur le progrès des arts et de l'esprit humain sous le règne de Louis XV*. Aux Deux Ponts: À l'Imprimerie Ducale, 1776.

Guyot Desfontaines, P. F. *Dictionnaire néologique*. N.p.: 1726.

Harrington, Sir John. *A New Discourse of a Stale Subject, Called the Metamorphosis of Ajax*. 1596. Ed. E. Donno. New York: Columbia University Press, 1962.

Hartkamp-Jonxis, Ebeltje. *Indian Chintzes*. Amsterdam: Rijksmuseum, 1994.

———. "Indian Export Chintzes." In K. Riboud, ed. *The Quest of Themes and Skills in Asian Textiles*. Bombay: 1989: 80–86.

Hautecœur, Louis. *Histoire de l'architecture classique en France*. 6 vols. Paris: Editions A. & J. Picard, 1948.

Havard, Henry. *Dictionnaire de l'ameublement*. 4 vols. Paris: Maison Quantin, 1890.

Havard, Louis. *La Maison salubre et la maison insalubre à l'exposition universelle de 1889*. Paris: Charles Noblet, 1890.

Hébrard, Pierre. *Caminologie, ou Traité des cheminées*. Dijon: F. Desventes, 1756.

Hellman, Mimi. "Furniture, Sociability, and the Work of Leisure in 18th-Century France." *Eighteenth-Century Studies* 32, no. 4 (1999): 415–445.

Hénissart, Jean-Félix. *Satyre sur les cerceaux, paniers, criards et manteaux volans des femmes.* Paris: C. L. Thiboust, 1727.

Héroard, Jean. *Journal.* Ed. M. Foisil. 2 vols. Paris: Fayard, 1989.

Herrmann, Wolfgang. "The Author of the *Architecture moderne* of 1728." *Journal of the Society of Architectural Historians* 18, no. 2 (May 1959): 60–62.

Hoog, Simone, ed. *La Manière de montrer les jardins de Versailles.* Paris: Réunion des Musées Nationaux, 1982.

Hunter-Stiebel, Penelope. *Louis XV and Madame de Pompadour: A Love Affair with Style.* New York: Rosenberg & Stiebel, 1990.

Hurtaud, Pierre and Magny. *Dictionnaire historique de la ville de Paris.* 4 vols. Paris: Moutard, 1779.

Inventaire général du mobilier de la couronne sous Louis XIV. Ed. J. Guiffrey. 2 vols. Paris: J. Rouam, 1886.

Irwin, John, and Katharine Brett. *Origins of Chintz.* London: Her Majesty's Stationery Office, 1970.

Janneau, Guillaume. *Les Sièges.* Paris: Editions de l'Amateur, 1993.

———. *Le Meuble léger en France.* Paris: Paul Hartmann, 1952.

Jarry, Madeleine. *Le Siège français.* Fribourg: Office du Livre, 1973.

Jaubert, Abbé. *Dictionnaire raisonné et universel des arts et métiers.* 5 vols. Paris: Didot Jeune, 1773.

Journal économique. 43 vols. Paris: Antoine Boudet, 1751–1772.

Kalnein, Wend Graf, and Michael Levey. *Art and Architecture of the 18th Century in France.* Trans. J. R. Foster. Harmondsworth, Middlesex: Penguin Books, 1972.

Kaufmann, Emil. "The Contribution of Jacques-François Blondel to Mariette's *Architecture française.*" *The Art Bulletin* 31, no. 1 (March 1949): 58–59.

Kimball, Fiske. *The Creation of the Rococo.* Philadelphia: Philadelphia Museum of Art, 1943.

Krafft, Jean-Charles, and Nicholas Ransonnette. *Elévations des plus belles maisons de Paris.* 1992. 2 vols. Paris: 1801–1812.

Laclos, Choderlos de. *Les Liaisons dangereuses.* 1781. Paris: Garnier/Flammarion, 1981.

Lafayette, Marie-Madeleine Pioche de La Vergne, Comtesse de. *La Princesse de Clèves.* 1678. Ed. J. Mesnard. Paris: Garnier-Flammarion, 1980.

———. *Correspondance.* Ed. A. Beaunier. 2 vols. Paris: Gallimard, 1942.

Laing, Alastair, et al. *François Boucher, 1703–1770.* New York: Metropolitan Museum of Art, 1986.

Lajer-Burcharth, Ewa. "Pompadour's Touch: Difference in Representation." *Representations* 73 (winter 2001): 54–88.

La Luzerne, Bishop César de. *Oraison funèbre de Louis XV, le Bien Aimé, roi de France et de Navarre, prononcée le 7 septembre 1774 à Notre-Dame.* Paris: Guillaume Desprez, 1774.

La Morlière, Charles Jacques. *Angola, histoire indienne.* Agra/Paris: 1747.

Langenskiöld, Eric. *Pierre Bullet the Royal Architect.* Stockholm: Almquist & Wiksell, 1959.

La Tour du Pin, Henriette-Lucy Dillon, Marquise de. *Journal d'une femme de cinquante ans, 1778–1815.* Paris: Mercure de France, 1979.

Laugier, Marc-Antoine. *Essai sur l'architecture*. Paris: Duchesne, 1758.

Law, John. *Oeuvres complètes*. Ed. P. Harsin. 3 vols. Paris: Librairie Sirey, 1934.

Le Camus de Mézières, Nicolas. *Le Génie de l'architecture*. Paris: Benoît Morin, 1780.

Le Grand d'Aussy, Pierre Jean-Baptiste. *Précis d'une histoire de la vie privée des Français dans tous les temps et dans toutes les provinces de la monarchie*. Paris: 1779.

Lemire, Beverly. *Fashion's Favourite: The Cotton Trade and the Consumer in Britain, 1660–1800*. Oxford: Oxford University Press, 1991.

————. "Domesticating the Exotic: Floral Culture and the East India Calico Trade with England, c. 1600–1800." *Textile: The Journal of Cloth and Culture* 1, no. 1 (2003): 65–85.

Le Muet, Pierre. *Manière de bâtir pour toutes sortes de personnes*. Paris: Melchior Tavernier, 1623.

Le Pautre, Pierre. *Cheminées à la royale, semblables à celles posées à la Ménagerie*. Paris: 1698.

Léribault, Christophe. *Jean-François de Troy, 1679–1752*. Paris: Arthena, 2006.

Le Roi, J. A. *Curiosités historiques*. Paris: Henri Plon, 1864.

Le Roux, Jean-Baptiste. *Nouveaux lambris de galeries, chambres, et cheminées*. Paris: Jean Mariette, c. 1710.

Lilley, Ed. "The Name of the Boudoir." *Journal of the Society of Architectural Historians* 53, no. 2 (June 1994): 193–198.

Lister, Martin. *A Journey to Paris in the Year 1698*. Ed. R. P. Stearns. Urbana-Champaign: University of Illinois Press, 1967.

Londeau, Chevalier de. *Traité du maintien du corps*. Paris: Lesclapart, 1760.

Loyer, François. *Paris au XIXe siècle*. Paris: Hazan, 1987.

Luynes, Charles Philippe d'Albert, Duc de. *Mémoires sur la cour de Louis XV (1735–1758)*. Ed. L. Dussieux and E. Soulié. 17 vols. Paris: Firmin Didot, 1860.

Marie, Alfred. *La Naissance de Versailles*. 2 vols. Paris: Vincent Fréal, 1968.

Mariette, Jean. *Architecture française*. Paris: Mariette, 1727–1738.

Mariette, Pierre-Jean. *Abecedario*. Ed. P. de Chennevières. 4 vols. Paris: Dumoulin, 1853–1854.

Marivaux, Pierre Carlin. 1713. *Le Spectateur français*. Paris: Bonnard, 1921.

————. *La Vie de Marianne*. 1728–1737. Paris: Garnier-Flammarion, 1978.

Massounie, Dominique. "L'Usage, l'espace et le décor du bain." In Rabreau, ed. *Paris, capitale des arts sous Louis XV*: 197–210.

Mercier, Louis Sébastien. *Tableau de Paris*. 1781. 9 vols. Amsterdam: 1783.

Miller, Lesley. "French Silks (1650–1800)." In J. Harris, ed. *Five Thousand Years of Textiles*. London: BMP, 1993: 180–184.

Mitford, Nancy. *Madame de Pompadour*. New York: Harper & Row, 1954.

Montesquieu, Charles Louis de Secondat, Baron de. *Les Lettres persanes*. 2 vols. Cologne: Pierre Marteau, 1721.

[Moreau, Jacob Nicolas]. *Examen des effets que doivent produire dans le commerce de France, l'usage et la fabrication des toiles peintes*. Paris: Veuve Delaguette, 1759.

Nemeitz, J. C. *Séjour de Paris*. 1718. 2 vols. Leiden: Jean Van Abcoude, 1727.

Neufforge, Jean-François de. *Recueil élémentaire d'architecture*. 6 vols. Paris: Author, 1757–1768.

Neuman, Robert. "French Domestic Architecture in the Early 18th Century: The Town Houses of Robert de Cotte." *Journal of the Society of Architectural Historians* 39, no. 2 (May 1980): 128–144.

Nietzsche, Friedrich Wilhelm. *Sämtliche Briefe*. Ed. Giorgio Colli and Mazzino Montinari. 8 vols. Munich: Deutscher Taschenbuch, 1986.

Noailles, Paul, Duc de. *Histoire de Madame de Maintenon*. 2 vols. Paris: Comptoir des Imprimeurs-Unis, 1849.

Palatine, Charlotte-Elisabeth, Duchesse d'Orleans, née Princesse. *Correspondance*. Ed. G. Brunet. 2 vols. Paris: Charpentier, 1857.

———. *Correspondance*. Ed. E. Jaeglé. 2 vols. Paris: Quantin, 1880.

———. *Lettres de Madame la Duchesse d'Orléans, née Princesse Palatine*. Ed. O. Amiel. Paris: Mercure de France, 1985.

———. *Mémoires*. Ed. Michaud and Poujoulat. 32 vols. Paris: 24, rue des Petits-Augustins, 1838.

Pardailhé-Galabrun, Annik. *The Birth of Intimacy: Privacy and Domestic Life in Early Modern Paris*. Trans. J. Phelps. Philadelphia: University of Pennsylvania Press, 1991.

Patte, Pierre. *Discours sur l'architecture où l'on fait voir combien il serait important que l'étude de cet art fait partie de l'éducation des personnes de naissance*. Paris: Quillau & Prault, 1754.

———. *Monuments érigés en France à la gloire de Louis XV*. Paris: Rozet, 1767.

Péricaut, Emmanuel. "La Seconde Place: Une speculation." In T. Sarmant and Luce Gaume, eds. *La Place Vendôme*. Paris: Action Artistique de la Ville de Paris, 1999: 69–73.

[Périer, Jacques, Constantin, and Auguste Charles]. *Prospectus de la fourniture et distribution des eaux de la Seine à Paris par les machines à feu*. Paris: Veuve Ballard, 1781.

Perrault, Charles. *Contes*. Paris: Gallimard/Folio, 1981.

Peyssonnel, Charles de. *Les Numéros*. 4 vols. Amsterdam/Paris: Rue et Hôtel Serpente [Gaspard Cuchet], 1782–1784.

Piganiol de La Force, Jean-Aimar. *Description historique de la ville de Paris et de ses environs*. *Nouvelle édition*. 8 vols. Paris: Thomas Legras, 1742.

Piton, C. *Marly-le-Roi*. Paris: C. Joanin, 1904.

[Pompadour, Jeanne Antoinette Poisson d'Etiolles, Marquise de]. *Lettres de la marquise de Pompadour*. 2 vols. London: Owen, 1776.

Procès-verbaux de l'Académie Royale d'Architecture: 1671–1793. 10 vols. Paris: Edouard Champion, 1913.

Rabreau, Daniel, ed. *Paris, capitale des arts sous Louis XV*. Paris: William Blake, 1997.

Recueil de différentes modes du temps. Paris: A. Hérisset, 1729.

Relations artistiques entre la France et la Suède: 1693–1718 (Correspondance entre Nicodème Tessin le jeune et Daniel Cronström). Stockholm: Egnellska Boktryckeriet, 1964.

Ribeiro, Aileen. *Dress in 18th-Century Europe: 1715–1789*. New York: Holmes & Meier, 1985.

———. *The Art of Dress: Fashion in England and France, 1750–1820*. New Haven and London: Yale University Press, 1995.

———. *Fashion and Fiction: Dress in Art and Literature in Stuart England*. New Haven and London: Yale University Press, 2003.

Rivarol, Antoine de. *De l'Universalité de la langue française*. Paris and Berlin: Bailly, 1784.

Roche, Daniel. *A History of Everyday Things: The Birth of Consumption in France, 1600–1800*. Cambridge: Cambridge University Press, 2000.

———. *The Culture of Clothing: Dress and Fashion in the Ancien Régime*. Cambridge: Cambridge University Press, 1994.

Ronesse, Jacques Hippolyte. *Vue sur la propreté des rues de Paris*. N.p.: 1782.

Ronfort, Jean Nérée. "Commandes pour le grand dauphin à Versailles." *Dossier de l'art* 124 (November 2005): 38–65.

Rosenfeld, Myra Nan. *Largillierre and the 18th-Century Portrait*. Montreal: Montreal Museum of Fine Arts, 1981.

Roubo, André-Jacob. *L'Art du menuisier*. 4 vols. Paris: Saillon & Nyon, 1769–1775.

Rykwert, Joseph. *The First Moderns: The Architects of the 18th Century*. Cambridge, Mass.: MIT Press, 1980.

———. *The Necessity of Artifice*. New York: Rizzoli, 1982.

Saint-Simon, Louis de Rouvroy, Duc de. *Mémoires*. Ed. Y. Coirault. 8 vols. Paris: Gallimard, 1983.

Salmon, Xavier. *Madame de Pompadour et les arts*. Paris: Réunion des Musées Nationaux, 2002.

Sassoon, Andrian, and Gillian Wilson. *Decorative Arts: A Handbook of the Collections of the J. Paul Getty Museum*. Malibu, Calif.: J. Paul Getty Museum, 1986.

Sauvage, Henri. "La Maison de rapport." *L'Illustration* (March 30, 1929): 38–43.

Savary des Bruslons, Jacques. *Dictionnaire universel du commerce*. 4 vols. Paris: J. Estienne, 1723–1730.

Schnapper, Antoine. "The Position of the Portrait in France at the End of the Reign of Louis XIV (1680–1715)." In Myra Rosenfeld, ed. *Largillierre*: 61–81.

Scott, Katie. *The Rococo Interior: Decoration and Social Spaces in Early 18th-Century Paris*. New Haven and London: Yale University Press, 1995.

———. "Framing Ambition: The Interior Politics of Madame de Pompadour." *Art History* 28, no. 2 (April 2005): 248–290.

Sellars, John. *The Art of Living: The Stoics on the Nature and the Function of Philosophy*. Hants, U.K.: Ashgate, 2003.

Sévigné, Marie de Rabutin-Chantal, Marquise de. *Correspondance*. Ed. R. Duchêne. 3 vols. Paris: Gallimard, 1972.

Showalter, English. *Françoise de Graffigny: Her Life and Works. Studies on Voltaire and the 18th Century*. Vol. 11. Oxford: Voltaire Foundation, 2004.

Soulavie, J. L. *Mémoires historiques et anecdotiques de la cour de France pendant la faveur de la marquise de Pompadour*. Paris: Arthus Bertrand, 1802.

Sourches, Louis de Bouchet, Marquis de. *Memoires du marquis de Sources sur le règne de Louis XIV*. Ed. Cosnac and Pontal. 12 vols. Paris: Hachette, 1889.

Spectator, The. Ed. D. Bond. Oxford: Clarendon Press, 1965.

Stein, Susan. *The Worlds of Thomas Jefferson at Monticello*. New York: Abrams, 1993.

Stratmann-Döhler, Rosemarie. *Jean-François Oeben: 1721–1763*. Paris: Perrin & Fils, 2002.

Swain, Margaret H. "Nightgown into Dressing Gown: A Study of Mens' Nightgowns." *Costume* 66 (1972): 10–18.

Tessin, Carl. *Tableaux de Paris et de la cour de France, 1739–1742: Lettres inédites de Carl Gustaf, comte de Tessin*. Ed. G. von Proschwitz. Paris: J. Touzot, 1983.

Tessin, Nicodemus. "Relation de la visite de N. Tessin à Marly, Versailles, Clagny, Rueil, et Saint-Cloud en 1687." *Revue de l'histoire de Versailles et de Seine-et-l'Oise* (1926): 150–167, 274–300.

———. *Traité de la décoration intérieure*. 1717. Ed. P. Waddy. Stockholm: Swedish Museum of Architecture, 2002.

Thornton, Peter. *Seventeenth-Century Interior Decoration in England, France, and Holland*. New Haven and London: Yale University Press, 1978.

————. *Authentic Décor: The Domestic Interior 1620–1920*. New York: Crescent Books, 1984.

————. *Upholstery in America and Europe from the 17th Century to World War I*. New York: Norton, 1987.

————, and Maurice Tomlin. *The Furnishing and Decoration of Ham House*. London: Furniture History Society, 1980.

Ursins, Anne-Marie de La Trémouille, Princesse des. *Lettres inédites de la princesse des Ursins*. Ed. M. A. Geffroy. Paris: Didier, 1859.

van Effen, Justus. *La Bagatelle*. 1718. 3 vols. Amsterdam: Michel-Charles Le Cene, 1722.

Velde, François de. "Government Equity and Money: John Law's System in 1720 France." *Federal Reserve Bank of Chicago Working Papers*, no. 2003-31.

Verlet, Pierre. *La Maison du XVIIIe siècle: Société, décor, mobilier*. Paris: Baschet, 1966.

Victoria, Anthony. *The Master Chairmaker's Art: France, 1710–1800*. New York: Frederick Victoria & Son, 1984.

Vigarello, Georges. *Concepts of Cleanliness: Changing Attitudes in France Since the Middle Ages*. Trans. Jean Birrell. Cambridge: Cambridge University Press, 1988.

Viollet-le-Duc, Eugène. *Dictionnaire raisonné de l'architecture française du XIe au XVIe siècle*. 10 vols. Paris: B. Bance, 1863.

Walpole, Horace. *Horace Walpole's Correspondence with Sir Horace Mann*. Ed. W. S. Lewis et al. 48 vols. New Haven: Yale University Press, 1954.

————. *Horace Walpole's Correspondence with Madame du Deffand and Wiart*. Ed. W. S. Lewis and W. H. Smith. 4 vols. New Haven: Yale University Press, 1939.

Watson, F. J. B. *The Wallace Collection: Furniture*. 5 vols. London: W. Clowes for the Trustees of the Wallace Collection, 1956.

————. *The Wrightsman Collection*. 3 vols. New York: Metropolitan Museum of Art, 1966.

Whitehead, John. *The French Interior in the 18th Century*. London: Lawrence King, 1992.

Wildenstein, Georges. *Le Salon de 1725*. Paris: Société de l'Histoire de l'Art Français, 1924.

————. "Les Tableaux dans l'hôtel de Pierre Crozat." *Gazette des Beaux-Arts* LXXII (1968): 5–10.

Willett, C., and Phillis Cunnington. *The History of Underclothes*. London: Michael Joseph, 1951.

Wright, Lawrence. *Warm and Snug: The History of the Bed*. London: Routledge & Kegan Paul, 1962.

————. *Clean and Decent: The Fascinating History of the Bathroom and the Water Closet*. New York: Viking, 1960.

Young, Arthur. *Travels During the Years 1787, 1788, and 1789*. 2 vols. London: W. Richardson, 1794.

Ziskin, Rochelle. *The Place Vendôme*. New York: Cambridge University Press, 1999.

ILLUSTRATION CREDITS

25 *Madame de Montespan in Front of the Château de Clagny.* Anonymous engraving based on a painting by Henri Gascard. c. 1675. Photograph: Bibliothèque Nationale de France.

53 *Plan du rez-de-chaussée d'un grand hôtel du dessein de Jacques-François Blondel, architecte du roy. Encyclopédie.* Photograph: Rare Books and Special Collections, Van Pelt Library, University of Pennsylvania.

56 Claude Prosper Jolyot de Crébillon (Crébillon fils). *La Nuit et le moment.* 1755. Anonymous engraving. Photograph: Rare Books and Special Collections, Van Pelt Library, University of Pennsylvania.

60 *Élévation d'un cabinet orné de pilastre avec armoires pouvant contenir des livres ou des morceaux d'histoire naturelle.* François Boucher the Younger. c. 1750. Bibliothèque Historique de la Ville de Paris. Photograph: Gérard Leyris.

71 *Le Plaisir de l'été.* Engraving: B. Pater/L. Surugue. 1744. Private collection.

72 J. C. de La Fosse, *Baignoire vue en face.* c. 1760. Photograph: Patrick Lorette for Joan DeJean.

74 Jean Mariette, *Décoration intérieure d'une chambre des bains. Architecture française.* 1732. Rare Books and Special Collections, Van Pelt Library, University of Pennsylvania.

78 A. J. Roubo, *Plans et élévations de différentes sortes de baignoires.* 1769. Bibliothèque Historique de la Ville de Paris. Photograph: Gérard Leyris.

79 *Le Baigneur.* Anonymous engraving. 1767. Bibliothèque Historique de la Ville de Paris. Photograph: Gérard Leyris.

85   J.-F. Blondel. *Plans et profils de la décoration des lieux à soupape. Architecture dans le goût moderne*. 1738. Bibliothèque Historique de la Ville de Paris. Photograph: Gérard Leyris.

88   J.-F. Blondel. *Lieux à soupape vus du côté du siège. Architecture dans le goût moderne*. 1738. Bibliothèque Historique de la Ville de Paris. Photograph: Gérard Leyris.

90   *Plans, coupes, et élévations de diverses chaises d'aisances*. Engraving by A. J. Roubo. 1769. Bibliothèque Historique de la Ville de Paris. Photograph: Gérard Leyris.

91   *A Convenience Armchair with All Its Accessories*. 1786. In Pierre Giraud, *Commodités portatives*. Photograph: Patrick Lorette for Joan DeJean.

96   Jean Mariette. *Décoration du côté de la cheminée de l'hôtel de Roquelaure, du dessin de M. le Roux architecte. Architecture moderne*. 1732. Bibliothèque Historique de la Ville de Paris. Photograph: Gérard Leyris.

98   Sectional drawing of Gauger's improved fireplace, set inside an ornamental mantelpiece. In Nicolas Gauger. *La Mécanique du feu*. 1713. Rare Books and Special Collections, Van Pelt Library, University of Pennsylvania.

106   *Les Grillons*. Engraving by Claude Gillot. 1719. Photograph: Patrick Lorette for Joan DeJean.

109   *Plans, coupe, et élévations d'un fauteuil en cabriolet*. Engraving by A. J. Roubo. 1769. Photograph: Patrick Lorette for Joan DeJean.

112   *A Duchesse*. Engraving by J. C. Delafosse. c. 1768. Photograph: Patrick Lorette for Joan DeJean.

112   *A Duchesse Broken in Three*. Engraving by J. C. Delafosse. c. 1768. Photograph: Patrick Lorette for Joan DeJean.

114   *Femme de qualité sur un canapé*. Engraving by Jean Dieu de Saint-Jean. 1686. Photograph: Patrick Lorette for Joan DeJean.

116   *Madame la duchesse de Bouillon en déshabillé négligé sur un sopha*. Engraving by Antoine Trouvain. c. 1690. Photograph: Patrick Lorette for Joan DeJean.

117   *Madame de *** en Magdelaine*. Engraving by Jean Mariette. c. 1690. Photograph: Patrick Lorette for Joan DeJean.

119   *Madame la princesse de Rohan*. Engraving by Antoine Trouvain. 1696. Photograph: Patrick Lorette for Joan DeJean.

123   *Tapissier. Intérieur d'une boutique et différents ouvrages. Encyclopédie.* Photograph: Rare Books and Special Collections, Van Pelt Library, University of Pennsylvania.

124   *Ottomanne.* Engraving by J. C. Delafosse. c. 1768. Photograph: Patrick Lorette for Joan DeJean.

125   *Canapé à joue dans le goût pittoresque.* Engraving by J. C. Delafosse. c. 1768. Photograph: Partick Lorette for Joan DeJean.

126   *Élévations de plusieurs grands sièges.* Engraving by A. J. Roubo. 1769. Bibliothèque Historique de la Ville de Paris. Photograph: Gérard Leyris.

133   *Élévations d'un buffet à vaisselle.* François Boucher the Younger. c. 1750. Bibliothèque Historique de la Ville de Paris. Photograph: Gérard Leyris.

137   *Plans, coupes, et élévations d'une table de toilette, et d'une table de nuit.* Engraving by A. J. Roubo. 1769. Bibliothèque Historique de la Ville de Paris. Photograph: Gérard Leyris.

143   *Canapé exécuté pour M. le Comte de Bieliński.* Designed by Juste Aurèle Meissonnier. Engraved by Gabriel Huquier. 1735. Bibliothèque Historique de la Ville de Paris. Photograph: Gérard Leyris.

148   *Décoration du haut d'une porte et de son couronnement.* Engraving by Babel. In C. E. Briseux. *L'Art de bâtir des maisons de campagne.* 1751. Rare Books and Special Collections, Van Pelt Library, University of Pennsylvania.

149   *Décoration d'une salle à manger vüe du côté du buffet.* Engraving by J.-F. Blondel. In *Architecture dans le goût moderne.* 1738. Rare Books and Special Collections, Van Pelt Library, University of Pennsylvania.

154   *Panneaux de menuiserie.* Engraving by Babel. In C. E. Briseux. *L'Art de bâtir des maisons de campagne.* 1751. Rare Books and Special Collections, Van Pelt Library, University of Pennsylvania.

157   *Détails de menuiserie.* Large-pane and small-pane windows. Engraving by Pierre Patte. In J.-F. Blondel. *Cours d'architecture.* 1771. Photograph: Rare Books and Special Collections, Van Pelt Library, University of Pennsylvania.

160   Versailles-style parquet. *Encyclopédie.* Photograph: Rare Books and Special Collections, Van Pelt Library, University of Pennsylvania.

168   *Décoration de la chambre de parade de l'hôtel d'Evreux.* Jean Mariette. *Architecture française.* 1732. Rare Books and Special Collections, Van Pelt Library, University of Pennsylvania.

169   *Décoration d'une chambre à coucher dont le lit à deux chevets est en niche.* Engraving by J.-F. Blondel. *Architecture dans le goût moderne.* 1738. Bibliothèque Historique de la Ville de Paris. Photograph: Gérard Leyris.

170   *Duchess bed. Encyclopédie.* Rare Books and Special Collections, Van Pelt Library, University of Pennsylvania.

171   *Niche bed. Encyclopédie.* Rare Books and Special Collections, Van Pelt Library, University of Pennsylvania.

172   *Turkish bed. Encyclopédie.* Rare Books and Special Collections, Van Pelt Library, University of Pennsylvania.

181   *Décoration de lambris avec un renfoncement en niche pour un boudoir.* François Boucher the Younger. c. 1750. Bibliothèque Historique de la Ville de Paris. Photograph: Gérard Leyris.

193   *Fountains in the Gardens of Versailles.* 1714. Hand-colored engraving. Pierre Le Pautre/F. Delamonce/G. Fontainier. Photograph: Patrick Lorette for Joan DeJean.

195   *Les Paniers.* Anonymous engraving. c. 1725. Photograph: Patrick Lorette for Joan DeJean.

196   *Mademoiselle des Mastins Dancing at the Paris Opera.* Engraving by Jean Mariette. 1680s or 1690s. Photograph: Patrick Lorette for Joan DeJean.

222   *Le Billet-doux.* 1755. Engraving by Louis Aubert/Pierre Duflos the Younger. Private collection.

224   Trade card of Jean Magoulet, embroiderer to the queen. Etched and engraved. Early 1690s. Photograph courtesy of Waddesdon Manor.

Color Plates

Jean-François de Troy. *The Declaration of Love.* 1725. Private collection.

Arthur Devis. *Mr. and Mrs. Richard Bull of Onger, Essex.* 1747 (?). Institute of Fine Arts, New York University. Photograph: Josh Nefsky.

Louis Tocqué. *Portrait of Maria Leszczyńska.* 1740. Museé du Louvre. Photograph: Réunion des Musées Nationaux/Gérard Blot/Christian Jean.

Armchair. 1705–1710. Made for Pierre Crozat. Unsigned. Museé du Louvre. Photograph: Réunion des Musées Nationaux/Daniel Arnaudet.

François Boucher. *Portrait of Madame de Pompadour.* Oil on canvas. 1756. Photograph: Alte Pinakothek. Munich/Pinakothek Blauel/Gnamm-Artothek.

Jean-François de Troy. *La Lecture de Molière*. 1728. Private collection.

A flying dress. c. 1730. Les Arts Décoratifs/Musée de la Mode et du Textile, Paris. Photograph: Laurent Sully Jaulmes.

Jean-François de Troy. *The Garter*. 1725. Private collection.

Painted and dyed cotton. India. Coromandel Coast. c. 1750. Collection Maison Georges Le Manach. Photograph: Alain Damlamian.

Painted and dyed cotton. India. Coromandel Coast. c. 1740. Collection Maison Pierre Frey-Braquenié.

Painted and dyed cotton. India. Coromandel Coast. c. 1750. Collection Maison Georges Le Manach. Photograph: Alain Damlamian.

Painted and dyed cotton. India. Coromandel Coast. Early 1700s. Corteilles. Collection Maison Pierre Frey-Braquenié.

Painted and dyed cotton. India. Coromandel Coast. Early 1700s. Collection Maison Pierre Frey-Braquenié.

La Valette. Collection Maison Pierre Frey-Bracquenié.